God Behind the Screen

"Here is a well-written, insightful and deeply engaging analysis of what interests readers most: the quest for human destiny. Whether we are reading novels, poetry or books on psychology, philosophy or spirituality, the overarching project is to figure out who we are, as individuals and a species. In *God Behind the Screen* we find a rich and multidisciplinary analysis to help us on our way. I found this book impossible to put down."

—Dana Sawyer, The Maine College of Art

This interdisciplinary study of literary characters sheds light on the relatively under-studied phenomenon of religious psychopathy. *God Behind the Screen: Literary Portraits of Personality Disorders and Religion* identifies and rigorously examines protagonists – in works from a variety of genres, written by authors such as Aldous Huxley, Jane Austen, Sinclair Lewis, and Steven King – who are both fervently religious and suffer from a range of disorders underneath the umbrella of psychopathy.

Janko Andrijasevic is a Professor of English Literature at the University of Montenegro. His areas of interest include Aldous Huxley, medical humanities, spirituality, and psychology in literature. He has published a monograph on religion in Aldous Huxley's work, as well as two short novels, all in Serbo-Croatian.

Routledge Interdisciplinary Perspectives on Literature

87 **From Mind to Text**
Continuities and Breaks Between Cognitive, Aesthetic and Textualist Approaches to Literature
Bartosz Stopel

88 **Attachment, Place, and Otherness in Nineteenth-Century American Literature**
New Materialist Representations
Jillmarie Murphy

89 **Shame and Modern Writing**
Edited by Barry Sheils and Julie Walsh

90 **Provincializing the Bible**
Faulkner and Postsecular American Literature
Norman W. Jones

91 **Avant-Garde Pieties**
Aesthetics, Race, and the Renewal of Innovative Poetics
Joel Bettridge

92 **Modern Political Aesthetics from Romantic to Modernist Literature**
Choreographies of Social Performance
Tudor Balinisteanu

93 **Spatial Modernities**
Geography, Narrative, Imaginaries
Edited by Johannes Riquet and Elizabeth Kollmann

94 **God Behind the Screen**
Literary Portraits of Personality Disorders and Religion
Janko Andrijasevic

For a full list of titles in this series, please visit www.routledge.com

God Behind the Screen

Literary Portraits of Personality Disorders and Religion

Janko Andrijasevic

Routledge
Taylor & Francis Group
New York London

First published 2019 by Routledge
52 Vanderbilt Avenue, New York, NY 10017
2 Park Square, Milton Park, Abingdon, Oxon OX14 4RN

First issued in paperback 2020

Routledge is an imprint of the Taylor & Francis Group, an informa business

Library of Congress Cataloging-in-Publication Data
CIP data has been applied for.

ISBN 13: 978-0-367-66541-8 (pbk)
ISBN 13: 978-1-138-33904-0 (hbk)

Typeset in Sabon
by codeMantra

Contents

Introduction

At any given moment, the reality of existence oscillates at multiple levels, both parallel and intersected. The multifaceted and interlaced levels of existence are too complex to be grasped rationally. This is why the history of thought and science consists only of probing into various cross sections and segments of reality, while the complete phenomenon in its fullness lies outside our reach. "All philosophies and perspectives are necessarily simplifications of the world, and as simplifications, certain things are necessarily omitted."[1] In science's attempt to research specific subject areas, the reductionist approach is frequently taken, in which the phenomenon under the microscope is isolated from the rich context it belongs to. Less often, the inclusive approach is applied, which involves an awareness of the context the subject matter is holistically embedded in. In the first case, we get a more detailed, and in the second, a more genuine, picture of things.

Certain phenomena have frequently been at the center of various studies (either analytical or synthetical), while others, for unknown reasons, have slipped out of focus, dwelling in the shadows like some exotic, endemic species, despite having been present in reality since time immemorial.

One insufficiently researched phenomenon in the field of greater humanities is how people with personality disorders mask their malfunctions with the semblance of religiosity. Or, more precisely, these are the cases in which a disordered psychological level of existence overpowers the spiritual one, which lies at a more profound depth; a pathological personality structure thus skews spirituality. As a consequence, there often emerges a person who believes in the righteousness of their own religious standpoints and practices, which, in fact, are immature, inauthentic, and unwholesome.

The belief in a system of reality that transcends the material world goes back to the birth of human society. However, in contrast to benign epiphanies about a higher ground that have been occasionally occurring, there have also evidently been forms of malign, distorted religiosity. Although hypotheses about the use and misuse of belief in early human societies belong to the realm of speculation, later history abounds in concrete instances of unwholesome religious states of mind: religious fanaticism, masochism, obsession, hypocrisy, and so forth.

Despite the aforesaid, deluded religiosity has so far been considerably neglected as one of the important areas of humanistic research. Psychology of religion is still a marginal branch of psychology, while religion and psychopathology represents only a minor portion of it. However, if we note that the latter is not only about bizarre religious experiences of certain individuals, but that throughout history it powerfully, and at times fatally, affected larger masses of humanity, it is surprising that religious psychopathology remains such a neglected area of research. There may be many reasons for this, but they lie beyond the scope of this book. Instead, this study is a modest contribution to the subject, with the hope that it might elicit greater academic interest in this field.

The initial motivation for this book was my primary curiosity about some basic aspects of our inner lives: the psyche, the spirit, the creativity, and how they interact. While it is generally agreed upon that the roots of all three lie deep down in the layers of our unconscious being, it might be more contentious to ask whether they emerge from the same plane of unconsciousness, or from unconscious planes that are qualitatively different? And if these planes are hierarchically structured, which one is at a higher, and which at a lower ontological level? How do they influence one another, if indeed they do? And do they bolster or corrupt one another, or is it that perhaps they do the former in some cases and the latter in others? These are some of the relevant epistemological questions this book will explore.

The theoretical focus in this study will be on the relationship between the psychological and the spiritual levels of being. The representation of the creativity level is mostly practical: to illustrate the interrelationship between the psychological and the religious, I have used exclusively the creative works of literature written in the English language. Creative works other than literary fiction are not referenced.

This book begins with considerations of the major levels of personality, touching upon several models that have been in psycho-scientific and religious circulation for several decades. According to some teachings, a human being is nothing but a mechanism, and consciousness merely a (by-)product of its functioning; therefore consciousness is inseparable from the physical. A somewhat wider and traditionally more accepted idea is that we have a body and a soul. The "soul" is sometimes considered to be monolithic, sometimes bipartite (psyche and spirit), and sometimes tripartite (psyche, soul, and spirit). In further analysis I am leaning mostly on the ontologic–anthropologic dimensionality as expounded by Viktor Frankl, whose personality model consists of three existential levels – the somatic, the psychic, and the noetic, all of which are intertwined and integrated with three levels of awareness – the unconscious, the subconscious, and the conscious. For the purpose of this book, most attention will be given to the interactive, two-sided influence between the psychic and the noetic existential planes.

The psychological and the spiritual are tightly interconnected. The cases where they complement and strengthen each other denote examples of development characterized by psychological and religious maturity, both of which will be described later. However, absolute maturity does not exist in real life. It is more of an ideal to be striven for. Hence, the manifestations of immaturity, either psychological or religious, are on much wider display at the scene of humanity, and easier to recognize. I will try to describe their characteristics, too. Maturity, immaturity, and morbidity are, of course, very complex phenomena, and they are used in this book only insofar as they highlight the psycho-spiritual literary analysis that is in the focus of this text. The category of mental disorders that best reflects the negative symbiotic relationship between psyche and soul are personality disorders, so they will be at the heart of psychological analysis.

Finally, the second and the third major parts of the book consist of adequate illustrative case studies of personality disorders and religion in novels and creative biographies in English, written for the most part in the twentieth century. I do believe that world literature captures overall human experience and that it overarches all situations and all states of mind or spirit experienced by human beings. By the same token, it must contain essential insights into the relationship between personality disorders and religion, and *God Behind the Screen* explores these very insights. However, the restriction to titles in English has been made due to my academic background, which is in English, not in world literature. Even so, my knowledge is inevitably fragmentary, and the selection of the books I have made incomplete and open for supplementation.

Note

1 Theodore Millon, *Personality Disorders in Modern Life*, Hoboken, NJ: John Wiley &Sons, 2004, p. 277.

Part I

On Personality and Spirituality

1 The Levels of Personality – *Corpus et Animam*

The idea that personality is at the same time characterized by integration and multifacetedness is very familiar to all those who ever ventured into examining their own selves, which most of us have done in one way or another. On the one hand, humans have an implicit awareness that beneath the somatic – the only tangible aspect of personality – there is an extensive and unexplored universe that plunges down into multileveled depths of our inner worlds. On the other hand, unless all these diverse threads are integrated into a structure that leaves an impression of a more or less solid monolith, we are speaking of either immaturity or, in more serious cases, decomposition of personality.

The ontological layers of being and their harmonic or disharmonic dynamics can only be tackled by using abstract terms, for they are not locatable in a physical, biological, or even energetic sense, despite the fact that they do permeate all the aforementioned aspects of human existence. The component parts of personality can thus only be dealt with within the domain of experience, ideas, and intuitive knowledge, while the world of solid facts and hard core science is not the most adequate frame of reference here. This does not mean that the manifestations of personality feats and the consequences of behavior stemming from personal idiosyncrasies cannot be analyzed and measured using different methodological means. However, this book is not taking an approach that can be qualified as strictly scientific.

"The metaphor of levels or layers or strata [of personality] seems most natural."[1] It is difficult to state how many inter-autonomous strata there are. The notion that most people are familiar with is the idea *corpus et animam*, which implies that we are composed of body and soul. The bodily level entails no serious dilemmas because it represents a proof in itself, being materially manifested in space and time. However, it cannot be claimed that some of its functional and regulatory aspects are still not a mystery. "Pages could be given to its wonders."[2] The soul, on the other hand, is much more challenging to discuss, for its physical non-manifestation, the subtlety characterizing its acts, and the huge influence it has leaves the ratio eternally perplexed. The structure of the "soul" is the bone of contention we have been chewing on and fighting over for millennia.

The utterly reductionist understanding of human as a machine, i.e. a dimensionally depleted, mechanic/materialistic being, is a rather common "current conception, which prunes nature to almost its quantifiable components."[3] Still, even when seen as mere mechanisms, human beings are not denied the instinctual psychodynamism, however narrowly understood. The problem with materialistically oriented scientific approach lies in the fact that the psychological (nonmaterial) level of personality is considered "to be a part of the body,"[4] a product or even a by-product of brain activity. For scientists of this orientation, conscious experiences are merely echoes of the biochemical processes in the brain, which narrows mental life down to the physical level. "Thus everything would be reduced to properties of matter."[5] According to other, more open and holistically oriented stances, the reality is diametrically opposite. Here the body is seen as a manifestation of the spirit, on which it entirely depends. It is impossible to offer concrete proof for either of these approaches. Huston Smith says that everything only "depends on [our] ontic sensitivity."[6]

In some spiritual traditions, the way of life of an individual based predominantly on bodily needs is compared to that of nonhuman animals and is considered essentially subhuman. In Hinduism, there are four principles that characterize basic animal behavior, namely "eating, sleeping, defending and mating."[7] If the overall actions of an individual do not exceed the four mentioned principles, it is believed that this person, put very bluntly, leads an animal life. Higher potentials of the personality, primarily spiritual ones (believed to be implicit in every individual) remain dormant in such cases.

Returning for a moment to the materialistic/behavioral personality model, even when speaking of humans as computers, the existence of some kind of a software platform is not denied. So, even the most extreme reductionist interpretations mention the body on one side and a kind of a "soul" on the other. Let us now move on to the considerations of the nature of the "soul."

The widely exploited term "soul" was used earlier in the roughest and broadest sense to denote that part of personality that is not identical with the body. It is the underpinning instigator of an individual life, and as soon as it separates from the body, we speak of death, i.e. of the negation of life. What is the nature of this constituent of personality, which components does it consist of, which laws is it bound to, what principles does it function by? These are some of the perennial questions that will remain largely unanswered. Still, each closer insight into the nature of the "soul," however inconclusive, bears enormous significance for humanity, because knowledge about the soul is commensurate with progress and progressiveness, while ignorance about it engenders stagnation and degradation.

In spiritual traditions, soul is generally not seen as a homogenous antipode of the body. The qualitative heterogeneity of the soul may be illustrated by the etymological description of the mythical Hellenic term "psyche" – "'the spirit or soul of man' and also 'the seat of the will, desires, and passions.'"[8] Or more vividly, in the same mythology, "psyche" is also a butterfly that goes through various painful metamorphoses until it reaches the final "transcendent glory."[9] The soul contains different components defined in a different way from religion to religion, from philosophy to philosophy, from psychology to psychology. The Christian tradition inherits the model of "a human as a trinity made of spirit, soul, and body,"[10] Hinduism endorses a similar concept of being, body, and Absolute Truth[11] (although this and other Far Eastern religions distinguish between several levels of identity), and other religions also offer their own configurations of the composite levels of the soul. Philosophers and psychologists suggest numerous models of multifaceted layers of personality, but delving into their similarities and differences would take us too far. This is why I choose to adopt the classification proposed by Viktor Frankl as a starting point and a guiding light in dealing with the tangled paths of inner life. I have great confidence in Frankl because he approached both religion and science in a pithy and undogmatic way, trying to correspond to the objective reality as much as possible. I have also largely drawn on the ideas of Huston Smith, which give a touch of additional precision to Frankl's model. Finally, whenever we are dealing with the modern understanding of the phenomenon of personality, it is impossible to avoid the contribution of the great twentieth-century psychologists – Freud, Jung, Fromm, Allport, Horney, and others, even though their ideas are in this study oftentimes present only implicitly.

Frankl's model of personality outlines the structure and dynamics of the main facets of human existence in a simplified, but functional manner. It combines two aspects of dimensional ontology: layers and strata.[12] Layers refer to the three basic levels of personality, very similar to the ones proposed by Max Scheler and Nicolai Hartmann: the somatic, the psychic, and the noetic. Strata regard three different degrees of consciousness, introduced into science by Freud: the conscious, the preconscious, and the unconscious. The levels of personality are graphically presented as three concentric circles – the somatic level is on the outside, the psychic is between the somatic and the noetic, and the noetic, or the spiritual, is at the core. If we imagine a three-dimensional projection of these circles as a cylinder, that cylinder could be immersed into triple strata of consciousness. The core of our personality contains "the spiritual center that is encompassed by the peripheral somatic and psychic layers."[13] This core is like an axis; it extends "throughout the unconscious, preconscious, and conscious strata."[14] So, "any human phenomenon, whether belonging to the personal axis or to the somatic-psychic layers, may occur on any level: the unconscious, preconscious, or conscious."[15] Besides this, the levels of personality are hierarchically layered. The higher dimension is the one that contains the lower one and overarches it at the same time. "Thus biology is overarched by psychology, psychology by noölogy."[16]

Let us now briefly dwell on the layers of personality named earlier. The somatic has already been noted, so more attention will be paid to the psychic and the noetic. Both belong to what we colloquially refer to as the "spirit" or the "soul," but since there is an essential difference between them, they need to be discussed in more detail.

Frankl sees the psychic dimension as lower than the noetic one. It is a level significantly permeated by the conscious, and it cradles emotions, sensations, instincts, passions, desires, the intellect, urges, talents, social impressions, and the learned behavioral patterns.[17] This region is governed by the forces of psychodynamism, which are frequently blind, but which possess the potential to be brought into the consciousness. Untamed and fragmented, these forces can lead one into chaos, but harmonized with the stronger and steadier forces originating from the noetic dimension (more profound and higher than the psychic one) they become but helping hands on the path to overall personal evolution.

In Frankl's vocabulary, the spiritual dimension is called noetic instead of spiritual for the sake of avoiding the religious connotation. Elsewhere, in various mythological and religious traditions, it was denoted as "*psyche*, *anima*, *sarira atman*, *nephesh*, *nafs*."[18] It is the deepest and at the same time the highest level of personality in which dwell the phenomena specific only to humans. The noölogical also represents "the final locus of our individuality."[19] Every human being possesses this kind of spirituality, but the decision whether to reach out toward it and channel it through a religious or some alternative belief or not is an individual and very private issue. The noetic phenomena include free choice, will, creativity, numinous/religious experiences, morality, conscientiousness, a sense of values and love, the potential to be awed, intuition, inspiration, search for meaning, and humor.[20] The noetic core lies deep within the being, and the more intense a contact an individual establishes with it, the more integrated and mature that individual is. Of course, the contact with the noetic forces within us is sporadic, it "flashes for a moment, now here, now there, only to withdraw."[21] Abraham Maslow considers this contact with the authentic noetic being to be a peak achievement in the actualization of the self, and adds that what characterizes those experiences is that they are "transitory and brief."[22] The reason for this being so is very simple: peak experiences are exhausting and we do not have enough strength to be exposed to them for more than fleeting moments.

Although we usually identify with our conscious being, the noetic dimension is much closer to our essence than the mind. The dynamism that is active at the noetic level of personality is pointing in two directions at the same time complementary and converging: toward the subject that we love, serve, and adore, and toward our own being and its development. Frankl claims that the noetic cannot be pathological. Instead, the extent of its healthy participation in one's life depends on the state of the individual's psychological setup, through which the noetic is being filtered into everyday life. "As the Jains say, a lamp's flame may be bright, but let its chimney be coated with dust or soot and the lamplight will be dim."[23]

In the already quoted book *Forgotten Truth* (1976), Huston Smith mentions the fourth personality level which he calls the "spirit." It is a transindividual level permeated with universal energy. In an upside-down funnel way, this energy connects us with the overall creation. Frankl speaks of this level as of an "unconscious god" within us, or the "ultimate meaning of life." Since the analysis of this potential mode of existence can easily lead into theologizing, the focus here will mostly be on the psychological and the noetic, as well as the complex interactions of the two.

An overview of the fundamental building blocks of human personality would be incomplete without mentioning two more aspects of Frankl's dimensional ontology – anthropological unity and deterministic openness.

The unity of different modes of personality, or "unitas multiplex" as Thomas Aquinas called it, is imminently human. Even though we analyze them separately, "somatic, psychic, and noetic modes of being [cannot] be separated from each other."[24] It is quite another matter how these modes are interconnected within their unity – to which extent they are harmonized and complementary, and to which they are disintegrated and disparate. This matter represents probably one of the central questions of the humanities in general.

The deterministic openness of the human being (even though the phrase may sound as an oxymoron) refers to the fact that we are conditioned by various factors that are outside of our control, but that still do not define us in entirety. On one hand, it is impossible to get away from the influence of the genes, the environment, life circumstances, etc., but, on the other, these determining factors are not completely decisive for how we will develop as persons. In case they were absolutely decisive, we would not have been speaking of determinism but of pan-determinism, which would not allow for any personal impact on our own development. We would be atomistic creatures locked up within strictly defined and unchangeable walls, and many a human endeavor would lose its meaning. Where environmental factors are concerned, their influence on certain aspects of human personality is indubitable: at the somatic level, "our dependence on outer influences is almost absolute," at the psychic level, it is "flexible and interchangeable," and at the spiritual, "there is always a free choice when we are faced with external situations."[25]

Hence, it seems that at the noetic level, we are open to the world around us as well as toward the inner potentialities that have the power to "make a Heaven of Hell, a Hell of Heaven."[26] This power lies in the depths of our beings, stretching beyond the biological, the sociological, or the psychological. By its essential bonds, it connects us with other people and with the whole of creation.

The Relationship between the Psychic and the Noetic

In the depths of our being, psychodynamic forces stir together with the authentic bits of the essential self. In other words, "the human and the divine"[27] mix within us. The platforms from which they depart, as described in the aforementioned text, are not placed at the same ontological level, and although in everyday life they are frequently grouped in the same category of phenomena, the distinction between the spiritual and the psychic is very prominent. The most significant difference lies in the nature of these two personality layers – while the psychic belongs to the dimension of psychophysical facticity (which means that it grants us no specific, distinguishing quality), the noetic is directly linked only with the ontological, with nothing psychogenetic in it. "Authentic existence is present where is a self is deciding for itself, but not where an id is driving it."[28] There may even be greater similarity between the somatic and the psychic – disregarding the fact that the somatic is manifested through matter and the psychic is not – than there is between the psychic and the noetic, despite the fact that neither are embodied in matter or even in energy ("Mind, if it were energy, would be measurable quantitatively"[29]). Frankl states that "within the realm of facticity the line between the somatic and the psychic cannot be drawn clearly."[30] When seeking the causes of certain neuroses, psychiatric practice oftentimes "knows very well how difficult it is to differentiate between psychogenic and somatogenic components."[31] On the other hand, the difference between the psychic and the noetic is clear and crucial.

The difference that is of somewhat lesser importance is the one between the conscious and the unconscious. The psychic and the spiritual (as well as the somatic) facts are manifested on both the conscious and the unconscious levels, in a shifting ratio that is undulating over the zone of the preconscious, like an ebb and a flow. "The border between the conscious and the unconscious is a very fluid one – it is permeable – for there is a constant transition from one to the other."[32] Accordingly, our authenticity cannot be sought in the domain of either the conscious or the unconscious, only in the domain of the noetic, "whereas it is relatively irrelevant whether it is conscious or unconscious."[33]

Why is it that the noetic level of existence includes, overarches, and surpasses the psychic level? Why is it holding the supreme position in the hierarchically layered structure of our being? The answer can perhaps be sought in the fact that this aspect of existence penetrates the deepest unconsciousness, where the most significant source of living lies. "The potentialities of development of human souls are unfathomable."[34] The spiritual lies deep within the core of the personality, while the layers of psychophysical factuality are being integrated and organized around it. "The spiritual core, and only the spiritual core, warrants and constitutes oneness and wholesomeness in man."[35] The noölogical is the source and the destination. The values and qualities it contains make the basis of *philosophie perennis.*

The urge of contemporary science to analytically and etiologically explain all phenomena cannot be satisfied where the nature of spiritual facts is concerned. They are the basic particles our personalities consist of and cannot be understood exclusively by the theoretical or the practical mind, but rather require the previously mentioned "ontic sensibility" and a developed spiritual intelligence.[36] The profoundest spiritual person is unavailable to reflection, cannot be analyzed or further reduced. Maslow called its properties "the value of 'being' [...] that is intrinsic and cannot be reduced to anything more basic."[37] It is a "true Urphänomenon, an irreducible phenomenon"[38] with which "we have to transcend the ontic plane toward the ontological dimension."[39] The overall, integrative growth of personality requires deep self-observation, and "after the integration (or the successfully completed psychological development) that can be attained through psychotherapeutic practice, the individual continues in the direction of spiritual development, towards transcending of the self."[40] According to the spiritual–humanistic understanding of human beings, "there is a relationship between the immanent self and a transcendent Thou."[41] I hesitate to call the "transcendent Thou" God, but even when I do, I have in mind, first of all, the metaphysical source that is experienced differently in different individual and collective acts of spiritual life.

Excessive self-consciousness, rationality, or control thwarts the contact with the inner transpersonal quality that abides in us. Even too eager a desire to discover one's spirituality can become frustrating. The most meaningful thing to do is to "let our uncertainties exist,"[42] for "spiritual activity so absorbs the person as the executor of spiritual acts that he is not even capable of reflecting on what he basically is."[43] By merging the spirit and the self, we achieve ultimate integration which, according to Daniel Helminiak,[44] represents the highest level of spiritual development. In it lies our essential authenticity. The examples of a superb fusion of spirit and self are called mystical in the religious jargon. Besides numerous other universalities that characterize human beings, we also share a quality based on which each of us is also a *homo mysticus.*[45]

In real life, however, the cases of harmonious integration of the psychic and the noetic in human individuals are much rarer than the cases of discord between these two inner dimensions of being. There is a line across which this discord transgresses into a serious disorder, and that represents the central theme of this book.

The even graver problem emerges when the noetic is being altogether ignored by certain schools of psychology or one-dimensional scientific approaches. The spiritual is thus either completely overlooked or studied using the methodology and instruments intended for phenomena at the psychical or the psychic levels of existence, and explained in their terms. However, Ludwig Biswanger, the Swiss psychiatrist and one of the founders of existentialist psychology, spoke about "'instincts and spirit' as 'incommensurable concepts,'"[46] which I agree with. If we try to project the higher level onto a lower one, the result can never be adequate. Noetic phenomena (conscientiousness, responsibility, intuition) are feelings that emerge from the spiritual dimension. "Feeling can be much more sensitive than reason can ever be sensible."[47] These phenomena "may never be projected from the spiritual level down to the lower psychic level without distortion."[48] To conclude, I take the approach to human nature which includes the proposition that its three basic layers are the somatic, the psychic, and the noetic, and that the psychic is hierarchically above the somatic, and the noetic above the psychic.

Personal Maturities and Immaturities

The incommensurability of the psychic and the noetic does not mean that these two modes of existence are not tightly interconnected. They condition each other strongly. Even though this may sound mechanistic, the psychic is a filter through which the noetic is being streamed into our everyday being. The degree of communication between our conscious ego and the unconscious spiritual depths largely depends on the extent of distortion, porosity, and wholesomeness of the aforesaid filter. Of course, this is just one simplified angle of looking at the relationship between the inner layers of personality. The noetic has a therapeutic effect on the psychic, and a harmonious connection of the two brings forth a synergic quality indispensable for the growth of being. The text that follows will attempt to establish what characterizes psychic health, or more precisely psychological maturity, and what is suggestive of psychological immaturity. Further in the book follows a general consideration of the term "religiosity," as well as its basic modalities – mature and immature faith. Combinations of personal (im-)maturity and the state of one's religiosity are in this book illustrated by the examples of characters described in works of fiction and creative nonfiction. However, the first step in the analysis for a better understanding of these phenomena is the description of psychological maturity.

Psychological Maturity

Has a breathing human being characterized by absolute psychological maturity ever lived? It is not easy to give an answer to this question. Some authors agree about the potential possibility of the existence of such a case, but they invariably emphasize that, even if some perfect humans were out there, "they are very small in number."[49] For others, "ideal normalcy is just an abstract term, and is not to be encountered in clinical practice."[50] Accordingly, "we shall be talking more about an *ideal* than about an actual person."[51] It is probably more realistic to accept the latter opinion, for we live in an imperfect world to which we are connected due to our imperfections (as Hindus or Buddhists would say, based on their belief in karmic consequences). Perfection is a characteristic of some other (potential) worlds. In this context, the distinction will be made between the relative degree of maturity and the relative degree of immaturity (for most humans possess elements of both). Another important aspect is the direction in which we as humans are going – whether our actions and strivings lead us toward psychological growth, whether we have fixed our development at a certain level and continue to stagnate, or whether we regress toward lower existential stages. "A large number of people display more or less certain deviations from 'ideal normalcy', some, on the other hand, display smaller or greater aberrations, while some make their environment suffer due to their disturbances. The smallest number display obvious signs of mental illness."[52] So, it seems that it is the extent of immaturity all of us share that matters greatly in the final run.

Psychological maturity is thus realizable only relatively. Although we laconically use the qualifications "mature" and "immature" in everyday life to pass judgments about other people, maturity in fact comprises a well-developed set of features of which "the distinctive richness and congruence [...] are not easy to describe."[53] The father of personality psychology, Gordon Allport, stresses that "maturity of personality does not have any *necessary* relation to chronological age"[54] and that "a well-balanced lad of eleven [...] may have more signs of maturity than many self-centered and neurotic adults."[55] Perhaps the previous quotes were unnecessary, for life experience has presented us with numerous instances confirming this. However, considering the fact that adults, usually parents or teachers, frequently attempt to establish their authority based solely on their age, the previous statement rightfully debunks such attitude.

What is it, then, that makes for psychological maturity? According to Freud, maturity implies the ability to work and love. This has already become proverbial. In Allport's opinion, it is in "the way of responding to the problems set by life,"[56] and for Erik Erikson, "such people stand on their own two feet and do not have too many requirements of others."[57] The founder of Gestalt psychology Fritz Perls thinks that "maturity means a transition from external supports and strongholds to inner ones."[58] Broadly, however, maturity includes a large number of aspects observable at various levels: emotional, intellectual, social, creative, ethical, and also spiritual. All of them are partly culturally conditioned. This book is written from the perspective of Western culture in a broadest sense, in which hopefully "there is considerable agreement on the norms for soundness, health, or maturity."[59] I also hope that the ideas expounded in this book contain a high level of universality.

Most humanistic thinkers of the twentieth century contemplated the criteria that constitute psychological maturity. Freud and the psychoanalysts dealt much more with mental illness than with mental health, but they also took into consideration the conditions for psychological wellbeing. The psychologists that came later paid much more attention to these conditions, including the already mentioned Allport, but also Abraham Maslow, Marie Jahoda, Erik Erikson, Charlotte Bühler, Harry Allen Overstreet, Martin Seligman, and many more. In fact, most psychological thinkers dealt with the issue of psychological maturity, either directly or indirectly. What follows is an attempt to give a cumulative overview of the elements of maturity the mentioned psychologists proposed and to show the great complexity of the quality of psychological maturity. Whenever a group of values is concerned, it is difficult – or rather, impossible – to present these elements hierarchically. Furthermore, they acquire a full meaning only when integrated and consistently manifested in the global functioning of an individual.

The description of mental maturity can begin at any of its individual aspects, just like *The Quran* can be read without necessarily following the order of the *suras*. Let the first step in this description be the degree of objectivity with which we observe and experience ourselves. It could also be called the degree of self-observation. It varies within a huge span from individual to individual. Some simply do not dare look themselves in the eye, mostly due to fear, pain, or the consequences such an encounter with themselves would inevitably produce. This path of least resistance, the way of ignoring and/or denying the objective self, leads toward imprisonment in an illusion we create about ourselves. The maintenance of this illusion requires enormous amounts of psychic and other kinds of energies. However, it never grants us a compensatory fulfillment in return. Better insight into one's own personality, no matter what one finds in it, is characteristic of a greater degree of maturity. In order to be able to make such insights, we need an openness to learn (which requires at least average intelligence), to clearly understand our problems, and to modify our own convictions. It is a mature thing to change one's stances in case experience shows that our old formulae and patterns were worn out and inadequate. This is not to say that opportunistic (particularly political) party switching is mature, but the abandonment of an untenable life philosophy is. A rigid and defensive adherence to a philosophical idea is not an infrequent occurrence, particularly among the jealous creators of such ideas. They are usually unable to admit the shortcomings of their theories, but continue to promote them even when solid facts start to contradict them. Apart from blocking the paths of the authors' personal growth, clinging to unwholesome theories frequently also has a destructive effect on others.

Since this book largely flirts with psychology, an example from its history can be mentioned here, concerning the lobotomy practice invented by Dr. Walter Freeman. Over the years of its practice, it irrevocably damaged large mental (and, overall, human) potential of numerous patients subjected to this controversial surgical procedure in the 1940s and 1950s. "Many of Freeman's patients were so damaged by the surgery that they needed to be taught how to eat and use the bathroom again."[60]

A less consequential but, in several cases, equally brutal and unsubstantiated idea, this time about psychosexual development, authored by Dr. John Money of Johns Hopkins University in Baltimore, proved tragic for the Reimer family from Canada.[61] This example of "the failure of [...] Raimer's gender reassignment [...] really stains Money's legacy."[62] One of the twin brothers from this family, David, suffered serious penis impairment as an infant on occasion of the Jewish ritual circumcision performed in the local hospital using the then-new technology powered by electricity. In accordance with Dr. Money's theory that a person will become a mature man or a mature woman dependent on whether the child is raised as either a boy or a girl from the age of three onward, the parents decided to raise little David as Brenda. Further development of the Reimer twins proved how insensitive and inadequate Dr. Money's theory was. However, even when the premature and tragic death of both brothers refuted his theory, the scientist did not show enough maturity to question his stances, but refrained from giving any comments on the whole case.

Consequently, objective self-observation requires not only intelligence (the mentioned scientist was in no way lacking it), but a readiness to objectively face oneself and one's ideas.

Nobler minds allow at least a grain of doubt about their stances. It is perhaps this very characteristic that makes them great, while it certainly makes them more mature. Even Freud, extremely sensitive to the criticism of his theories (from which Alfred Adler was the first to secede, which was never forgiven), admitted by the end of his life that he had dealt only with certain aspects of human personality, ignoring other ones. In a letter to his contemporary Roberto Assagioli, a psychologist of a psychosynthetic orientation, he wrote: "I am interested only in the basement of the human being,"[63] thus indirectly admitting to have probably neglected some other premises in the edifice of personality.

On the other hand, Viktor Frankl offered his logotherapeutic ideas on meaning only as a framework to be supplemented and reworked by other thinkers and practitioners in accordance with the requirements of objective reality. His followers today reproach many proponents of the currently popular positive psychology for failing to recognize Frankl's contributions to this field, the fundaments of which he set in the books written as early as 1930s. However, Frankl himself probably would not have made a great fuss about whether or not his name was mentioned as long as useful ideas helped people realize their potential. This supposition was confirmed to me in a private communication with Alex Vessely, the grandson of Viktor Frankl, himself a psychologist and film director.[64]

Objective self-observation is, thus, one of the aspects of maturity that helps us approach essential authenticity. In order to achieve it, we need the continual freshness of evaluation, healthy criticism, and spontaneous openness for new experiences. Understanding of the self should be based on a combination of one's own experience and on how others experience us. Apart from the fact that by self-observation we are able to see ourselves and our shortcomings in a clearer light, it also helps us see others more clearly and understand their standpoints better (the more aware we are of our own imperfections, the less prone we are to adopt the projection mechanisms[65]).

Allport offers an interesting positive correlation between self-observation and humor – the better we know ourselves, the readier will we be to make jokes at our own expense (children almost never do this), in a healthy, therapeutic, and benevolent way. When we love and accept an object with all its absurdities and inconsistencies, we are able to laugh about it (not at it). At the beginning of this chapter, it has been stated that there is practically no such thing as absolute maturity of a living human being, which means that everyone carries in oneself a certain measure of absurdities and inconsistencies. The ability to recognize, accept, and laugh about them expresses a high degree of personal maturity.

A relatively objective insight into one's own personality is needed for the achievement of psychological maturity, but maturity also requires a relatively objective view of the environment and the reality around us. It implies seeing things as they are, with as high a degree of objectivity as possible. It is clear that we do not have X-ray eyes, but we also do not have to go around blindfolded. The principle of reality is important because it snaps us out of cherishing unrealizable desires, which make us miss out on true life. It also makes our position in reality optimally pleasant, neither unrealistically euphoric nor gloomily isolated.

Since life largely is a struggle, it is not always easy to maintain an objective attitude toward reality. We see things in a darker light than they really are when the life struggle exhausts us, or in a rosier light when we are experiencing happiness. What is important, though, is to make sure that our daily diet does not consist only of sour grapes or sweet lemons. We should not completely lose track of time as measured by clocks, or see threats in unfamiliar landscapes just because we do not know them. In case we manage to make an objective relationship with the surrounding world, its transience and uncertainty will not push us into existential despair. The need for absolute certainty in things that essentially cannot offer such certainty is unrealistic and represents an anteroom for serious neurosis. "The attempt to dominate things and keep them tightly under control can be aggressive and self-destructive, for in this way we force ourselves to deny our own experience and manipulate it, and alter whatever does not fit into the 'favurable' image we have of ourselves."[66]

In every darkness, there's a grain of light; in every light, there's a grain of darkness (the Taoist *yin-yang*). Our relationship with ourselves and the world around us cannot be mature if it is surgically sharp and does not allow for a dose of illusion to mix in with our reality. A measure of healthy illusion is required just for the sake of avoiding the quicksand of pessimism. Paradox is, in a way, the natural state of our innermost noetic self, so the idea that our wellbeing depends also on a portion of illusion, though sounding paradoxical, reflects some genuine truths about living. "In a study done with a video game, depressed people who played for half an hour knew just how many little monsters they had killed; the undepressed people guessed four to six times more than they had actually hit. Freud observed that the melancholic has 'a keener eye for the truth than others who are not melancholic.'"[67]

This illusion can be understood as a hope, a desire to be better than we currently are, and to live in better conditions than we currently do, as a motivating tension between the usually gray reality and the desire to ennoble it. Without a healthy dose of tension, we would dissipate into the homeostatic inertia. The most important element here is the measure itself, i.e. the balance and roundedness of the dynamics between the opposing principles. What exactly that measure is, and how to strike a perfect balance, are, alas, the questions to which no precise answer can be given. The inability to decide the ideal measure is just one of the instances of numerous life factors that inherently contain a quality of uncertainty. The only thing that can be said is that a golden balance is not stricken easily, and that the path toward it, as formulated in the ancient Upanishadic wisdom, leads across "a razor's sharp edge."[68]

Rational objectivity is not the only element necessary for mature self-observation and acceptance of self. What is also needed is emotional benevolence and warmth. Instead of ungrounded anxiety, unconquerable fear of danger and death, pronounced feelings of unrest and uncertainty, disproportionate reactions to fragments of emotional experiences, surrender to segmental urges, abhorrence of the human body (Jonathan Swift was notoriously famous for this[69]) – instead of all these, the signs of a higher degree of maturity are emotional balance, observance of one's own feelings and the feelings of others, and the "frustration tolerance."[70] There must be no fear in expressing one's own authentic emotionality, nor a sense of threat when we are in touch with emotional expressions of others.

One should love oneself in a tolerant and non-egoistic way. Although a forced order cannot be given to love someone or something (love belongs to those phenomena that withdraw before conscious intention), to love oneself comes naturally and easily. When we do not feel love for our own being, it probably implies some inner barrier that should be therapeutically removed. Lay people usually equate love for self with narcissism, but narcissism essentially lacks warmth and sincere feelings for oneself, and adopts selfishness as a compensatory principle. If mature love for oneself were not a supreme value, Jesus Christ would not have instructed to love our neighbors *as ourselves*.

The degree of self-observation and self-acceptance directly reflects on our attitudes to others. In order to be ready for mature interpersonal interaction, an individual usually needs to sort out the intrapersonal domain first. How one relates to others perhaps represents the best indicator for identification of personal shortcomings. A mature person has the ability to understand others, to empathize with their life situations and identify with them. Such a person is ready to love others and reciprocally share ideas, joys, problems, and material values. The mere number of friendships and acquaintances is not relevant for evaluation of one's degree of maturity. What is relevant is the ability to deepen the relationships with certain, adequately chosen individuals. Another important element is a healthy (i.e. benevolent) criticism toward others, as well as a sensitivity to detect manipulative intentions, emotional and energetic vampirism, negative motives for which others chose to be in our company. It is a mature thing to protect oneself from being used or exhausted in toxic relationships (symbiotic relationships suit only those who have their own share of serious personal shortcomings). Casting pearls before swine is not a sign of either wisdom or good will, but of a lack of judgment. Being in a toxic relationship usually means the blockade of the opportunities for further personal growth.

The principle of one's attitudes to others also reflects on their attitude to the wider environment. The desire to put in an effort and contribute to the advancement of the environment is quite natural, as well as the frustration when this desire is thwarted. Maturity does not lie in either uncritical glorification or deprecation of any familiar or foreign environment. A balanced and benevolent critical judgment is again the key to maturity when speaking about an individual's relationship with the social and natural world around us.

Reaching out to beings and objects outside of ourselves is a normal need of every healthy personality. Allport calls this need an "extension of the sense of self,"[71] while Frankl calls it self-transcendence ("meaning must not coincide with being; meaning must be ahead of being. [...] Existence falters unless it is lived in terms of transcendence toward something beyond itself"[72]). In childhood, we have a natural inkling to enjoy socialization, animals, play, and fairy tales. There is not an overly wide range of ways in which we actualize the meaning of existence. Small children across the globe tend to engage in similar activities up to a certain age. Variations ensue only later. As adolescence kicks in, the process of questioning one's own tendencies starts, as well as the discovery of "which facts and roles are for him propriate, which peripheral, or not suited at all to his lifestyle."[73] This is a period of finding or, more accurately, of fine-tuning into one's own identity, which needs to continue all the way on the path to self-transcendence. Knowing oneself is a prerequisite for surpassing oneself. This is why Erik Erikson considers finding one's true identity as a crucial developmental attainment, without which there is no maturity. Its opposite, the so-called identity diffusion, which might be an outcome of the unsuccessfully resolved developmental stage of the teenage years, implicitly undermines the foundations of further wholesome functioning of the personality.

The extension of the sense of oneself can go in the direction of love for another person ("the welfare of another is *identical* with one's own"[74]), friendship, belonging to a social group, profession, fight for justice, and spiritual involvement. Briefly, this particular "criterion of maturity [...] calls for authentic participation by the person in some significant spheres of human endeavour."[75] The feature opposed to self-transcendence is self-love, which is an "inescapable factor in every life [...] but only self-extension is the earmark of maturity."[76] If people do not show an interest in anything outside of themselves, they "live[...] closer to the animal level than to the human level of existence."[77]

Animal life, however, is inherent in human life. All the Darwinian acts toward survival that we acquired and preserved during the evolution process are meaningful in the contemporary context, too. One of them is adaptability. The environment we live in inevitably changes, with changes being more rapid today than at any time in the past (at least in the technological sense). Life circumstances also incessantly fluctuate, at times quite sharply and intensely. Changes invariably represent a source of stress. To adapt to changes means to develop a greater level of resistance to stress. The more vitality, adaptability, and resourcefulness[78] we have, the more maturely do we grapple with life's requirements. Although this category of features comes instinctively to nonhuman animals, in humans, besides being instinctive, it sometimes also gets distorted by the entangled complexities of an individual psychology. Hence, it is sometimes necessary to relearn this skill, or at least sharpen the inborn adaptive impulses.

At a social level, a mature person "shows adaptability coherent with the social environment."[79] On one hand, it means that the person is not isolated from society and is willing to compete for and share in social values, and on the other, they show resistance to conformist trends in society. Without the preservation of "personal integrity even under group pressure,"[80] there is no self-conscious personality. Similarly, maturity cannot be attained if a person is not ready to "substitute outer control with auto-control."[81]

In psychoanalytic terms, the generalized conclusion on adaptability is that it is achieved when "the primary 'Me' of instincts and pleasure develops into a secondary mature 'Me' (of reality), that has cast off the pleasure principle and adapted to reality."[82]

Work is also an evolutionary achievement characteristic of humans. Just like in the case of adaptability (or any other basic action, like eating, sexual activity, etc.), the impulse to work may be skewed in various ways. Maturity is reflected in those who organize their work successfully and who are focused on the problem and the aim they want to achieve. That aim may be either pragmatic, lucrative, pleasurable, or just a time-filler, but the important thing is that it exists. Without a task to be completed and an effort that needs to be put in an assignment, we fall into "existential frustration,"[83] i.e. "existential vacuum,"[84] which is an incubator for various types of psychopathology. Furthermore, work has a therapeutic effect, for "egoistic impulses of drive-satisfaction, pleasure, pride, defensiveness can all be forgotten for long stretches while a task takes over."[85]

The attitude a mature person takes toward her or his work, toward other people, and toward the environment they circulate within is one of reliability and seriousness. Such a person is able to endure and make sacrifices in order to attain an aim deemed valuable, expressing all the while a high degree of responsibility. Existential psychologists see responsibility as a crucial feature of a mature personality.

Responsibility is a corrective and a landmark of another significant humanistic value – the freedom of choice. Freedom without responsibility turns into whimsical egotism. Genuine freedom is not regulated by conventions, but by conscientiousness and responsibility to someone or something. As Maslow was saying, freedom requires "independence of culture and environment,"[86] and life between freedom and responsibility exacts great courage. This is why some existential thinkers assert that the bottom line of maturity reflects in how much bravery we have in facing numerous moral dilemmas and challenges of existence.

Psychologists have listed many other characteristics as signs of higher personal maturity. They vary in a wide range from economic maturity[87] (which implies a well-balanced relationship with money and an ability to resist the challenges of rushing after it) to the acceptance of the inevitable fear of suffering and death. Within this range of characteristics are optimism, creativity, individuality, the occasional need for solitude, benevolent humor, and spontaneity. A mature person cannot be distressed out of one's mind by a piece of criticism or euphorically enthralled by a praise (or even worse – by flattery). Psychoanalysts would add that maturity cannot be attained without a successful resolution of the Oedipal complex (which cannot be objected to) and without the completion of total intercourse with a person of the opposite sex (which is a much more contested idea in contemporary psychology). "There are innumerable instances of celibates, both male and female, and even of sexual deviants, whose accomplishments and whose conduct are so outstanding that we cannot possibly consider them as 'immature.'"[88] By "sexual deviants," Allport probably meant homosexuals (not those with paraphilias such as pedophilia or the like), who, in the early 1960s, when he was writing hisbook *Pattern and Growth in Personality*, were still considered mentally ill.

The attainment of a high level of personal maturity does not mean that all individuals who achieve it go in the same direction. Personality styles and values that we cherish vary considerably. Of course, an understanding of the hierarchy of values is an inescapable criterion of maturity. For example, a person who inconsolably cries over a dead cat but has no empathy whatsoever for humans (like Mother Imelda, a nun in Karen Armstrong's[89] autobiographical book *Through the Narrow Gate*) does not reflect any kind of emotional balance or an understanding of the hierarchy of values.

On the other hand, however, there is not only one category of values at a single level of the hierarchy. There are more of them. In Hinduism, the religion that has traditionally shown sensibility for various types of psychological personality types, there are multiple paths to salvation through various forms of yoga (or, more precisely, of getting in touch with the metaphysical source: "The word *yoga* derives from the same root as does the English word yoke, and yoke carries a double connotation: to unite (yoke together), and to place under disciplined training"[90]. There are four dominant ways of yoga: through knowledge (*jnana*), through devotion (*bhakti*), through work (*karma*), and through psychophysical exercise (*raja*). At a certain level, all of these different ways are valid. The same holds true for the values pursued by a psychologically mature person. In the life of such person, these values exist as goals toward which most of the activities and life efforts are driven. Allport calls these framework values "the unifying philosophy of life,"[91] because all of these individual aspects of maturity are being integrated in a concrete manner and directed in a certain way. Charlotte Bühler uses for this the German word *Bestimmung*, which is difficult to translate but means something along the lines of general direction. Some people only have one goal toward which they direct their potential; some have several smaller goals. Psychologists do not agree on whether there is a definite number of such unifying life philosophies or not. Bühler does not propose any specific number, while Eduard Spranger lists six basic types people strive toward: theoretic (the question of truth being the main preoccupation), economic (usefulness), aesthetic (shape and form), social (love for people), political (power), and religious (unity).[92]

Thus, in its practical form, maturity does not represent an abstract diffusion, but a concrete orientation toward a goal-deemed valuable.

In order for all of the previously described values and characteristics of psychological maturity to get inner cohesion and unity around a meaningful kernel, the character of the individual necessarily needs to be ethically integrated. Without morality, there is no normality. If a person possesses prominent qualities in the domain of the intellect, creativity, or whatever else, but is "unsure about the difference between right and wrong in daily living,"[93] that person cannot be called mature in the full psycho-ethical sense. Although it is natural for a human being to have moral dilemmas instead of moral certainty in many life situations, due to complex variations and dynamics of different values at a given moment, a mature person has a relatively clearer sense of what is good and what is not. In the social context, this implies a high degree of tolerance for the different, primarily in an ethnic, religious, political, sexual, racial sense. For Maslow, "ethical certainty" and "democratic character structure"[94] are unavoidable categories of healthy personal roundedness. Just like a self-realized *brahmin*[95] sees in every living entity the qualitatively identical spiritual soul, so Maslow considers that a mature person shows "respect to any human being just because he is a human individual."[96]

The ethical dimension belongs to the cluster of higher dimensions of being. Any relativizing of moral values (not the traditionalistic, but essential ones) is a short-lived affair, despite the fact that the history of humankind abounds in such endeavors.

Even though morality is usually treated as a category separate from spirituality, perhaps "the development of autonomous morality [...] could be the 'link' that connects and enables the continuation of growth, i.e. the transition from the psychological to the spiritual sphere of development."[97] Lawrence Kohlberg, a psychologist who, in the mid-1980s, set the principles of the (so far) most widely accepted psychological theory of the six levels of moral development, subsequently introduced the seventh level, calling it "religious orientation."[98] Ethical questions "are not eventually answered by logic or reasoning,"[99] hence the necessity to introduce the "cosmic" or the perspective of "eternity" into their resolution. Not all of us decide to move on from the moral to the spiritual level, "such a perspective is a matter of aspiration."[100] The most important thing is to respect the decisions of those who decide to explore their spirituality as well as of those who do not.

Reality spreads through multiple landscapes, some of which are covered by the fog of the inexplicable. Several of us pause before those landscapes and decide not to go further on, while others muster enough adventurousness to explore the misty counties. In other words, some decide not to tackle the indecipherable questions of spirituality, while some decide to plunge into them. Whether this decision, to let into one's life the questions of spirituality or not, is a criterion of personal maturity is very difficult to say. Psychologists are also divided on this matter, with attitudes ranging from Freud's famous conviction that religion "comprises a system of wishful illusions together with a disavowal of reality"[101] and an "individual obsessional neurosis"[102] (basically meaning that anyone who is religious in fact has mental problems), to the stance that "some kind of spiritual life is necessary for psychic health."[103] Although I slightly side with the idea that mature religiosity contributes to the richness and integrity of an individual, I do not want to pass any judgments of one kind or the other, simply because I am not completely sure that my attitude is the right one. My task here is to describe a mature, and particularly an immature, person and her or his spirituality, not to make qualifications whether theism is more adequate than atheism, or vice versa. Both can be either mature or immature, and the particular interest of this book is the description of both types of immaturities. If psychologically mature, neither an atheist nor a believer will come into a conflict. Viktor Frankl thinks that a believer has gone one step further and that it is he or she who, from a higher position, should tolerantly accept those who decide not to admit spirituality as an important dimension into their lives. "Human freedom extends greatly and the Creator made humans so free that this freedom includes even the freedom to deny God, and that a human being is free to be against their Creator, that they can negate God."[104]

Abraham Maslow gave quite a poetical name to one of his criteria of maturity: "limitless horizons." It implies a "concern with the ultimate nature of reality"[105] and gives the individual a "mystical," "religious," i.e. an "oceanic" hue of maturity. The nature of religious maturity, whether seen as a necessary element of overall maturity or not, will be discussed in a later chapter.

A mature person is not a slave of inhibitions and conflicts and "does not manifest abnormal instinctive urges or hypertrophied and pathological superego."[106] Such a person is less defensive, egoistical, mistrustful, and does not show developmental standstills, fixations, or regressions. Generally, maturity implies personal integration ("a harmony among impulses, tendencies, desires, thoughts, etc., within the psyche"[107]). All the aforementioned characteristics amalgamate in a person, with inter-dialectics that are always syncretic, never atomistic.

The most mature individuals in history (some psychologists, like Maslow, Bühler, and Erikson, studied their psychological portraits) were still not completely devoid of inner contradictions, nor did they possess perfect self-control in every moment, or a crystal clear insight into objective reality. "Minor foibles and foolishness existed in even the most clearly self-actualizing lives."[108] On the path toward greater maturity fallouts are integral parts of the process, and the absolute ideals are ultimately unattainable, but what indubitably makes us human is the potential to actualize a certain extent of maturity in our lives.

Psychological Immaturity

Human nature incorporates a large number of psychic characteristics, all of which stretch throughout their own wide gamut ranging from the positive to the negative end on the continuum of that characteristic. To make things even more complicated for the analysis of human nature, these characteristics extend through dimensions of existence that largely abide in the lightlessness of the unconscious. Hence, it seems impossible to identify every single trait of an individual character. Still, if we imagined that a comprehensive and exact overview of the elements that comprise personality were possible, we are coming upon a second, seemingly even more insurmountable obstacle – how to grasp all the complex interrelationships and dynamics of individual elements that comprise a human character, and how to understand the principles based on which these elements round up in a single whole. Lucid insights in the psychological wisdom of human nature in the last hundred odd years contributed to the drastic improvement in our understanding of it, but the unresolvable remnants will always be there to confuse and surprise us.

The knowledge of the nature of personality is relative, conditioned, and partly intuitive. This is why any conclusion drawn from this knowledge is unavoidably either equally or perhaps even more relative, conditioned, and intuitive. The aforesaid holds true for the points on psychological maturity examined in the previous section, but also for the points of psychological immaturity that are to follow in this one. The two mentioned concepts may sound like opposites, but in real life, it would be difficult to find a concrete mature psychological profile that stands as an antipode to another concrete immature psychological profile. Rather, we are talking about relative maturity and relative immaturity, because the boundaries between them are elastic, imprecise, and porous. This is why it makes sense to introduce terms such as "zones of maturity" and "zones of immaturity," two partly overlapping, though insufficiently sharply defined, sets of characteristics. The zones of immaturity may at a certain point start to transgress into "zones of abnormality," with reduced functionality and communication with the outside world. The extreme cases of psychotic mental illness, however, are not in the focus of this book.

The terms maturity and immaturity imply genesis. Maturity is a degree attained when, after some time, the conditions for the transfer to a higher qualitative level are met (they exist as potentialities in human nature), and immaturity means either stagnating at the same qualitative level for a long time or attaining insufficient levels of quality. Environmental factors are very important. An apple ripening in the sun grows larger, juicier, more sweet-scented than the one hidden under the leaves in the middle of the treetop. However, people depend less on the factors of the natural environment than other living entities, and the extent and the nature of environmental influences are not predictably clear.

Children are naturally egoistic, manipulative, and dependent, while these same features in an adult represent marks of immaturity. For certain reasons, such people did not manage to traverse the path "from possessiveness to the stage of unselfishness, from dependence to autonomy, from egocentrism in relating with others to socialization."[109] Psychology usually seeks reasons for this in a person's early childhood and in the relationship of the parents with the child. If they live in an atmosphere of fear, danger, and insecurity, children may well develop what Karen Horney calls "basic anxiety."[110] Children try to look for a way out of this basic anxiety, but since their capacities are not developed, the "solutions" they come up with are mostly inadequate. "Despite his own weakness and fears he unconsciously shapes his tactics to meet the particular forces operating in the environment. In doing so, he develops not only *ad hoc* strategies but lasting character trends which become part of his personality."[111] Such people undergo neurotic distortions on the psychic level and have to deal with its consequences for the rest of their lives. The impulse toward neutralization of inner conflicts and attainment of personal unity is natural, for unity enables better functioning in the world. However, if the conflict is not resolved at the root level, but an attempt is made to eliminate it by improvization, it only grows more powerful, more destructive, and more unconscious. "A spurious tranquillity rooted in inner dullness is anything but enviable."[112]

The question of absolute maturity frequently comes to the fore when ideal psychological health is considered, but it is inconceivable to ask about absolute immaturity, perhaps because it is not a goal to be striven for. Most frequently, immaturity is characteristic only for certain personality domains, "unlike the rest of the psyche that sometimes 'grows' disproportionately, based on a compensatory principle."[113] At times, these hypertrophied components of personality may point to an immaturity at the core. With immaturity, just like with maturity, it is much more difficult to talk about an all-encompassing interaction of its individual segments than about the segments themselves (which this modest undertaking does not even pretend to achieve). What follows are descriptions of separate characteristics of psychological immaturity.

The description of an immature personality can also start at any given feature, because it is difficult to single out which trait of immaturity is more important and which one is more marginal. Selfishness is certainly among the most prominent ones. Selfish individuals do not expand beyond strict boundaries of what belongs to them. "His church, his lodge, his family, and his nation make a safe unit, but all else is alien, dangerous, to be excluded from his petty formula for survival."[114]

Although such closeness from the other and the different is an express sign of immaturity, it can frequently be encountered in daily life. In certain undemocratic societies, it is even officially reinforced and encouraged. A person whose interaction with the world is barren "might become very competent at work, or attain high positions in politics, art, or in the religious field,"[115] but such success is primarily of outward nature, while inner growth is stunted.

Universal fears of danger and death remain raw and unprocessed in immature people. They most frequently repress them into the opaqueness of the unconscious, from which these fears surreptitiously perform their dysfunctional acts. The fear of death may be manifested in a number of ways, such as the neurotic need for absolute certainty, control, obsession with "the danger of knives, of high places, with health foods and medicines, with self-protective superstitions and rituals."[116] Only facing these fears and trying to accept them can unblock the basic neurotic situation. "Those who leaned to know death rather than to fear and fight it become our teachers about *life*."[117]

The way people love those close to them, and the way they treat others, reveals a lot about their degree of personal maturity. The most mature among us are those who are able to love selflessly and sanely, to show respect to others, and to find understanding for them. Personal immaturity is best and most frequently reflected in the very playfield of social relationships. An immature person's love contains pathological admixtures of possessiveness, control, jealousy, and authority over the person they love. They are not ready to love unconditionally. In many cases, personal shortcomings and inner conflicts are sought to be resolved through romantic relationships instead of at the individual level. Such situations make a partner more of an instrument than as an object of love.

At an even more serious level of immaturity, there is no readiness for more profound affective relationships at all. Such people function only within the domain of superficial acquaintances and poor emotionality toward those they are closely related to. When immaturity crosses the threshold of sociopathy, the individual is completely devoid of the capacity to love; they show emotional coldness and a lack of empathy and understanding. The lack of love for others unavoidably reflects on the inability to love oneself.

In more general social relationships, the functioning of immature individuals shows variegated maladaptation, ranging from social isolation on one side to clinging manipulation and dependency on the other. What characterizes such people are mistrust, inconsistency, unreliability, irresponsibility, stereotypy, absence of valid ethical judgment, great expectations and demands of others, and relying on other people's potentials. Depending on the personality style, social maladaptation acquires various specific variations.

An immature person is prone to overly complain and is frequently disproportionately critical of other people and social phenomena. At the same time, they find it hard or impossible to accept any criticism on their own account, but instead expect admiration, compliance, justification, and protection. They also do not possess a capacity to joke at their own expense, and their sense of humor is likely to be unsophisticated and "consists usually of absurdities, horse play, or [...] the degradation of some imagined opponent."[118] An objective attitude to either time or money is lacking, as well as concern for the social and physical environment. An immature person is sometimes passive, listless, aimless, with decreased or extinct creativity, devoid of productive tension, without social initiative, while sometimes all of these features are hypertrophied in an opposite direction. Due to their neurotic and defensive patterns, overly immature people generally miss out on essentially valuable life experiences, all the while perpetuating unrealizable dreams. An immature human being sometimes loses the capacity "to wish for anything wholeheartedly because his very wishes are divided, that is, go in opposite directions"[119] (which is a reflection of the conflict of opposing, usually unconscious neurotic traits in the depth of the psyche[120]). Such people are generally closed off to new experiences, because the notion of stirring the heart of the neurosis in any way causes them fear and panic.

Strongly neurotic individuals are neither able to see the world around them in an objective way nor to see their own selves objectively. One of the most unfortunate consequences of the frustrated process of maturation is the failure of these people to know their true selves. Without communication with the most intimate and genuine emotions, ideas, and needs, or, in other words, with the noetic core, we see ourselves as strangers. In order to tolerate such inner captivity, we dress this unknown, frightening, and generally hated person in a rationally tailored suit of what we should look like and, finally, who we should be. We lose empathy and love for ourselves, and once we cut ties with our own genuine personality, we are simply unable to hold anyone else in great esteem, either. "When we deny our feelings, we deny that others feel."[121] Instead of an organic connection with the core of our personality, we try to present a picture of ourselves that we have created in our minds. In these attempts, genuine emotions and character traits only represent obstacles, so we replace them with fabricated surrogates. We endorse affectation instead of emotionality and express inauthentic intellectual, aesthetic, social, spiritual interests, thus trying to manipulate others' perception of us. However, "the affected person is not aware that his deception is transparent or that his pose is unbecoming."[122] Only a mature person "knows that he cannot counterfeit a personality."[123]

Certain characteristics of immaturity are specific for certain personality types only, or even for only a concrete individual, since "every clinical case is a world of its own."[124] Still, if we were to point out some common tendencies of immaturity along with the previously described ones, the following could be added to the list: pronounced urges, inner conflicts, inhibitions, and defensiveness. Whatever personality elements people possess, they attempt to use what they have in order to construct a unified entity, which represents "the practical necessity to function in life"[125] and is quite natural. The problem here lies in the fact that this unity is built upon unhealthy foundations, and due to strong defensiveness, these foundations are never reexamined, but endlessly perpetuated.

"Neurosis [...] is always a matter of degree."[126] The difference "between an ill and a healthy person lies only [...] in the degree, not in the kind, i.e. it is a quantitative not a qualitative difference, since every normal person is only approximating normality, for they are also bearers of psychopathology, to a greater or lesser extent."[127] The boundaries are not easily defined; this is why it might make sense to talk about the zones of illness and health. What determines psychopathology is "the level and intensity [...] of immature kernels."[128] In regular circumstances, people sometimes manage to maintain functionality despite inner pathological content, but amid circumstances of heightened stress or trauma, this stability is usually decomposed, and it oversteps into the zone of a higher degree of dysfunctionality.

Although the idea of imprecise boundaries between health and illness has been mentioned several times, it is still possible to identify "some clear elements of abnormality,"[129] such as irrationality, maladjustment, unpredictability, aggressiveness, and many more. When all of these "become more intense and rigid so as to thwart (in part or in total) the communication with the outside world,"[130] we can speak of more serious mental illness. This book will be less about such forms of psychopathology, because religiosity of a person who does not communicate with the world is inevitably hermetic and pathological (even though such statements could be contested[131]). More attention will be paid to cases of personality disorders in which it is trickier to recognize pathological religiosity. Such religious morbidity that is more difficult to discern has a more devastating effect than the obviously pathological, both for the person who perpetuates it and for others. Here we can include people with serious immaturities as well as those with personality disorders, who "range within the wide area between mental sanity and illness."[132]

Notes

1 Gordon Allport, *Pattern and Growth in Personality*, New York: Holt, Rinehart and Wilson, 1961, p. 140.
2 Huston Smith, *Forgotten Truth*, New York: Harper Colophon, 1977, p. 63.
3 *Ibid.*, p. 68.
4 *Ibid.*, p. 63.
5 Sir John Eccles, as quoted from: *Ibid.*, p. 65.
6 Huston Smith, *Forgotten Truth*, p. 64.
7 *Bhagavad Gītā As It Is*, purported by Swami Prabhupada, New York: Collier Books, 1972, p. 365.
8 William S. Haubrich, *Medical Meanings: A Glossary of Word Origins*, Philadelphia, PA: American College of Physicians, 2003, p. 195.
9 *Ibid.*

10 "coveka kao trojstva duha, duse i tela," Snezana Milenkovic, *Psihoterapija i duhovnost*, Belgrade: Cigoja stampa, 2002, p. 260.
11 See: *Bhagavad Gītā As It Is*, p. 365.
12 See: Viktor Frankl, *Man's Search for Ultimate Meaning*, New York: Basic Books, 2000, p. 34.
13 *Ibid.*, p. 35.
14 *Ibid.*
15 *Ibid.*, p. 36.
16 Viktor Frankl, quoted from: Ann V. Graber, *Viktor Frankl's Logotherapy*, Lima, OH: Wyndham Hall Press, 2010, p. 46.
17 See: *Ibid.*
18 Huston Smith, *Forgotten Truth*, p. 74.
19 *Ibid.*
20 See: Ann V. Graber, *op. cit.*, p. 29.
21 Huston Smith, *Forgotten Truth*, p. 79.
22 "prolazna i kratka," Abraham Maslow, *O zivotnim vrednostima*, tr. Aleksandar Dimitrijevic, Belgrade: Zarko Albulj, 2001, p. 99.
23 Huston Smith, *Forgotten Truth*, p. 87.
24 Viktor Frankl, *The Will to Meaning*, New York: A Meridian Book, 1988, p. 22.
25 "nasa zavisnost od spoljasnjih uticaja je skoro apslutna [...] fleksibilna i zamenljiva [...] postoji slobodan izbor kada smo suoceni sa spoljasnjim situacijama," Elisabeth Lukas, quoted from: Snezana Milenkovic, *op. cit.*, p. 73.
26 John Milton, *Paradise Lost*, *The English Poems of John Milton*, Ware: Wordsworth, 2004, p. 143.
27 "ljudsko i duhovno," Snezana Milenkovic, *op. cit.*, p. 8.
28 Viktor Frankl, *Man's Search for Ultimate Meaning*, p. 32.
29 Sir Charles Sherrington, quoted by Huston Smith in: *Forgotten Truth*, p. 67.
30 Viktor Frankl, *Man's Search for Ultimate Meaning*, p. 33.
31 *Ibid.*
32 *Ibid.*, p. 32.
33 *Ibid.*
34 William James, *The Varieties of Religious Experience*, Harmondsworth: Penguin, 1987, p. 357.
35 Viktor Frankl, *Man's Search for Ultimate Meaning*, p. 34.
36 Danah Zohar and Ian Marshall are among the most important contemporary scholars who write about the SQ factor, i.e. the spiritual intelligence
37 "vrednostima 'bica' [...] koje su intrinzicne, koje se ne mogu svesti na nesto temeljnije," Abraham Maslow, *op. cit.*, p. 17.
38 Viktor Frankl, *Man's Search for Ultimate Meaning*, p. 39.
39 *Ibid.*, p. 36.
40 "nakon integracije (uspesno okoncanog psiholoskog razvoja) koja se može postici kroz praksu psihoterapije, pojedinac nastavlja put dalje u pravcu duhovnog razvoja, u pravcu prevazilazenja, transcendiranja selfa," Snezana Milenkovic, *op. cit.*, p. 217.
41 Viktor Frankl, *Man's Search for Ultimate Meaning*, p. 68.
42 "dopustiti nasim neizvesnostima da postoje," Snezana Milenkovic, *op. cit.*, p. 204.
43 Viktor Frankl, *Man's Search for Ultimate Meaning*, p. 36.
44 Daniel Helminiak is a Catholic priest, theologian, and professor of Transpersonal Psychology at the University of West Georgia.
45 A phrase also used by Jung's student and disciple Erich Neumann, see: Snezana Milenkovic, *op. cit.*, p. 107.

46 Ludwig Biswanger, quoted from: Viktor Frankl, *Man's Search for Ultimate Meaning*, p. 32.
47 Viktor Frankl, *Man's Search for Ultimate Meaning*, p. 44.
48 "nikad ne moze, bez nasilja, iz prostora duhovnosti projicirati na nizu razinu psihicnosti," Viktor Frankl, *Bog podsvesti*, tr. D. Petrovic, Belgrade: Zarko Albulj, 2001, p. 55.
49 "je njihov broj mali," Srboljub Stojiljkovic, *Psihijatrija, sa medicinskom psihologijom*, Belgrade, Zagreb: Medicinska knjiga, 1979, p. 159.
50 "idealna normalnost samo jedan apstraktan pojam, i ne srece se u klinickom iskustvu," a footnote in: Giacomo Dacquino, *Religioznost i psihoanaliza*, tr. Silvana Trosanski-Mircevic, Belgrade: Plato, 2005, p. 92.
51 Gordon Allport, *Pattern and Growth in Personality*, p. 277.
52 "Velik broj ljudi pokazuje izvesna manja ili veca odstupanja od 'idealnog normalnog', drugi, pak pokazuju manje ili vece nastranosti, treci dovode svoju okolinu u situaciju da trpi od njihovih nastranosti, a jedan, znatno manji broj ispoljava upadljive znake dusevnih poremecaja," Srboljub Stojiljkovic, *op. cit.*, pp. 159–160.
53 Gordon Allport, *Pattern and Growth in Personality*, p. 276.
54 *Ibid.*, p. 277.
55 *Ibid.*
56 *Ibid.*, p. 279.
57 "takva licnost stoji na sopstvenim nogama i ne postavlja preterane zahteve drugima," quoted from: Srboljub Stojiljkovic, *op. cit.*, p. 161.
58 "zrelost znaci da smo od oslonaca i uporista koja smo trazili i nalazili spolja presli na one unutrasnje," quoted from: Snezana Milenkovic, *op. cit.*, p. 232.
59 Gordon Allport, *Pattern and Growth in Personality*, p. 276.
60 Howard Dully and Charles Fleming, *My Lobotomy*, New York: *Three Rivers Press*, 2008, p. 67.
61 See: John Colapinto, *As Nature Made Him: The Boy Who Was Raised as a Girl*, New York: HarperCollins, 2013.
62 Timothy F. Murphy, "Experiments in Gender: Ethics at the Boundaries of Clinical Practice and Research," *Ethics and Intersex*, ed. Sharon E. Systma, Dordecht: Springer, 2006, p. 146.
63 John Firman and Ann Gila, *Psychosynthesis: A Psychology of the Spirit*, Albany: State University Of New York Press, 2002, p. 19.
64 In his latest biography *Becoming Myself*, Irvin Yalom gives a slightly different view of Frankl, describing him as someone who was extremely interested in accentuating his legacy and personality
65 See: Gordon Allport, *Pattern and Growth in Personality*, p. 292.
66 "Pokusavati da gospodarimo stvarima i drzimo ih cvrsto pod kontrolom moze biti agresivno i samodestruktivno, jer na taj nacin silimo sebe da negiramo i manipulisemo vlastitim iskustvom, koje se ne uklapa u 'pozeljnu' sliku o sebi samima," Snezana Milenkovic, *op. cit.*, p. 204.
67 Andrew Solomon, *The Noonday Demon*, New York: Scribner, 2001, p. 433.
68 "Katha Upanisad," *Upanisads*, tr. Patrick Olivelle, Oxford: Oxford University Press, 1996, p. 240.
69 See the fourth part of *Gulliver's Travels,* depicting the land of horses, or Houyhnhnms, and their human-like servants, Yahoos: Jonathan Swift, *Gulliver's Travels*, London: Penguin, 1994, pp. 240–329.
70 Gordon Allport, *Pattern and Growth in Personality*, p. 288.
71 *Ibid.*, p. 283.
72 Viktor Frankl, *Psychotherapy and Existentialism*, New York: Washington Square Press, 1967, p. 12.

73 Gordon Allport, *Pattern and Growth in Personality*, p. 283.
74 *Ibid.*
75 *Ibid.*, pp. 283–284.
76 *Ibid.*, p. 285.
77 *Ibid.*, p. 283.
78 See: *Ibid.*, p. 279.
79 "pokazuje adaptaciju koherentnu drustvu," Giacomo Dacquino, *op. cit.*, p. 90.
80 "licnog integriteta i pod pritiskom grupe," *Ibid.*, p. 91.
81 "zamenjivanje ambijentalne kontrole autokontrolom," *Ibid.*
82 "primarno 'Ja' instinkata i zadovoljstva razvija u sekundarno zrelo 'Ja' (realnosti), koje je odbacilo princip zadovoljstva i adaptiralo se na stvarnost," *Ibid.*, p. 92.
83 Viktor Frankl, *The Unheard Cry for Meaning*, New York: Touchstone, 1979, p. 23.
84 *Ibid.*, p. 82.
85 Gordon Allport, *Pattern and Growth in Personality*, p. 290.
86 Abraham Maslow, quoted from: *Ibid.*, p. 280.
87 See: Gordon Allport, *Pattern and Growth in Personality*, p. 290.
88 *Ibid.*, p. 287.
89 "They celebrate when one of their sisters dies, but look at the emotion produced when something happens to a cat! There was something wrong here. Something I did not want to understand." Karen Armstrong, *Through the Narrow Gate*, London: Flamingo, 1998, p. 226.
90 Huston Smith, *The World's Religions*, New York: Harper One, 2009, p. 27.
91 See: Gordon Allport, *Pattern and Growth in Personality*, p. 294.
92 See: Eduard Spranger, *Types of Men: The Psychology and Ethics of Personality*, Halle: M. Niemeyer, 1928, pp. 109–240.
93 Abraham Maslow, quoted from: Gordon Allport, *Pattern and Growth in Personality*, p. 281.
94 See: *Ibid.*
95 One of the four major castes in Hinduism; "priests and the teachers of religion" ("svestenici i učitelji religije"), K. M. Sen, *Hinduizam*, tr. Vesna Mladenovic, Belgrade: Decja knjiga, 1990, p. 36.
96 Abraham Maslow, quoted from: Gordon Allport, *Pattern and Growth in Personality*, p. 281.
97 "razvitak autonomne moralnosti [...] mogao da bude ona 'kopca' koja povezuje i omogucava nastavak razvoja, odnosno prelazak iz dusevne u duhovnu sferu razvoja," Snezana Milenkovic, *op. cit.*, p. 81.
98 Marion Smith, "Religious Education," *Lawrence Kohlberg: Consensus and Controversy*, ed. Sohan Modgil and Celia Modgil, New York: Routledge, 2011, p. 280.
99 *Ibid.*
100 *Ibid.*
101 Sigmund Freud, *The Future of an Illusion*, tr. and ed. James Starchey, New York: W. W. Norton, 1961, p. 43.
102 *Ibid.*
103 "neka vrsta duhovnog zivota neophodna za psihicko zdravlje," Snezana Milenkovic, *op. cit.*, p. 81.
104 "Covjek je do te mjere slobodan i od Stvoritelja tako slobodnim stvoren da ta sloboda ide do slobode nijekanja i da se stvor moze odluciti protiv svog Stvoritelja, da moze Boga poreci," Viktor Frankl, *Bog podsvesti*, p. 56.
105 Gordon Allport, *Pattern and Growth in Personality*, p. 280.
106 "ne pokazuje abnormalne instinktivne nagone ili hipertroficno i patolosko Nad-ja," Giacomo Dacquino, *op. cit.*, p. 91.

107 "harmoniju izmedju nagona, teznji, zelja, misli, itd. unutar psihizma," a footnote in: Giacomo Dacquino, *op. cit.*, p. 91.
108 Gordon Allport, *Pattern and Growth in Personality*, p. 276.
109 "od posesivnosti do stadijuma davanja, od zavisnosti ka autonomiji, od egocentrizma prema relaciji sa drugima i ka socijalizaciji," Giacomo Dacquino, *op. cit.*, p. 118.
110 Karen Horney, *Our Inner Conflicts*, Abingdon: Routledge, 2001, p. 41.
111 *Ibid.*, p. 42.
112 *Ibid.*, p. 28.
113 "za razliku od ostatka psihizma koji 'raste', cesto i prekomjerno, zbog kompenzacije," Giacomo Dacquino, *op. cit.*, p. 119.
114 Gordon Allport, *Pattern and Growth in Personality*, p. 286.
115 "cak moze biti veoma sposoban na poslu, i dostici visoke pozicije u politici, umetnosti ili na religioznom polju," Giacomo Dacquino, *op. cit.*, p. 123.
116 Gordon Allport, *Pattern and Growth in Personality*, p. 288.
117 Elizabeth Kübler-Ross, *On Children and Death*, New York: Touchstone, 1997, p. xiii.
118 Gordon Allport, *Pattern and Growth in Personality*, pp. 292–293.
119 Karen Horney, *Our Inner Conflicts*, p. 37.
120 See: *Ibid.*, p. 19.
121 Alexander Lowen, *Narcissism, Denial of the True Self*, New York: Touchstone, 2004, p. 49.
122 Gordon Allport, *Pattern and Growth in Personality*, p. 294.
123 *Ibid.*
124 "svaki klinicki slucaj gradi svet za sebe," Giacomo Dacquino, *op. cit.*, p. 121.
125 Karen Horney, *Our Inner Conflicts*, p. 54.
126 *Ibid.*, p. 28.
127 "izmedju bolesne i zdrave osobe postoji samo [...] u stepenu, a ne u vrsti, tj. kvantitativna a ne kvalitativna razlika, posto je svaka normalna osoba takva samo priblizno, jer je i ona nosilac psihopatologije, u manjoj ili ve'oj meri," Giacomo Dacquino, *op. cit.*, p. 121.
128 "nivo i intenzitet [...] nezrelih jezgara," *Ibid.*
129 James Butcher et al., *Abnormal Psychology*, Boston: Pearson, 2004, p. 5.
130 "dobiju takav obim i rigidnost da sprecavaju (delimicno ili potpuno) komunikaciju sa svetom," Giacomo Dacquino, *op. cit.*, p. 122.
131 Some authors accept the possibility of healthy religiosity even in patients with severe psychotic illnesses. Viktor Frankl calls this potential the "psycho-noëtic antagonism which is an inherent capacity in a human being – that is, man's faculty as a spiritual being to freely take a stand toward inner as well as outer conditions." Viktor Frankl, *The Doctor and the Soul*, New York: Vintage Books, 1973, p. 260.
132 "u sirokoj oblasti izmedju dusevnog zdravlja i dusevne bolesti," Srboljub Stojiljkovic, *op. cit.*, p. 162.

2 Generally on Religion

Dilemmas and uncertainties underlie everyday life, from the most banal to the most subtle aspects of existence. There are very few things we can be absolutely sure about, if any. An urge for absolute certainty in as many things as possible represents a classical sign of neuroticism. Doubting is natural; there is just one thing absolutely no one should have any doubts about (although in reality some people do), and that thing is a certain dose of mystery in life. "Human experience combines 'nature' and 'spirit,' and people function simultaneously in these two dimensions."[1] There are not only Darwin's, Marx's, or Freud's games in the world's courtyard.[2] All that belongs to the sphere of "spirit" is largely inexplicable, ineffable, and unprovable. Of course, rationalistic minds think that reason can explain everything, and if there is currently no rational explanation for certain phenomena, the answers will most certainly be reached in the future. Many of them probably will, but to negate everything that is inexplicable is not mature. Such a stance based on oversimplification and, in essence, psychological defensiveness disregards a whole chunky slice of reality. The reader who thinks that everything in this world is explicable better drop this book right away to avoid being irritated by the standpoint that lies at the heart of it – the standpoint that mystery undeniably exists. Or, more precisely, in an all-encompassing reality, overly abundant with facts of diverse nature, distributed on various levels, there is a certain set of elements that does not let the X-rays of our reason through, and "that seem[s] always to have been an essential component of the human experience of this beautiful yet terrifying world."[3] Let us imagine that we lived in an idyllic landscape, dotted with woods and pastures, log cabins and hillocks, and that in the midst of this landscape, there was a lake, dark blue and clear and immeasurably deep. This lake gives life to all of us, stirs our imagination, brings us together, frightens us, and is an inexhaustible source of stories, legends, and dreams. Such a lake exists in the life of every human being and is lodged at that remnant which represents reality outside of time and space, and which is the raw material of every religion.[4]

In this book, the term mystery does not imply only rare and exotic phenomena such as the Bermuda Triangle or crystal skulls. Primarily it refers to the edges of reality that rub off on our lives in passing by day in day out, and which, unlike the solid but temporary elements of this world, are immersed in eternity. The ultimate Truth, if it exists (and I lean more toward the idea that it does than that it does not), includes both the finite and the infinite. Besides, truth "is something indivisible... Hence, the intellect, which is not truth, never comprehends truth so precisely that truth cannot be comprehended infinitely more precisely."[5]

The finite domain, although in itself infinitely complex, might be approachable to the human intellect, though not to the intellect of a certain individual (for no single person is able to possess the totality of material knowledge) but to that of the human collectivity. However, "Human beings cannot fully know the Infinite. Intimations of it seep into us occasionally, but more than this we cannot manage on our own."[6] Phenomena of infinity cannot be approached using the logical–rationalistic methodology, but a methodology based on instruments of numinous–intuitive nature. Religion is the sphere that deals with the aspects of the infinity of the spirit, and more or less directly with all other forms of infiniteness, too.

The elasticity and the indestructability of the religious thought throughout human history, despite radical scientific breakthroughs, corroborate the fact that the world in its essentialness is "marbled with inconsistency, paradox, and contradiction,"[7] and that this elusive heart of the world is in fact a mystery which we are "neither able to resolve nor to abandon."[8] The reason "had never been able to provide human beings with the sense of significance they seemed to require."[9] All those who set sail for the discovery of the inner worlds are explorers in their own right as great as Columbus or Cook,[10] or perhaps even greater, for the territories they explored were enshrouded in "dazzling obscurity,"[11] and the only compass to navigate through "experiences that are obscure and ineffable"[12] was their intuition and subjective experiences of sailing towards Truth. Of course, if there were no objective correlatives and clear guidelines, a journey into madness might also be mistaken for a discovery of oceans in fog. These correlatives and guidelines are discussed a little later in this book.

We continue the analysis of personal religiosity without taking into consideration the scholarly attempts at defining religion as a phenomenon, because the search for the most adequate definition could be endless. Besides, the ambition of this book is not to deal with religion *per se*. Even the most approximate definition (for a perfect one does not exist) would not give a particularly significant contribution to the aims of this book. Some authors who examine religion *per se* think that "the study of religion requires no *universal* definition,"[13] and "scholars have [...] largely abandoned the effort to do so."[14] Hence, it will suffice to say that in this work, religion is understood as a "a generic concept, designating the totality of all belief systems,"[15] which has an aim to "widen understanding, give meaning, provide solace, promote loving-kindness, and connect human being to human being."[16] The importance of the ability to face suffering and death must also not be forgotten, as well as ethical questions (although religion is "more than morality, but if it lacks a moral base it will not stand"[17]). On the other hand, many of its aspects will simply have to be omitted, due to the complexity of religiosity in an individual life. It must be pointed out that the only approaches unacceptable for this book are the reductionistic and the mechanistic ones (which is quite clear from the aforementioned). Rather, we side with Mircea Eliade's qualification that religion is autonomous, i.e. "in its origin and function it is not a byproduct of other systems (for example, economy or society), it does not depend on them, and does not generate them."[18] Of course, the heart of religion is immersed in the unavoidable mystery mentioned at the beginning of this chapter. If we were to sublimate religion into a single word, that word would most likely have at its base the Greek term *musteion*, which means "to close the eyes or the mouth."[19]

"Religion in its purest form is a vast work of poetry."[20] This comparison is based on the notion that the sources of religion and poetry originate in the profound noetic layers of personality. Since the noetic content cannot be revealed to the rational mind in its fullness, what reaches the reason are only the echoes and circuitous brushes. This is why poetry (or rather overall art) and faith have similar roots – elusive, symbolic, powerful. Just as poetry marches on for centuries tirelessly talking about love, so religion in the same way does not tire of the idea of God. Neither of them explains what love or God is. Religion "encompasses a great diversity of phenomena, even within a single tradition,"[21] and God denotes "a whole spectrum of meanings, some of which are contradictory or even mutually exclusive."[22] What God represents in one generation, in "one set of human beings could be meaningless in another."[23] When an idea of God is worn out, it is "quietly discarded and replaced by a new theology."[24] Only "a fundamentalist would deny this."[25] The very elements that hard science has been choking on for a long time (religion's immensity and indeterminancy, among others) carry for spirituality an inexhaustible potential of energy adaptable and applicable to all people and all individuals at every single point in place and time.

Despite the feeling that the "soft voice of religion [is] stifled in postmodern cacophony,"[26] it still exists, as it has been existing from the very moment human beings "became recognizably human."[27] In case we do not have an inkling toward religious faith, we are prone to believe in some other ideal, but if we cease to be *homo religiosus* in the widest possible sense of the word (even in case we were atheists), we become *homo pathologicus*.

Religion, on the other hand, did not vanish "under the cascade of factual knowledge"[28] of contemporary science, because it is fueled by that which science, as generally accepted today, does not have a clear insight into. Not only that religion resists challenges such as scientific analyses, technological advances, individualized interpretation by every single believer; it also outlives peoples, religious traditions, and churches.[29] It seems impossible to run away from the fact of "the universal occurrence of religion in history,"[30] an idea easily corroborated by hard facts. However, the most important question that has been paradoxically neglected when discussing religion's significance is the way in which we endorse it, what we turn it into, and whether our individual interpretation of religion (which is an inevitability) resonates with religion's healthy core or not.

In his book *The Individual and His Religion*, Gordon Allport states that there are "as many varieties of religious experience as there are religiously inclined mortals upon the earth."[31] Perhaps we might boldly increase this number by abolishing the phrase "religiously inclined." Allport gives a vivid illustration of this idea using a picture of numerous believers who go to mosques on Fridays, "bending low in the direction of Mecca. The wave of conformity is like that of a vast impersonal tide. Yet, from the point of view of subjective religion, the significance of the devotion is different for each Moslem."[32] In some religions, such as, for example, Hinduism, theology emphasizes the idea that god "may appear differently to different people."[33] Every individual possesses "a personal system of metaphysics,"[34] and "each of us by nature is a *fabricator deorum*, a maker of gods."[35] A parallel can be drawn with the idiosyncrasy of each individual psychology, and psychiatrists would probably add psychopathology, too. Still, to insist only on religious differences is a short-sighted act when a wider picture of the meaning of existence is taken into account.[36] All personal metaphysics are "similar to small brooks that run into one another in order to meet God (Hari), who is like an ocean."[37]

External differences among religious traditions are great. Both scholars in religious studies and laymen sometimes claim that there is no common thread running through different religions and that "no generalization can conceivably apply to the full variety of its [religion's] expression."[38] In their opinion, "major world religions view the term God quite differently; to suggest that they are all talking about the same thing is to homogenize the concept of God illegitimately."[39] However, I am much more inclined toward the stance that all religions share the same nucleus, immersed in the lake of *mysterium tremendum*.[40] This idea has been substantiated throughout history by some of the greatest authorities in the area of religious studies, such as William James ("there is a certain composite photograph of universal saintliness, the same in all religions"[41]) Erich Fromm ("the human reality, for instance, underlying the teaching of Buddha, Isaiah, Christ, Socrates, or Spinoza is essentially the same"[42]), Mircea Eliade ("*all* religions are maps of the human mind [...] and this is why religions have so much in common"[43]), Karen Armstrong ("working in isolation from one another, and often in a state of deadly hostility, they had come up with remarkably similar conclusions"[44]), as well as many other thinkers and writers. Those who see irreconcilable differences among religions are probably under exaggerated influence of the various aspects that certain traditions emphasize. Allport called these aspects "cognitive poles,"[45] and they include deities, soul, values, freedom, sin, immortality, prayer, good deeds, dogma, and tradition.[46] The noetic reality within a being is not homogenous, and various traditions tend to pay more attention to some of these basic aspects due to historical, cultural, geographical, biological, and other reasons. It may be that some of these segments are somewhat neglected in certain religions, but they are never completely ignored.

Taking into account the historical fact of numerous enmities between religions (even though the cause of enmity is never essentially religious, but only masked by religious discourse), the question is sometimes raised whether it would be best if there only were a single, universal religion. In that case there would be no ground for religious wars. However, this idea is too naïve, the solution of the problem oversimplified, and it oversees the inevitable cultural and traditional elements that the enormous number of believers associate a certain religion with. This would also cancel out the possibility of religious diversity, as well as precious religious eclecticism. Finally, there are too many differences among people's inner needs that only one religious initiative would be sufficient for them all. The hypothetical idea of a universal religion did not sit well with many of the scholars who considered it, such as Allport, Huston Smith, Aldous Huxley, William James, and Viktor Frankl.

Every religion has a pure and healthy potential at its root, which the followers may get in touch with within themselves and move upward toward spiritual and general human development. However, in its historical experience, believers in every religion also show the tendency to distort, narrow down, and misuse the essential religious teachings. This is why it is not possible to say that there is only one true religion.[47] All of them are potentially good, and all of them can be perverted. Still, claiming "salvation as the monopoly of any one religion is like claiming that God can be found in this room but not the next, in this attire but not another."[48] As will be seen later, attitudes that religions are incompatible are characteristic of religious immaturity.

Whether we approach religion as a universal phenomenon depersonalized and homogenized at an abstract level (for methodological reasons), or we study individual religious traditions (either one or more of them), we will inevitably come across "one great partition which divides the religious field. On the one side of it lies institutional, on the other personal religion."[49] What aspects of religious life belong to institutional, and which to personal, religiosity?

Even though establishing a clear-cut distinction between the extrinsic (organized, institutional) and the intrinsic (personal, inner) religion is an "overly complex [...] and multidimensional task,"[50] it is still possible to draw a rough line between the two. The domain of the extrinsic religion covers "worship and sacrifice, procedures for working on the dispositions of the deity, theology and ceremony and ecclesiastical organization,"[51] as classically put by William James. Using more contemporary terms, James P. Carse identifies extrinsic religion in intellectual schemes, historical narratives, mythology, community, martyrs, symbols, rituals, and sites.[52] It offers the believers "answers to questions of religious character, such as those referring to the meaning of life, continuation of existence after death, what ensues after bodily demise, etc."[53] Briefly, extrinsic religion incorporates the cultural, intellectual, and social aspects of a religion.

Intrinsic religion, on the other hand, has to do with the personal (or rather private) relationship between an individual and what they perceive as the metaphysical source. Instead of a structure organized around rational principles, inner religion (sometimes also referred to as spirituality) is more of "a species of poetry,"[54] an "inward leap [...] into the unintelligible,"[55] and requires "editing out ego" for "an essential [...] religious experience."[56] Most descriptions of intrinsic religion apostrophize the redundancy of the rational and the essentialness of the supr-arational. Instead of a philosophy, that has a lot to do with extrinsic religion, spirituality relies on pure experience, germinating from "the inner dispositions of man himself which form the centre of interest, his conscience, his deserts, his helplessness, his incompleteness."[57] It seems that intrinsic religion takes root only in a mind decluttered of logical constructions and rational debris. Various religions use various methods to cleanse the mind – prayer, meditation, asceticism, hard work, absurd. The idea is to probe into the noetic core of being and tap into the inner reservoir of meaning. The deeper one goes, the higher one ascends. There is "one unsuspected depth below another"[58] and, paradoxically, or rather proverbially, "as without, so within" – the innermost ontological depths overlap with the uppermost metaphysical peaks.

The "outer" and the "inner" aspects of religion cannot be compared. They belong to qualitatively different realms. This is not to say that there is no connection between them – they are buckled up at their core. It is difficult to set up a strict division between the two, and they are usually mixed up in an individual life. Some lean more toward the extrinsic, others toward the intrinsic. The extreme margins accommodate those to whom personal religion is unknown but are loud in their religiousness, as well as those who are not involved in any form of external religious behavior but are spiritual in their own idiosyncratic way. "A participant in institutional religion may manifest either intrinsic or extrinsic religiousness, as may a nonparticipant."[59] In religious studies, schemes of development from the extrinsic toward the intrinsic have been suggested, which might be true for many believers, but real life experiences sometimes prove that those schemes are actually not working.

Bearing the aforesaid admixture of the inner and the outer in mind, what is it that finally distinguishes good religion from bad? The impossibility to claim that institutional religion is bad *per se* is clear. Can we, in the same vein, claim that intrinsic religion is impossible to be bad? Here, ay, is a tiny rub. Personal religion can go awry, but then it gets dubbed immature or, at more advanced levels of distortion, pathological. It still remains personal, but it cannot be called intrinsic any longer, because factors other than spiritual ones are at play here (primarily psychological, cultural, etc.). Besides, religious immaturity is mostly linked with the extrinsic aspects of religion. What, then, is an indicator of a good religion? Paradoxically simple (concerning all the numberless tangles of religiosity), but unarguably meaningful, is Karen Armstrong emphasis that "compassion is the test of true spirituality."[60] In case "practical compassion"[61] is missing, all other achievements of a religious lifestyle are not worth much. "All faiths insist"[62] on it, at least in their unalloyed versions. It is difficult to disagree that things are as simple as that. Beliefs can be whatever they want to be – their wholesomeness is judged only by how they are manifested in real time and how they affect real people, as well as the animate and inanimate environments.

Instead of delving deeper into the nature of religion, which is not the aim of this book, or arguing about its un/necessity in the lives of individuals, we rather just accept it as a phenomenon that has existed since the dawn of history. What is being pointed out here, though, is the criticism of both aspects of religion described earlier. This book is permeated with the criticism of intrinsic religion, or more precisely with those instances in which inner religion gets corrupt. Intrinsic religion *per se*, in its pure form, hardly deserves any criticism. Not so with the extrinsic religion. Most of the complaints people have ever addressed to religion are largely directed at its institutional aspects. Let us name but a few.

Objections against religion have been numerous, whether they come from sharp-eyed critics or from dogmatic atheists. Their diverseness might roughly be clustered into smaller categories, such as psychological, cultural, ethical, intellectual, and historical.

Where psychological shortcomings are concerned, extrinsic religion sometimes cherishes and imposes principles the psychological equivalents of which are considered utterly detrimental. Early on in religious education, children are oftentimes pumped with the "mechanisms of guilt that would probably haunt them all their lives."[63] Aldous Huxley remarked that "if children suffered agonies from the process of mental distortions at the hands of their pastors [...] we should by this time have learned something about right education."[64] In some religions, guilt is frequently imposed in connection with the body and its functions, seen as impure. The early psychoanalysts must have reacted against religion somewhere along these lines. Instead of accepting libidinal energy as an unavoidable strand in the weaving of a human being, or at least pointing to the possibility of its sublimation into spiritual energy, some religions obsessively dwell on sex as a working of the devil. Discouraged by religion to integrate sexual impulses into the framework of morality, and encouraged to repress them physically, these impulses take a life of their own subliminally, and, deemed unacceptable, distort the minds and behaviors of many.

It is no news that in many religious communities, change is equated with heresy. In the description of psychological maturity in the previous chapter, change has been mentioned as one of the adaptability prerequisites. Fear of change and of "upsetting the tranquil undemanding rhythm of our everyday lives"[65] reinforced by the urge to "quell all inner doubts"[66] is seen in psychology as a barren attempt at resolving inner conflicts that only exhausts and never resolves anything. On the other hand, in extrinsic religion, it is unquestioningly considered the right thing to do. Change is being dispelled by "absolute certainty in the truth"[67] of a particular religious dogma, which is an obvious absurd. Even the most fundamental adherents to a religion will claim that the spiritual is shut away from the tentacles of reason, but at the same time be ready to take (and more rarely to give) life for the dogmatic construct of their religion that reason alone has created. Absolute obedience and intellectual conformity are insisted upon, disregarding the hard fact that every single founder of a religion had been a nonconformist. Instead of an authentic individual search for the spiritual, people "take over the ancestral religion much as they take over the family jewels,"[68] even though the ancestral religion, if often oversimplified, infused with magical thinking, discriminatory, and alike. When people grow up under the unquestioning influence of an extrinsic religion, they come to the paradoxical situation to be "terrified by genuine expressions of religion."[69] What they find unbearable to witness is the wide display of feelings and ideas they had buried in the unapproachable depths of their psyches. This is reminiscent of the neurotics' fear of experiencing genuine emotions due to layers upon layers of defenses and avoidant ways out of the heart of neurosis. In a religious context, the "immature urgencies arising from unconscious forces"[70] feed fanaticism, which can be seen as a form of religious psychopathology.

Instead of encouraging free communication and dialogue in matters as elusive as spirituality, institutional religions more frequently address the world in the form of "broadcasting [...] or airing, or loudspeaking."[71] The standardized content of belief and traditionalistic features of maturity are thus imposed on the congregation of individuals as heterogenous (at least in psychological and spiritual terms) as are the flowers in a spring meadow. Individual attempts to question the handed-down dogmas are looked down upon, or even severely punished. Such attitudes have been more prominent in the past, but are not unfamiliar even in the most contemporary democratic societies today. Suffice it to quote a sentence from the Republican Party of Texas 2012 political platform: "We oppose the teaching of [...] critical thinking skills and similar programs that [...]

focus on behavior modification and have the purpose of challenging the student's fixed beliefs and undermining parental authority."[72] Conservative politics and conservative religion go hand in hand, with a common goal of thwarting critical thinking and preserving "fixed beliefs," thus apotheosing the letter (or literalism) and ignoring the spirit of Paul the Apostle's words that "the letter killeth, but the spirit giveth life."[73] True knowledge can never be "knowledge *against*";[74] it is inclusive, not exclusive, as extrinsic religion frequently does present it.

The pressure from religious authorities to conform finds excellent response among the masses. "Once a doctrine, however irrational, has gained power in a society, millions of people will believe in it rather than feel ostracized and isolated."[75] In such religion, the "inner demand is absent."[76] Neither do the believers show genuine spiritual needs, nor does the organized religion stoop to fulfill them. Interests of both remain at the ego level, and the requirement to present one face while privately living another breeds boundless bigotry and exposes human inconsistency – further characteristics of obvious psychological immaturity. "The pious medieval nobleman who, in church, believed in forgiving enemies and turning the other cheek, was ready, as soon as he had emerged again into the light of day, to draw his sword at the slightest provocation."[77] The modern version of medieval crusaders could be the members of mafia, for whom religion more often than not plays an important part in their overall iconography.

From the epistemological point of view, extrinsic religion's presentation of knowledge fails to offer a full picture and a key that unifies all strands. Instead, organized religion often ignores substantial elements of reality. Similar to reductionist psychological approaches, religion also tends to leave out "whole regions of experience,"[78] the only difference being the content that is left out.

Having touched upon some of the major faults authentic soul-seekers find with traditional religions, it becomes clearer that instead of cherishing peace and love, religions have had their finger in the pie of numberless wars and other nasty episodes in history. With so many malignant holes in the fabric of religious functioning, the tragic events dotting our history begin to make sense. Again, the faults are not addressed at the intrinsic religious dimension, or even at religion as a phenomenon, but to "the spirit of politics and the lust of dogmatic rule [that] are apt to enter and contaminate the originally innocent thing."[79]

Religious Maturities and Immaturities

Religious Maturity

Projecting positive and negative criticism of religion from the general onto the individual level, we will now briefly deal with the features of mature and immature personal religiosity. Positive characteristics regarding all domains of humanity are usually more uniform and less suited for artistic representation, while negative ones, being more idiosyncratic and intriguing, are presented in art more frequently and generally more strongly, hence the popularity of villains in literature and film on one side, and the paleness of highly moral characters on the other. However, popularity is not a value in itself, as it appears to undifferentiated eyes. Values lie in maturity.

Religious maturity is not necessarily related to how religious an individual is, but rather to the extent of their psychological maturity, since religiosity is "always conditioned by psychological problems."[80] This is not to say that neurosis, or in extreme cases even psychosis, "must be detrimental to the religious life of the patient."[81] Personal spirituality lies deep within and is essentially untouched by pollution from more superficial levels. However, when skewed psychological structures interlock religiosity within their distortion, it becomes contaminated, reduced, instrumentalized, nominal, and removed from religious essentialness.

There is a whole range of "degrees of religious faith [...] from high to low,"[82] and anybody at any of these degrees may be either mature or immature, depending on how well their religiosity sits within their own life economies. It probably is a long stretch to include mature atheists into the category of the religiously mature, but even though they are not religious, at least they have a mature attitude toward religion – are not irritated by it, do not have the constant urge to deny or denigrate it, and do not go ballistic at the mention of God. Viktor Frankl states that, since religiosity's kernel lies in the haziness of the unconscious, some people simply halt before the gates of this mysterious abyss, choosing to lead moral lives without plunging into spirituality. A mature atheist and a mature believer will never become involved in a conflict. "What counts first and more than anything else is the utmost sincerity and honesty. If God really exists he certainly is not going to argue with the irreligious persons because they mistake him for their own selves and misname him."[83]

Leaving atheists aside, we now turn to what comprises mature religiosity. In a simplified overview, the developmental line of healthy belief goes roughly from being spiritually and philosophically open, through engaging in inner change, to manifesting ever subtler and more compassionate attitudes toward people and environments. However, this developmental itinerary incorporates many different events that enfold in the depths of personality, and that may be identified separately, but that are necessarily unified within a complex structure of a religiously mature person.

Authentic religiosity is always intimate and thoroughly personal. Genuine spiritual insights are reached only though inner processing (conscious or unconscious), and are absolutely owned by the individual. This ownership makes individuals certain about their attitudes – certain in the sense that they are not easily swayed by outer influences. On the other hand, people who borrowed religious ideas from others and did not arrive at them through an internal process necessarily lack a sense of security in them and live in fear of losing these ideas (which would leave them suspended over a precipice of meaninglessness) – hence the fanatical urge to defend their beliefs, whether or not they make spiritual sense. "The more weakly one stands on the ground of his belief the more he clings with both hands to the dogma which separates it from other beliefs."[84] Mature believers are not frantically defending their religion, but, quite contrary, are wonderfully open about it.

Openness about one's religion, as stated earlier, does not exclude certainty about it. However, the kind of certainty mature believers have is not absolute, since they know they are in an evolving state in which every new minute can bring in more richness and depth. Instead of maintaining isolationist religious ideas disconnected from reality, they cherish knowledge that "conforms with sense perception, with reason, and with the beliefs of others."[85] The developmental path of mature religiosity is not straightforward – there are ups and downs and abrupt turns like on any adventurous journey. Being called the cradle of paradox, spirituality's adventures might even be the most unpredictable ones. Sometimes the rivers run underground, and suddenly epiphanies spout, geyser-like, on the surface of consciousness. However, there is continuity in this growth, in which each stage brings a "new meaning and new motive."[86] When believers close themselves off from these steps ahead (which can go on indefinitely), they deprive themselves of one of religion's main aims – change.

Mature openness embraces elements completely unacceptable in sectarian religiosity. Doubt is certainly the most prominent one. "The believer is often closer to the agnostic than we think."[87] Such an attitude accounts for absolute sincerity, which is a key ingredient in any authenticity. Besides, doubt enables seeing through all the religious dross listed in the previous chapter.

Another unorthodox attitude to God and religion is humor. A mature believer does not shy away from the "laughing God," but enjoys joking with him. This quality "is said even to be a divine attribute."[88] Humor can also have psychotherapeutic effects, since it is "man's principal technique for getting rid of irrelevancies."[89] It lies in the noetic dimension of human (and divine) existence. Frowning upon laughter and merriment, as is well known, is a landmark of some religions, which automatically smothers a whole strain of healthy spirituality.

Entrenchment makes us "lose our vision altogether: what is seen over and over again ceases to be seen."[90] This is why a constant shift is needed to keep our spiritual perception keen. Departing from a given platform of a religion (without abandoning it) and not clinging to it is the way which allows for inner growth and guides us through the layers of religious meaning – which starts with the literal, goes on through the ethical and the allegorical, and preferably ends in the anagogic – i.e. the capacity of a religion "to inspire us."[91]

Inspiration breeds action and change. If there is no change, there is no meaningful religion. It is "erroneous to maintain that religious attitude necessarily makes for passivity."[92] Gordon Allport expressly stated that "the most important of all distinctions between the immature and the mature religious sentiment lies in this basic difference in their dynamic character."[93] As the founder of personality psychology, he was well aware of the resistance of character to change after early developmental stages. Still, he took it as "the obvious fact that, when intense, religious belief is able to transform character."[94] The transformation implied goes in the direction of enlargement of one's personality by adjusting to "the supreme context,"[95] frequently at the cost of some "loss and pain,"[96] but nevertheless so rewarding that no cost seems too high. The results that the inner change brings about are rewarding in themselves, because new perceptions, new sensibilities, and new philosophies, much subtler that the earlier ones, are acquired. "When larger ranges of truth open, it is surely best to be able to open ourselves to their reception, unfettered by our previous pretensions."[97]

Religious people regularly pray, but "if nothing be really transacted while it lasts; if the world is in no whit different for its having taken place,"[98] then prayer is just one of the empty motions the religious dutifully perform. The same holds true for repentance. It should generate "*getting away from* the sin, not groaning and writhing over its commission,"[99] in which case such repentance represents "deleterious and evil passions"[100] because it involves no change. "Man can recognize the forgiveness of Heaven for a sin only by his never committing this sin again."[101] Even when they do change a person within, clinging to self-punishing thoughts of remorse is unwholesome, as Shakespeare noted in *The Winter's Tale*: "Do as the heavens have done, forget your evil; / With them forgive yourself."[102]

Even changes taking place at the level of extrinsic religion may be positive, if motivated by mature reasons. Apostasy is hardly a positive religious decision, but if made out of an individual's desire to align their formal religious status with what they authentically feel within, sometimes even at the risk of their lives, it must be accepted and respected as a mature decision of a self-aware individual. In comparison to this, religious conversion (again, if done for genuine reasons) should seem like a benign redirection of religious guidance toward the same destination. Historically, however, conversion has been and in some societies still is considered an unacceptable treason. Such attitudes point to a high level of religious immaturity. Viktor Frankl, on the other hand, stated that religious conversions (calling them "inner revolutions"[103]) are but matters of free choice to change the position toward our own destiny.

Mature inner evolution steers away from selfish self-love and self-interest both in a psychological and in a religious sense. During psycho-social development, the natural egocentrism of a young child is supposed to be overcome and the first lessons of empathy learned. Some individuals practically never outgrow the egocentric phase and continue to bind their interests and emotions only to the ego, neglecting the deeper self. The process of maturation makes a person "less swayed by paltry personal considerations"[104] and more open to the positions of others in an understanding and charitable way. The "biased self-love"[105] has as a consequence "only a partial and distorted knowledge of both the self and of the world of things, lives, minds and spirit."[106] The similarity between psychological and religious development in this respect is identical.

What are the life props that reinforce our religious maturity? Has material wealth got anything to do with it? Most truth-seekers find material riches hindering and burdensome, and gladly choose to dispose of them. A wealthy religious leader provokes immediate suspicion. Sometimes, however, "wealth gives time for ideal ends and exercise to ideal energies,"[107] enabling the development that poverty would have thwarted. "But wealth does this only in a portion of the actual cases,"[108] which is why people do not trust it when religion and money go hand in hand. Giving up luxury is a sign of selflessness and of proper positioning of values, while those who make use of their wealth for desirable spiritual ends probably did learn how to avoid the alluring traps of materialism (be it money, power, sex, or whatever else) and apply the resources at hand to higher goals.

Detachment from wealth should be accompanied by detachment from other facts of life that constantly weigh on our being, such as pain and pleasure, luster and gloom, injustice, illness, and that ultimate challenge – death. "Man has to be reconciled to his finiteness, and he also has to be enabled to face the transitoriness of his life."[109] What is being advocated in such messages is, of course, not indifference toward life, or an abnegation of it, but a transcending of its rubs and snares through "inner wisdom"[110] and "higher excitement."[111] To go into details of this kind of theological transcendence would be too exacting for our purposes.

The practical consequence of detachment from overly worrying about worldly concerns is an attitude of genuine tolerance toward others – irrespective of the group they belong to, or what they believe in, or whether or not they believe at all. Rising above the mundane irrelevancies opens up vistas into matters more essential in the context of eternity, the result of which is a self-emerging, humbling acceptance of others. In this context, "the impulse to sacrifice"[112] and turn the other cheek makes more sense than it does for "the men of this world."[113] History showed that saints were sometimes ready to "cut off [their] own survival"[114] by showing no resistance to evil rather than engaging in acts of violence. There is even a literary example of this at the end of Aldous Huxley's good utopia *Island*, in which the spiritually minded people of the fictional island Pala succumb without defense to the militaristic invasion of the materially contaminated island kingdom of (again fictional) Rendang. From the perspective of worldly justice, nonresistance to evil is madness and voluntary acceptance of victimhood, while from the perspective of eternity, active resistance (which generally involves violence) is likely to defile the soul and take it down the drain toward devolution. However, such instances expose "the complexity of the moral life, and the mysteriousness of the way in which facts and ideals are interwoven."[115] In terms of religious maturity, it might be that those who lean toward reluctance "to take arms against a sea of troubles" are more spiritually sensitive than those who have no doubts about whether to fight back or not when feeling endangered, but since the survival instinct is involved here, it makes things even more complex and ambiguous.

The previous passage might give the reader a false impression that mature religiosity promotes passivity. When it comes to using violent methods, it perhaps does, but when it comes to relating to others and the world in general "in behalf of social betterment,"[116] it certainly does not. It might even be said that there is no authentic religiosity if there is no selfless striving to help others. "We must not attempt to live outside the world, which is given us, but we must somehow learn how to transform it and transfigure it. Too much 'wisdom' is as bad as too little wisdom."[117] Being created by the same hand, all living entities deserve respect and love. Spiritually advanced individuals know that their own person is neither more nor less worthy than the person of anybody else, and so both are entitled to equal treatment. It was Confucius who was "the first to promulgate the Golden Rule,"[118] which has been reverberating throughout religious and nonreligious contexts ever since, but had certainly been present as a principle even before Confucius worded it. The issue of whether our charity extends only to humans or includes nonhuman beings too differs in various theologies, but it probably is common sense that the larger the scope of our charity, the higher the reaches of our spirituality. What matters most is that our actions have "the consistency of its moral consequences"[119] and that we "must find a way of being in this world while not being of it."[120]

A truly religious person avoids talking about God all the time. The relationship of an individual with the divine is probably the most intimate relationship. The religious who cram God into every fitting and non-fitting context have probably not yet experienced the spiritual mystery, which shuts our lips in secrecy. "It's bad taste to be always talking about God. Like wearing all one's pearls all day long, instead of only in the evening when one's dressed for dinner."[121] Going on publicly about intimate things that are naturally nestled within a bower of protective shyness might be a sign that they are not yet authentically experienced.

Lying underneath all separate features of religious maturity is "a comprehensive philosophy of life"[122] that an individual has embraced. Without it, religious maturity is incomprehensible. Reason alone is unable to control every single event taking place in our world of our ideas and behaviors. Those who are just outwardly religious are transparent in their falseness. No matter how superb their religious presentation be, at least some small incongruence will expose their fragmented inauthenticity. Only a religious philosophy "that does not constitute a separate sector of behavior, but is integrated in the global structure of personality"[123] manages to act as a unifying force that governs our actions in the direction of spiritual evolution. That philosophy is not "something artificially added,"[124] but a system of knowledge that "respects personality itself"[125] and involves "responsible choices."[126] No ready-made philosophy can thus be expected to be a perfect fit for individual systems infinitely diverse due to numberless combinations of personality traits. Hence, people do not adopt *in toto* the explanation offered by any one master theologian but require their own interpretations, in order to construct eclectic or, better still, synergic philosophical systems that guide them. However, this should provoke no fear, at least as long as the major requirements of religious maturity are met, because, though different, separate spiritual endeavors do rise, and "everything that rises must *converge*."[127] Huston Smith adds, "When the virtues converge at the top of the pyramid [...] absolute perfection reigns."[128]

Maturity, whether psychological or religious, enfolds along similar lines, and in some cases, the two may be indistinguishable from one another. A psychologically mature person does not necessarily have to be religious (though some would argue that they need to be spiritual), but, on the other hand, "religious maturity does indicate the state of psychological wellbeing."[129]

Religious Immaturity

Religious immaturity is perhaps even more susceptible to gradation than its mature counterpart. The unhealthy attitudes to religion may vary from neurotic atheism to contorted religiosity of the psychotic, with numerous subtypes and levels in between. In fact, there might be as many different religious neuroticisms as there are individuals with psychological problems. The focus of this book is less on intolerant atheists and far gone psychotics and more on the cases of literary characters whose religiosity is paired with a disordered personality, somewhere between health and mental illness. This is in line with the historical position of personality disorders, a category in itself not easily classifiable and quite debatable. A common functionality of people with these disorders frequently masks their structural pathology. Just because people with personality disorders easily sneak into positions of social prominence, their influence is much more toxic than the one of the obviously psychotic. When they practice their versions of religiosity (whether they be ordinary citizens or highest religious leaders), they invariably impose it on others. In cases when "religious leaders [are] clearly borderline psychotics,"[130] there is a huge risk that the masses will uncritically take over the leaders' skewed religious views. The toxicity of the influence of people with personality disorders thus rises exponentially.

There is another segment of religiosity described in literature that this book will keep away from. Without naming any of the authors or titles, a large section of popular religious/spiritual literature will be left out due to an oversimplified, or, less euphemistically, dilettante rendition of spirituality, which lacks a philosophical background of any standing and is based on stereotypes, inauthenticity, and pretentiousness. Such books are neither psychologically nor religiously convincing, and the spirituality in them cannot be called either mature or immature, but trivial. It pains to see the positions such books make on bestseller lists worldwide.

Tracing out an opposite line to the one used in the description of religious maturity, its immature variant might also be roughly outlined along three stages: the one of closeness, the refusal to change, and the ramifications of such rigid and intense attitudes on other people and the world at large.

Close- and open-mindedness have been accepted as terms with opposite connotations – the first is negative, the latter positive. Despite the fact that such demarcation is quite clear-cut, many stay close-minded about their religion and other areas of life. It probably gives them a feeling of security universally yearned for, which is understandable, but at the same time deprives them of the fullness of reality. No close-minded person would probably ever admit to this fact, because their defensive rigidity is subconscious. Where a religious context is concerned, close-mindedness manifests in various ways.

The first step in erecting barriers around our religiosity is its absolute subordination to reason. Being a phenomenon that essentially belongs to the noetic layer of existence (even though it does stretch across the psychological and the somatic, too), religion becomes devoid of its heart where *mysterium tremendum* abides if observed only through the binoculars of reason, which ontologically belongs to a hierarchically different, psychological dimension of personality. It is as if we tried to determine the type of bacteria that infected an organ using reading glasses. The religion reduced to an exclusively rational thing becomes a set of rigid (but oftentimes inconsistent) rules, and a hardcore "obsession with the literal,"[131] including all its damaging effects. While more mature believers lean toward narrative theologies and the anagogic potential of sacred texts, "fundamentalist [...] prides himself on believing every word in the Bible."[132]

Fundamentalism and fanaticism are probably the most dangerous offshoots of immature religiosity. Unlike the more general area of ecclesiogenic neuroses, which "the psychology of religion has not yet directly touched upon,"[133] fanaticism and fundamentalism have been in the scope of scientific research, though usually analyzed within psychological, social, and political frameworks, since they wreak most havoc in these areas. However, this is primarily a psycho-religious occurrence, characterized by a blind urge to exclude from one's religion anything that counters the ramshackle religious construction some inadequate rationalistic minds have erected. "They will claim it even where the facts most patently pronounce its folly"[134] and "impose [it] as a test of maturity upon all other views."[135] Thereby, instead of being aware of their arrogant attitude of "put[ting] human understanding above God's,"[136] they will fool themselves into believing that they are following in the divine footsteps, and coerce everybody else to do the same. The individuals who attain higher and subtler spiritual insights represent threats to fundamentalists and are ruthlessly persecuted.

The term immaturity constantly used in this book implies the notion of developmental arrest. Just as psychologically immature people fail to grow out of attitudes and beliefs characteristic of early developmental stages, the same might be applied to religious immaturity. In many cases, it resembles the religiousness of a child, which is more fairy-tale-like than rooted in a theology. Gordon Allport used many adjectives to describe this kind of "primitive credulity,"[137] such as childish, authoritarian, superstitious, irrational, spasmodic, segmented, unreflective, oversimplified, wish-fulfilling, egocentric, magical, creature comfort, prone to self-justification and gratification of "the drives and the desires of the body."[138] It is also characterized by "anthropomorphic concreteness,"[139] an absence of dialogue (since children's language is "an egocentric one consisting of monologues"[140]), and an escapist way out of facing discomforting facts. Children know they depend on the outer world due to their physical weakness. Immature believers take this attitude, too. They have "an unconscious desire to be weak and powerless; they tend to shift the center of their life to powers over which they feel no control, thus escaping from freedom and from personal responsibility."[141]

Even a superficial glance at the closed-off, underdeveloped religiousness suffices to make conclusions about its fragmentariness and lack of the potential to "integrate[...] with the deeper life of the subject."[142] Sometimes, immature religiosity "excludes other positive personal and social values,"[143] and people falsely attribute every single facet of life to extrinsic religion. Generally, such attitudes are not profound enough to unify the intellect, the experience, and the emotions of an individual. Hence, they give the person no genuine spiritual context, but serve as just another tool in a naive act of childishness. They resemble Nick Bottom's playing of Pyramus in *A Midsummer Night's Dream*, which makes Hippolyta say, "Indeed he hath played on his prologue like a child on a recorder; a sound, but not in government."[144] Religion, like so many other things, is oftentimes used without the slightest idea of what its true purpose is and without the sensitivity about its inner life.

Stagnant religiousness gathers not only moss, but also thorns and briars. They grow in order to protect the stance about spirituality the person is unwilling to question or change. Emphatically speaking, it is easy to understand where the reluctance to change comes from. Embarking on a religious life is a major redirection of personal energies which exacts the abandonment of the old system of values, ideas, and relationships. Few are ready for such a drastic change. "There are two lives, the natural and the spiritual, and we must lose the one before we can participate in the other."[145] Some are honest about the unreadiness to take over the responsibilities a religious life requires and choose to remain atheists or agnostics. Some, on the other hand, gradually manage to embrace whatever religious life implies. However, many try to keep the best of both worlds, which is implausible in practice. In order to keep up their religious appearances, they must activate defenses in order to keep fooling themselves and others. To a mature observer, though, such pretenses are easily seen through.

"A defensive ruling-out of disturbing evidence"[146] keeps cognitive dissonances, abundant in a religiously immature life, under the surface of consciousness. Any kind of criticism or reconsideration of beliefs would be experienced as a threat to the established religious scaffolding of an individual. The same principle holds true for personality disorders. Personality structures are difficult to reassemble, just like distortedly healed skeletons are difficult to set right. Instead of accepting religion in heuristic terms, people with immature religiosity accept it as "a kind of uncritical abandon,"[147] and probably apply a similar attitude "to their parents, to political issues, to social institutions."[148]

The major test of maturity in general is the attitude an individual takes toward other people and animate as well as inanimate entities in the environment. As Confucius believed, "we need [...] friendly interaction to achieve maturity."[149] How do spiritually underdeveloped people present themselves and address others and the world in general?

Relational maturity begins with the attitude toward one's own self. Most of our interactions with the outside entities are directly affected by what kind of relationship we have with ourselves. Neglecting the spiritual self and overidentifying with the ego often lie at the core of both psychological and religious pathologies, and relational problems, too. Hindu theology clearly distinguishes between the false ego (represented by the body and all human attributes that are transient) and the true nature, which is intransient and identical with higher levels of spiritual existence, or *brahman*. Psychology generally uses the term "ego" for the false and the term "self" for the genuine sense of personhood. Overattachment to the ego is problematic since it is being placed at the throne of overall personality, despite originating from a lower ontological level than the self. Instead of open vistas emerging from the true self, the principal perspective of the ego "is designed to conserve self-interest,"[150] which, in turn, blocks religious maturation. "As long as the false self is 'in power', people are victims of their own convictions and emotions."[151] Higher spirituality coming from the noetic dimension is simply being ruled out.

A direct manifestation of superficial relationship with one's own self is superficiality in relationships with others. In the religious context, it most frequently takes the form of bigotry and hypocrisy. At the rational level, hypocrites know that their true motives are selfish, so they try to mask them up with religious discourse and empty motions. Sometimes, though, when people are deeply immersed in self-deceptions and deadened to reality, their hypocrisy might be unconscious. "However, the lack of awareness of one's own religious hypocrisy does not make it any less dangerous."[152] Probably one of the most unappetizing human characteristics, two-facedness, causes a lot of harm. Where religion is concerned, it has ignited fierce criticism throughout the centuries. Unfortunately, it has also driven religion away from many who might have benefitted from it were they equipped to look beneath the corruption at religion's surface. Fundamentalism is based on fear and ignorance, hypocrisy on selfishness and spiritual crudeness, and bigotry on blind prejudice.

The higher bigots and hypocrites stand hierarchically within a religious community, the graver the harm that they do. Leaving aside catastrophic historical evidence of misuse of religion in political, economic, and other kinds of ways, where the encouragement of genuine spiritual development of an individual is concerned, which should be religion's major goal, religious institutions sometimes perversely represent "danger for authentic religiosity."[153] Unwilling to stand any criticism, "religious institution may crudely eliminate those who start to question its establishment."[154] In the minds of the spiritually immature, coarse matters of this world have preeminence over anything truly spiritual.

The unreligious ways and methods of some religious leaders (or rather bureaucrats, as Abraham Maslow called them) are principally uniform, with slight differences that are mainly cultural. Instead of nourishing the fragile potential of the believers to be awed before the divine (a faculty that abides in the noetic dimension), they stir an atmosphere of fear, one of the most primitive "old brain" emotions. The frightened are easily manipulated. Besides, "fear casts out love. And not only love. Fear also casts out intelligence, casts out goodness, casts out all thought of beauty and truth."[155] The disciples are made to fear a punishing God who withdraws their pie in the sky for being disobedient and sinful, and generously welcomes them to the vast array of infernal pastimes in the netherworld. As Karen Armstrong remembers the sermons from her childhood, "Hell seemed a more potent reality than God."[156]

Believers belonging to certain religious denominations are also made to fear (and dislike) members of other religious groups, however similar their religions might be. In fact, in many cases, the more similar the religions, the fiercer the conflict between them. Opening up toward strangers, sharing spiritual insights, connecting on the noetic level, are the aims of true religion. Although there are strands in almost every spiritual tradition inclined toward connecting with the 'outsiders', a more common image to be encountered in the world today is of believers who "have retracted into denominational ghettos and erected new barriers of orthodoxy against the 'other.'"[157]

Religion is also frequently equated with nationality, in which case the conundrum of xenophobia rises to an even higher schizophrenic level. Such "piety is the mask, the inner force is tribal instinct."[158] In a tribal organization, it is legitimate to wish for as large a number of members as possible, to impose standardized values on every single person, to discourage and punish individuality, and to demonize the ways and members of other tribes. Tribalism is supposedly a form of social organization belonging to earlier evolutionary stages, yet, in numerous religious practices, the crude tribal spirit is wholeheartedly inherited and maintained, to the detriment of the spiritual element in these religions.

The effects of such dilettante engagements in such a powerful phenomenon as religion are *per forza* disastrous. On the social level, bias against different modes of religious practice is automatically connected with national, racial, class, and various other forms of prejudice that lead to discrimination, enmity, conflict, and war. Religions are frequently not choosing to do the ethical thing in conflicting situations, just in order to preserve their privileges. Sometimes, they even perversely come up with religious justifications of inhuman treatment of others.

On the psychological level, in immature believers, "hostility, anxiety, prejudice, are detectible by psychological methods."[159] Their inner worlds remain fragmented, and they are not equipped to cope with adversity when it comes along. The ornamental religious elements in their lives serve to reinforce their psychological defenses and mask their personality flaws. On the spiritual level, there is no development and no plunge into the noetic source hidden deep within, but rather an existence splattered away at the surface that involves inevitable and progressive spiritual devolution. All the basic targets of religion are missed. "Religion in many lives seems merely symptomatic of fear and frustration."[160]

Religious Psychopathology

The subtitle of this book states that it is a study of literary portraits of "personality disorders and religion." The original phrase was "religious psychopathology," but it was discarded because its use in scientific literature has been rather scarce and the phrase itself is insufficiently clear.

Still, in the light of the overall topic of the book, it might be useful to cast some light on it. All the authors who use it feel the need to explain what they mean by it. Frequently it is referred to "casually and without an in-depth analysis."[161] I will try to clarify how I understand this polymorphous phrase.

Religious psychopathology (in the context of this research) predominantly refers to psychological disorders that are "best expressed in religious language."[162] In other words, it refers to those cases where people with mental illnesses disguise and intermesh their shortcomings with religious beliefs and behavior. They show "skewed forms of belief [... and] a neuroticized understanding of God."[163] However, religion *per se* has got nothing to do with their disorders, the roots of which lie at the psychological level. "The link between religion and psychopathology is only accidental,"[164] for religion "does not engender mental illness."[165] Viktor Frankl would argue that "a dimensional difference"[166] is at play here, and that the problem "moves along that great divide which separates not psyche from soma, but psyche from spirit."[167]

The proverbial privacy and mistery of the relationship between a person and the divine is a thing not to be discussed or criticized unless it starts having negative effects on others, or in some cases the very person in question. The characteristics of one's pathological interpretation and introjection of religion are observable in many contradictions the person displays – "excessive naivety and rationalism; moral hyperconscientiousness and lascivity; enraging formalism (or ritualism) and abandonment of religious duties; rejection of physicality and hypochondria; aggressiveness towards religious (or Divine) authority and servility, a tendency of exposing or withdrawing; the need for admiration or pitying; and first of all the equation 'instinct = guilt.'"[168] Attempts have been made at establishing a typology of religious psychopathologies, but there is still much to be done in this regard. In this book, the classification used overlaps with the classification of personality disorders.

There have been a few more related terms in scientific circulation, such as ecclesiogenic neuroses and noogenic (as opposed to psychogenic or somatogenic) neuroses. The first refers to "neuroses induced by the clerical institution,"[169] while the latter implies "the tension of a conflicted conscience, or [...] the pressure of a spiritual problem, or [...] the midst of an existential crisis."[170]

Ecclesiogenic neurosis is a particular subclass of religious psychopathology in which religious duties are experienced as overly exacting for the person who does not feel strong enough to respond to them. The requirements of the church that can be overwhelming for an individual are "orders, prohibitions and threats of punishment, [...] excessive moral demands and control."[171] A tension ensues when the rules of extrinsic religion are out of tune with the developmental stage the person has attained at a particular moment. This lack of subtlety by religious institutions in taking into account individual spiritual potentials and needs often bears neurotic fruit.

Noogenic neuroses originate from the noological level and can be caused either by spiritual or any other specifically humanistic phenomena abiding in the noetic depth. Some authors claim that there are "no 'religious' but only 'ecclesiogenic neuroses,'"[172] while others allow the possibility of problems arising from the deep ontological core of being, which in itself is never flawed. The conflict is again created by the mismatch between the spiritual/noetic energy that "can appear suddenly and dramatically leading to immense confusion, anxiety, and sometimes impaired functioning"[173] and the psyche insufficiently strong to integrate this surge from the spiritual level. The term used for such instances characterized by emphasized intensity is "spiritual emergency."[174]

The complex relationships between the psychological and spiritual planes of existence might be reduced to four basic combinations, solely for methodological purposes, while in reality clear distinctions between these two major modes of being, both physically unquantifiable, are practically impossible. The proposed classification to four types includes cases in which:

a maturity has been reached at both the psychological and the spiritual levels;
b maturity has been reached neither at the psychological nor the spiritual level;
c maturity has been reached at the psychological but not at the spiritual level; and
d maturity has been reached at the spiritual but not at the psychological level.

The rarest instances among common humankind are those people who are psychologically mature and who at the same time cherish mature religiosity. Advancing far ahead on their developmental journey toward integrative self-actualization, they represent beacons for the myriad of struggling souls and minds. Writers sometimes describe such personalities as examples of the possibilities of human attainment that might stir the readers' own upward move. Goodness and maturity, however, are not nearly as fruitful sources for the works of art as are badness and immaturity, because positive traits are stereotypically experienced as bland and lifeless. It is true that some of the characters who belong to this category are too ethereal to be convincing blood-and-flesh humans, but literary masters know that the good ones have their surprising idiosyncrasies just as the bad ones do. The next chapter describes Larry Darrell, one of the literary characters who ticks both maturity boxes discussed here.

Even though all propositions for mental hygiene have been "expressed with venerable symbols in some portion of the world's religious literature,"[175] and "spiritual life includes previously resolved [...] problems from the sphere of mental [...] life,"[176] there are instances in which a person's psyche is ill, but the spiritual domain seems pure and healthy. This is not difficult to grasp if we believe that the spirit within can never be spoiled. "Religion is indestructible and indelible. Even psychosis cannot destroy it."[177] Furthermore, "a neurotic is religious or irreligious irrespective of being a neurotic."[178] However, spirituality partnered with a malfunctioning psyche and untouched by it is a very occurrence.

Sometimes, strange expressions of religiosity are interpreted as mental illness. "There can be some unusual and troubling spiritual experiences associated with the spiritual journey, and clinicians are faced with the prospects of differentiating such spiritual experiences from major psychoaphology."[179] This includes various mystical experiences that are sometimes manifesting as psychologically disordered functioning, so clinicians should be aware of the differences between the two. William James attributed the following characteristics to mystical experiences: ineffability, noetic quality, transiency, and passivity.[180] Unlike psychotic episodes, "some memory of their [mystical state's] content always remains, and a profound sense of their importance. They modify the inner life of the subject between the times of their recurrence."[181] The literary character of Mrs. Dempster is taken in this book as an example of a person with a strong spirituality encroached upon by psychological illness.

The zest of this book, however, are the good old villains, in this case those with a religious streak. They are underdeveloped both psychologically and spiritually, but for some quirky reason they believe themselves to be religiously superior. Most of the time they perpetuate pseudoreligion instead of religion. The third part of the book is dedicated to characters that display a wide range of different psycho-religious distortions.

The only category without representatives in this volume is the one of the psychologically and morally mature, but spirituality underdeveloped. Spirituality and religion play no major roles in their lives, so they are not of great interest for this study. However, this is a legitimate variant, because religiosity is a matter of deepest personal choice. What really counts is morally responsible behavior. Whether atheists or latent believers, they do not rage against the religious, like neurotic atheists do. Even though frequently despised by the immaturely religious, atheism in those with a high level of psychological maturity is much healthier than corrupt religiosity of any kind.

Notes

1 "Ljudsko iskustvo kombinira 'prirodu' i 'duh', a covjek funkcionira istovremeno u obje te dimenzije," Reinhold Niebuhr, quoted from: Rollo May, *Psihologija i ljudska dvojba*, tr. Anita Sujoldzic, Zagreb: Naprijed, 1980, p. 19.

2 See: Sisirkumar Ghose, *Mystics and Society*, London: Asia Publishing House, 1968, p. 7.
3 Karen Armstrong, *A History of God*, New York: Ballantine Books, 1994, p. xix.
4 See: Michael Cox, *Mysticism, The Direct Experience of God*, Wellingborough: The Aquarian Press, 1983, p. 25.
5 Nicolas of Cusa, a fifteenth-century German cardinal and philosopher, quoted from: James P. Carse, *The Religious Case against Belief*, London: Penguin, 2008, p. 15.
6 Huston Smith, with Jeffrey Paine, *Tales of Wonder, Adventures Chasing the Divine*, New York: Harper One, 2009, p. 193.
7 James P. Carse, *op. cit.*, p. 145.
8 *Ibid.*, p. 202.
9 Karen Armstrong, *A Short History of Myth*, Edinburgh: Canongate, 2005, Kindle edition, e-book.
10 See: Alan Hull Walton, "Introduction," *Ashvaghosa – The Awakening of Faith*, tr. Timothy Richard, New Hyde Park: University Books, 1961, p. 10.
11 William James, *The Varieties of Religious Experience*, Harmondsworth: Penguin, 1987, p. 420.
12 Karen Armstrong, *A Short History of Myth*.
13 James P. Carse, *op. cit.*, p. 136.
14 *Ibid.*, p. 147.
15 David M. Wulff, *Psychology of Religion, Classic and Contemporary Views*, New York: John Wiley & Sons, 1991, p. 4.
16 Huston Smith, *Tales of Wonder*, p. 175.
17 Huston Smith, *The World's Religions*, New York: Harper One, 2009, p. 29.
18 "po svom poreklu i funkciji nije nusproizvod drugih sistema (na primer, ekonomije ili drustva), ne zavisi od njih i ne generise ih," Mircea Eliade, *Vodic kroz svetske religije*, tr. Andjelka Cvijic, Belgrade: Narodna knjiga, Alfa, 1996, p. 14.
19 Karen Armstrong, *A Short History of Myth*.
20 James P. Carse, *op. cit.*, p. 111.
21 David M. Wulff, *op. cit.*, p. viii.
22 Karen Armstrong, *A History of God*, p. xx.
23 *Ibid.*
24 *Ibid.*
25 *Ibid.*
26 Huston Smith, *Tales of Wonder*, p. 97.
27 Karen Armstrong, *A History of God*, p. xix.
28 James P. Carse, *op. cit.*, p. 30.
29 See: Herman Hesse, *Moja vera*, tr. Jasmina Burojevic, Belgrade: Narodna knjiga – Alfa, 1999, p. 110.
30 Erich Fromm, *Psychoanalysis and Religion*, New Haven: Yale University Press, 1955, p. 26.
31 Gordon W. Allport, *The Individual and His Religion*, New York: Macmillan, 1962, p. 27.
32 *Ibid.*, p. 26.
33 "razlicitim ljudima moze razlicito prikazati," K. M. Sen, *op. cit.*, p. 50.
34 Aldous Huxley, "Foreword," Hubert Benoit, *The Supreme Doctrine*, (Psychological Studies in Zen Buddhism), New York: Pantheon Books, 1955, p. xi.
35 Jacques Calvin, quoted from: James P. Carse, *op. cit.*, p. 133.
36 See: Sisirkumar Ghose, *op. cit.*, p. 89.

37 "kao mali potoci, zajedno se krecu da bi sreli Boga (Hari), koji je kao okean," K. M. Sen, *op. cit.*, p. 122.
38 James P. Carse, *op. cit.*, p. 2.
39 Mark Knight, *An Introduction to Religion and Literature*, New York: Continuum, 2009, p. 3.
40 See: Rudolph Otto, *The Idea of the Holy*, Oxford: Oxford University Press, 1958, pp. 12–25.
41 William James, *op. cit.*, p. 271.
42 Erich Fromm, *Psychoanalysis and Religion*, p. 63.
43 "*sve* religije su mape ljudskog uma [...] zbog cega religije imaju toliko mnogo zajednickog," Mircea Eliade, *op. cit.*, p. 19.
44 Karen Armstrong, *The Spiral Staircase*, London: Harper Perennial, 2005.
45 Gordon W. Allport, *The Individual and His Religion*, p. 60.
46 See: *Ibid.*, pp. 60–61.
47 See: Herman Hesse, *op. cit.*, p. 85.
48 Huston Smith, *The World's Religions*, p. 73.
49 William James, *op. cit.*, p. 28.
50 "isuvise kompleksan i [...] multidimenzionalan posao," Stipe Tadic, paraphrased in: Vladimir Bakrac, *Religija i mladi: Religioznost mladih u Crnoj Gori*, Podgorica: Narodna knjiga, 2013, p. 64.
51 William James, *op. cit.*, p. 29.
52 James P. Carse, *op. cit.*, pp. 32–33.
53 "odgovor na pitanja religijskog karaktera, kao sto su pitanja koja se odnose na smisao zivota, te da li smrt znaci i kraj zivota, sta slijedi nakon smrti, itd," Vladimir Bakrac, *op. cit.*, p. 65.
54 Karen Armstrong, *The Spiral Staircase.*
55 James P. Carse, *op. cit.*, p. 126.
56 Karen Armstrong, *The Spiral Staircase.*
57 William James, *op. cit.*, p. 29.
58 *Ibid.*, p. 189.
59 Andrew Reid Fuller, *Psychology and Religion: Eight Points of View*, London: Littlefield Adams, 1994, p. 116.
60 Karen Armstrong, *Twelve Steps to a Compassionate Life*, London: The Bodley Head, 2011, p. 1.
61 Karen Armstrong, *The Spiral Staircase.*
62 Karen Armstrong, *Twelve Steps to a Compassionate Life*, p. 1.
63 Karen Armstrong, *Through the Narrow Gate*, p. 198.
64 Aldous Huxley, *Proper Studies*, London, Chatto and Windus, 1927, p. 91.
65 Michael Cox, *Mysticism, The Direct Experience of God*, p. 17.
66 Karen Horney, *Our Inner Conflicts*, p. 15.
67 James P. Carse, *op. cit.*, p. 33.
68 Gordon W. Allport, *The Individual and His Religion*, p. 52.
69 James P. Carse, *op. cit.*, p. 210.
70 Gordon W. Allport, *The Individual and His Religion*, p. 65.
71 James P. Carse, *op. cit.*, p. 187.
72 "2012 Republican Party of Texas Report of Platform Committee," word document downloaded from: https://talkingpointsmemo.com/muckraker/texas-gop-s-2012-platform-opposes-teaching-of-critical-thinking-skills, accessed at 10 July 2014, p. 11.
73 2 Corinthians 3.6.
74 James P. Carse, *op. cit.*, p. 60.
75 Erich Fromm, *Psychoanalysis and Religion*, p. 33.
76 Gordon W. Allport, *The Individual and His Religion*, p. 52.

77 Aldous Huxley, *Proper Studies*, p. 1.
78 Gordon W. Allport, *The Individual and His Religion*, p. 54.
79 William James, *op. cit.*, p. 335.
80 "uvek uslovljena psiholoskim problemima," Giacomo Dacquino, *op. cit.*, p. 94.
81 Viktor Frankl, *The Will to Meaning*, p. 132.
82 Gordon W. Allport, *The Individual and His Religion*, p. 138.
83 Viktor Frankl, *The Unheard Cry for Meaning*, p. 63.
84 Viktor Frankl, *Psychotherapy and Existentialism*, p. 85.
85 Gordon W. Allport, *The Individual and His Religion*, p. 138.
86 *Ibid.*, p. 64.
87 *Ibid.*, p. 73.
88 Viktor Frankl, *The Will to Meaning*, p. 17.
89 Gordon W. Allport, *The Individual and His Religion*, p. 92.
90 James P. Carse, *op. cit.*, p. 81.
91 Huston Smith, *Tales of Wonder*, p. 193.
92 Viktor Frankl, *The Doctor and the Soul*, p. 59.
93 Gordon W. Allport, *The Individual and His Religion*, p. 63.
94 *Ibid.*, p. 65.
95 *Ibid.*, p. 142.
96 William James, *op. cit.*, p. 45.
97 *Ibid.*, p. 333.
98 *Ibid.*, 465.
99 *Ibid.*, p. 128.
100 *Ibid.*
101 Viktor Frankl, *The Doctor and the Soul*, p. 59.
102 William Shakespeare, *The Winter's Tale*, http://shakespeare.mit.edu/winters_tale/full.html, e-book, accessed at 13 July 2014.
103 Viktor Frankl, *The Doctor and the Soul*, p. 59.
104 William James, *op. cit.*, p. 45.
105 Aldous Huxley, *The Perennial Philosophy*, London: Chatto & Windus, 1946, p. 96.
106 *Ibid.*
107 William James, *op. cit.*, p. 368.
108 *Ibid.*
109 Viktor Frankl, *Psychotherapy and Existentialism*, p. 32.
110 William James, *op. cit.*, p. 361.
111 *Ibid.*, p. 363.
112 *Ibid.*, p. 303.
113 *Ibid.*, p. 355.
114 *Ibid.*
115 *Ibid.*
116 Gordon W. Allport, *The Individual and His Religion*, p. 67.
117 Aldous Huxley, "Shakespeare and Religion," *Aldous Huxley, A Memorial Volume*, ed. Julian Huxley, London: Chatto & Windus, 1965, p. 174.
118 Karen Armstrong, *A Short History of Myth*.
119 Gordon W. Allport, *The Individual and His Religion*, p. 65.
120 Aldous Huxley, "Shakespeare and Religion," p. 174.
121 Aldous Huxley, *Time Must Have a Stop*, London: Chatto & Windus, 1945, p. 214.
122 Gordon W. Allport, *The Individual and His Religion*, p. 67.
123 "ne konstituise odvojeni sektor ponasanja, vec je integrisana u globalnu strukturu licnosti," Giacomo Dacquino, *op. cit.*, p. 94.

124 "nije nesto vestacki dodato," *Ibid.*
125 "postuje samu licnost," *Ibid.*, p. 95.
126 "odgovorne izbore," *Ibid.*
127 Teilhard de Chardin, quoted in: Huston Smith, *Tales of Wonder*, p. 191.
128 Huston Smith, *Tales of Wonder*, p. 191.
129 "religioznost jeste i pokazatelj psihickog zdravlja," Giacomo Dacquino, *op. cit.*, p. 96.
130 Gordon W. Allport, *The Individual and His Religion*, p. 83.
131 Huston Smith, *Tales of Wonder*, pp. 193–194.
132 Gordon W. Allport, *The Individual and His Religion*, p. 119.
133 "psihologija religioznosti jos zapravo nije izravno ni dotakla," Simun Sito Coric, *Psihologija religioznosti*, Jasterbarsko: Slap, 2003, p. 20.
134 William James, *op. cit.*, p. 333.
135 Gordon W. Allport, *The Individual and His Religion*, p. 53.
136 "ljudsko shvacanje iznad samog Boga," Simun Sito Coric, *op. cit.*, p. 266.
137 Gordon W. Allport, *The Individual and His Religion*, p. 122.
138 *Ibid.*, p. 63.
139 "antropomorfisticka konkretnost," Simun Sito Coric, *op. cit.*, p. 104.
140 "egocentricni jezik koji se sastoji od monologa," *Ibid.*
141 Erich Fromm, *Psychoanalysis and Religion*, p. 54.
142 Gordon W. Allport, *The Individual and His Religion*, p. 59.
143 "iskljuci druge harmonicne osobne i drustvene vrijednosti," Simun Sito Coric, *op. cit.*, p. 159.
144 William Shakespeare, *A Midsummer Night's Dream*, www.shakespeare-online.com/plays/mids_5_1.html, e-text, accessed at 21 July 2014.
145 William James, *op. cit.*, pp. 166–167.
146 Gordon W. Allport, *The Individual and His Religion*, p. 65.
147 *Ibid.*, p. 58.
148 *Ibid.*, p. 59.
149 Karen Armstrong, *Twelve Steps to a Compassionate Life*, p. 122.
150 Gordon W. Allport, *The Individual and His Religion*, p. 16.
151 "Sve dok je lazni self 'na snazi', osobe su zrtve vlastitih uverenja i emocija," Snezana Milenkovicć, *op. cit.*, p. 137.
152 "Medjutim, manjak svijesti o vlastitoj vjerskoj hipokriziji ne cini je manje opasnom," Simun Sito Coric, *op. cit.*, p. 160.
153 "opasnost za autenticnu religioznost," *Ibid.*, p. 42.
154 "vjerska institucija moze grubo ukloniti onoga tko pocne dovoditi u pitanje njezin establishment," *Ibid.*, p. 42.
155 Aldous Huxley, *Ape and Essence*, London: Chatto & Windus, 1978, pp. 36–37.
156 Karen Armstrong, *A History of God*, p. vii.
157 Karen Armstrong, *Twelve Steps to a Compassionate Life*, p. 134.
158 William James, *op. cit.*, p. 338.
159 Gordon W. Allport, *The Individual and His Religion*, p. 59.
160 *Ibid.*, p. viii.
161 "najcesce usputno i bez detaljne analize," Ilija Zivkovic, Suzana Vuletic, "Ekleziogene neuroze u psihopatoloskim oblicima religioznosti," Zagreb: *Drustvena Istrazivanja*, 2007, Vol. 6, No. 92, p. 1263.
162 Gordon W. Allport, *The Individual and His Religion*, p. 83.
163 "iskrivljene forme vjerovanja [... i] neurotizovanom poimanju Boga," Simun Sito Coric, *op. cit.*, p. 244.
164 "veza izmedju religije i psihopatologije je samo slucajna," Giacomo Dacquino, *op. cit.*, p. 137.

165 Gordon W. Allport, *The Individual and His Religion*, p. 83.
166 Viktor Frankl, *The Will to Meaning*, p. 143.
167 Viktor Frankl, *The Doctor and the Soul*, p. 273.
168 "vanredna naivnost i racionalizam; moralna hipersavesnost i lascivnost; razdrazljivi formalizam (ili ritualizam) i napustanje religioznih duznosti; odbijanje telesnosti i hipohondrija; agresivnost prema religioznom autoritetu (ili Bozanskom) i servilnost; tendencija ka izlaganju ili skrivanju; potreba za divljenjem ili sazaljevanjem; pre svega postoji jednacina 'instinkt = krivica,'" Giacomo Dacquino, *op. cit.*, p. 137.
169 "neuroza uvjetovanih crkvenom institucijom," Ilija Zivković, Suzana Vuletic, *op. cit.*, p. 1263.
170 Viktor Frankl, *On the Theory and Therapy of Mental Disorders*, tr. James M. Dubois, New York: Brunner-Routledge, 2005, p. 151.
171 "zapovijedi i zabrana i prijetnji kaznom, [...] prezahtjevna moralna trazenja i pretjerana kontrola," Simun Sito Coric, *op. cit.*, p. 143.
172 "nikakve 'religiozne' vec tzv. 'ekleziogene neuroze,'" *Ibid.*, p. 145.
173 Len Sperry, "Integrating Spiritual Direction Functions in the Practice of Psychotherapy," *Journal of Psychology and Theology*, 2003, Vol. 31, No. 1, p. 7.
174 Stanislav Grof with Hal Zina Bennett, *The Holotropic Mind*, New York: Harper Collins, 1993, p. 14.
175 Gordon W. Allport, *The Individual and His Religion*, p. 86.
176 "sam duhovni zivot pretpostavlja prethodno razresenje [...] problema iz sfere mentalnog [...] zivota," Snezana Milenkovic, *op. cit.*, p. 81.
177 Viktor Frankl, *The Will to Meaning*, p. 138.
178 *Ibid.*, p. 137.
179 Len Sperry, "Integrating Spiritual Direction Functions in the Practice of Psychotherapy," p. 7.
180 See: William James, *op. cit.*, pp. 380–381.
181 *Ibid.*, pp. 381–382.

Part II

Portraits of Religious Maturity

3 The Constant Seeker

Larry Darrell and Mature Religiosity

One of the bestselling novels on the eve of World War II on both sides of the Atlantic was Somerset Maugham's *The Razor's Edge* (1944), a book about the spiritual meanderings of Larry Darrell, a young American determined to abandon the materialistic allure of his homeland and plunge into a dicey search for perennial truths. Even though the novel abounds in different characters and themes, and even though "Maugham was a much more effective satirist than he was a describer of religious experience,"[1] it is the thread following Darrell's spiritual development that has, over the years, emerged as the novel's focal point.

Maugham had an idea to write a book like *The Razor's Edge* "for over twenty years,"[2] but what prompted him to get down to actually doing it was his visit to India in the late 1930s. He needed "a vehicle in which to set forth impressions of Indian mysticism and mystics and to restate many observations on religion, evil, God, punishment, and spiritual exaltation."[3] Aldous Huxley and Gerald Heard, both of whom also traveled to India and got deeply involved with the teachings of Vedanta, apparently had a significant impact on Maugham. Another British contemporary associated with the Huxley and Heard circle, Christopher Isherwood, is said to have inspired the character of Larry Darrell,[4] despite the fact that Isherwood was not very happy with it, feeling that "the fictional portrait [...] seemed to denigrate Vedanta and diminish the seriousness of his quest for oneness with God."[5] Despite harsh criticism that Maugham's rendition of Darrell's religious conversion has received from various sources, it is not so much the nature of Darrell's religion that is examined here, but rather Darrell's attitude to religion, which seems to meet the essential criteria of religious maturity as set up in a previous chapter.

Somerset Maugham is himself one of the characters in this first-person narrative novel. He meets Larry occasionally and, intrigued by the young man's life, makes Larry's story one of the major strands in the book. Their first meeting took place in Chicago, where Maugham was invited to dinner with an old friend, Elliott Templeton. Larry was also there, as his fiancée Isabel was Elliott's niece. He was a tall, agreeable, rather shy but pleasant young man with an unorthodox outlook on life. The major difference that set him apart from his peers was his unwillingness to either go to college or take up a job, even though he was offered a lucrative position in business. He wanted something else, but did not know exactly what that was. His subsequent search becomes the axis that unifies other characters and events described in the novel.

A Brief Biography of Larry Darrell

Larry Darrell remained an orphan at a young age. His mother, who "was a Philadelphian of old Quaker stock,"[6] died in childbirth, and his father, "an assistant professor of Romance languages at Yale,"[7] passed away when Larry was twelve. After that, the boy was brought up in a small town near Chicago by his father's friend Nelson, a doctor. They got along rather well, without arguments, because Larry was not prone to rebellion. Still, he did whatever he liked, since his foster father did not have a lot of authority over him. Larry blended in smoothly with other children. He had no particular talents, but there was one thing that fascinated him more than anything else – aviation. As World War I was breaking out, he ran away from home, lied that he was eighteen, and enlisted in the Air Corps. Apparently, he had done well in the war, where he received only a minor wound. Upon his return to Chicago, based on his success in the war, "several business men offered him positions."[8] He refused them all. His plans, though vague about what he wanted, were very clear about what he did not want.

What ensued in his life were over a dozen years of traveling through various foreign countries before his final decision to go back to America and settle there for good. First he spent two years in Paris, without a clear idea of what the purpose of his stay there was. Isabel agreed to wait for him after he assured her that two years in Paris was just what he needed, even though, in his own words, he was just "loafing" there. Instead of going back to America when the two years were up, he instead broke off his engagement and moved along on his wandering spree. A series of odd sojourns ensued: working in a mine in the north of France, spending some time as a farmhand in Germany, living in Spain, Italy, and then again in Germany. After staying in Bonn for a year, he spent three months in a German monastery. At a certain point, Europe apparently offered only limited philosophical resources, so he resumed pursuing his experience in China, Burma, and India. Instead of only three days in India as was his initial plan, he ended up staying there for five years – longer than anywhere else on his travels. India was the final foreign land he lived in before going back to America. Something took place there that put an end to his urge for "loafing."

Larry Darrell's Personality Traits

Before a more detailed clarification of the nature of his quest, let us briefly discuss his personality. Even though he does change throughout the bildungsroman thread of this novel, most of his personal characteristics are fairly consistent. Maugham introduces him as a young man freshly out of adolescence, with his character and identity largely formed. It is his spiritual, not psychological, identity that undergoes a major metamorphosis during the years of his search, which affected his character only by strengthening the already existing personality characteristics. The psychological substratum for his religious maturation was relatively healthy, as we shall see, and thus represented no obstacle on his way, as frequently is the case with people with a less wholesome psychological setup.

Based on a few remarks by Dr. Nelson about teenage Larry, who eventually did only what he pleased, it may be concluded that Larry had a comparably accentuated streak of independency from an early age. Being orphaned probably propped the development of his self-consciousness and individuality, which remained characteristic of him throughout later life and became one of the most salient features in his being in the world. The first step toward independent thinking is nonconformism, an attitude Larry took most of the time. Unlike other young men with undeniable intellectual potential, he did not want to go to college, and unlike the majority of the human race, who would unthinkingly grab the first opportunity of a lucrative job in business, Larry did not want that either. Instead, he chose to go abroad in search of something he could not define but felt strongly and intuitively drawn toward. Once in Paris, he avoided moving in higher social circles, even though Isabel's uncle kept inviting him to dinners and luncheons. What he found more than satisfying was "a scrubby little room in a hotel."[9] Generally, he was a very undemanding person in a materialistic sense. He never ate much and was not fussy about his food; he did not drink alcohol, and he absolutely did not care about money. When forced to take up a temporary job, it was no problem for him to be a farmhand, a carpenter, a mechanic, a deckhand on ship, a taxi driver, or to work in a coal mine or a garage, despite the extraordinary range of intellectual and spiritual knowledge that he possessed. Or just because of it.

The unlikely choices that Larry made in life testify about his free will. Turning away from careers that are regarded as superb in modern society, leaving his home country for "loafing" in Europe and Asia, getting rid of all his money in order to feel free from its bondage – all of these suggest that his choices were independent from anyone or anything external. Independent choices exact a high degree of bravery. In Larry's case, he was abandoning a very secure position in life for an extremely vague quest in a geographical, spiritual, emotional, intellectual, and all other senses, which is the journey of a hero, not a coward.

After returning from the Far East, Larry would not mind appearing before his friends with "a mop of dark brown hair that badly needed cutting" and in "a frayed shirt, without a tie, a brown, threadbare coat and a pair of shabby grey slacks."[10] However, such attire was not meant to make a statement, for the next day, being reminded of the social norms in the West, and essentially not wanting to be antagonistic,[11] "he looked not only neat, but well-groomed."[12] This individuality, or "a very singular detachment,"[13] as Maugham puts it, speaks of a greatly independent person "who can go no other way than their own."[14]

In his singularity, Larry spends a lot of time on his own, but is not a recluse, for he also needs to stay in touch with other people. In both of these relationships, i.e. to his own self and to others, he shows genuineness and depth.

Relating to his own self, he was driven by what many people choose to ignore – the desire to know himself. He responded fully to both aspects of this process, i.e. the discovery and the willful choice, and he went to great lengths to learn as much about himself as possible: read many books on psychology, philosophy, science, and mysticism, with "his evident power of concentration,"[15] learned five or six languages, traveled, engaged in manual labor, spent time on spiritual retreats, etc. Working in a German mine for a while was intended, in his own words, "to sort my thoughts and come to terms with myself,"[16] as were all other adventures and all loafing. Knowing oneself to the fullest extent is a prerequisite for self-perfection, which Larry considered "the greatest ideal man can set before himself."[17]

Larry's inner character reflected on the physical level, too, for the noetic–psychic–somatic components were well integrated within his overall personality compound. "He had a smile [...] that lit his face as with an inner light."[18] Even though he was particular in his ways and to some appeared perhaps stubborn and irresponsible, he was anything but egotistic: "modest and friendly and gentle,"[19] as well as unwilling "to talk about himself."[20] In psychodynamic terms, his ego was not a victim of either the superego or the id. Though not prone to hedonism, he was not ascetic either. When a situation presented itself, he would use it to consume a passion, for it is "foolish not to take delight in it while we have it."[21] One of his lovers explained, "He had [...] natural human instincts, but he was like a man so preoccupied that he forgets to eat, but when you put a good dinner before him he eats it with appetite."[22]

Productivity, another significant indicator of a healthy and fruitful relationship with oneself, was seemingly missing for some time in Larry's life. However, after years of quest for deeper knowledge, Larry summed up part of his ideas in a book of essays that he wrote on famous people: Rubens, Goethe, the Lord Chesterfield of the Letters, the Roman general

Sulla, the Mogul conqueror Akbar, etc. All of them achieved great successes in life, and Larry "was curious to see what in the end it amounted to."[23] The underlying motive was not to achieve fame, for ambition in a worldly sense was completely uncharacteristic of him. "To become anything of a public figure would be deeply distasteful to him."[24] He only wanted not to remain in a protective shell but to reach out at least to a handful of people drawn to his idea "that ultimate satisfaction can only be found in the life of the spirit."[25]

Larry does indeed tick most of the boxes of a psychologically mature person, at least where his relationship with his own genuine self is concerned. The only thing that seems to be lacking is a dose of humor on his own account. Maugham, himself somewhat grimly tempered, does not depict Larry laughing at all. However, since perfection is but an ideal, our hero, though imperfect, is still closer to it than most literary characters or real people one encounters.

On the other hand, where Larry's relationship to other people is concerned, the situation is slightly more ambiguous.

However, let us first consider some of the unambiguous qualities that characterize Larry's interaction with others. What is immediately noticeable are the warmth and benevolence that he radiates. This is observed multiple times in the novel, whether in the description of his voice ("wonderfully melodious"[26]), his smile ("as sweet as honey"[27]), or his overall character ("an angel of sweetness"[28]). He was always a careful listener and he smiled "as though he thought what you'd said funny, though it isn't funny at all."[29] When he spoke, "the pleasantness of his voice [...] invested even his most casual utterances with persuasiveness,"[30] and when playing with children he resembled a child himself.

Even though the relationship between Larry and Isabel was strained and their engagement was broken off in the end, the love they felt for one another was never doubted, from the days when it was still young, through the difficult time when Larry decided to leave for Paris (Isabel: "he does love me; Mama. I'm sure of that."[31]), to the very decision to go separate ways. The day after they passed that decision, they were supposed to meet at a family lunch. "Not only had Larry come to lunch [...], but he had acted as though his position were unchanged. [...] He treated Isabel with the same comradely affectionateness with which he had always treated her. [...] Nor did Isabel appear dispirited."[32] Of course, a romantic relationship involves complex emotions, and all that threatens its stability, which in this case was Larry's decision to move on on his own, is experienced as a catastrophe. Still, the non-egoism and the benevolence of the motives that were underlying his decision made Isabel accept and, to an extent, even understand the bleak situation. This same benevolence, "the peculiar strength and sweetness of his character,"[33] the lack of didacticism or reproach, had an unfailingly positive effect on others. In his presence "they calmed down,"[34] which is an impact only a highly developed and integrated person has on those around him.

Another quality that was characteristic of Larry was the seriousness and respect with which he approached people and situations. When others talked, he "appeared to take part in the conversation without opening his mouth,"[35] and he listened "not with his ears, but with some inner more sensitive organ of hearing."[36] When he spoke, he used no "gesticulation of any kind" but "looked you in the face with a pleasant, often whimsical expression in his dark eyes."[37] He also did not impose himself on others by talking too much, "but it didn't matter, his company was sufficient conversation."[38] Although his seriousness was never referred to as grim, but, quite contrary, "so pleasantly cheerful,"[39] the impression is that he is somewhat too sensible and hardly ever prone to antics, which might diminish the roundedness of his character.

The book of essays Larry wrote was an expression of the urge to share with others the achievements he had attained in his personal development. That was one of the reasons why, in the end, he returned to the United States after all. Even though Americans were described in the novel as "restless, busy, lawless, intensely individualistic,"[40] and his attempt to change them as viable as holding "back the waters of the Mississippi with your bare hands,"[41] Larry was not deferred. "I can try. It was one man who invented the wheel."[42] He believed that his personal example, without placing himself in the forefront, was the best he could do, and that those who sought truth would be naturally drawn to those who have achieved higher levels of purity and integrity.

Larry's altruistic personality style was corroborated by the concrete actions of sacrifice he was undertaking in order to help those he thought needed help. Thus he offered shelter and sustenance to Suzanne, a destitute lover of Parisian artists, and her little daughter, renting a country house for them. Furthermore, he also gave them his affection, time, even shared the bed with Suzanne, but left in the end when his help was no longer essential. In Spain, he let a pregnant eighteen-year-old girl live with him for a while, and the most selfless act of sacrifice was his proposal to marry Sophie, a desperate American girl addicted to alcohol and drugs, and thus save her from complete decline. The enterprise did not work out in the end, but his heroism is no lesser for it. Isabel did not consider his actions unconditionally heroic, for she thought he had an "urgent, clamorous need to save [...] soul[s]."[43] To pass a judgment on the nature of such altruistic acts, not too frequently to be found among humankind, is a delicate matter. Even though there might be some base in Isabel's stance, it is much easier to criticize than to perform such acts.

The ambiguous slant of his relating to others was his uncatchableness and superficial irresponsibility. One of the habits he retained from his adolescence was to keep secret where he lived, and to disappear and reappear completely unexpectedly. "He never liked telling people where he lived,"[44] and he was "with you one moment and without explanation gone the next. It was so abrupt; it was almost as if he had faded into the air."[45] There was also some kind of detachment and evasiveness about him that it was difficult for anyone to feel genuine intimacy with him. When talking to people, he would employ his "cordial frankness, but so vaguely as not to tell [...] much."[46] It was as if "he withheld in some hidden part of his soul something"[47] that set him apart. Maugham, a character in the novel, even compared him to "a great actor playing perfectly a part in a trumpery play."[48]

The comparison of Larry with an actor in a play does not give credit to his psychological maturity, for it is mostly disordered personalities who do not live authentically but under the dictate of a construct they created about how they should be. Isabel, who loved Larry and tried to understand him, which love in its essence is all about, was somewhat milder in her judgment. She too agreed that there was an untamed element in Larry's person, but she attributed this quality to something he was unconsciously guarding deep down – "a tension, a secret, an aspiration, a knowledge."[49] Taking into account that she was the one who was most hurt by Larry's unconventionality, her words bear greater significance and somewhat justify Larry's evasiveness.

One of the greatest tests of maturity is responsibility. Was Larry able to pass it? Looking at his behavior from the superficiality of social norms, he behaved in an unreliable manner, particularly when his engagement to Isabel was concerned. He shunned the responsibility he had taken over. However, it was not irresponsibility that was the reason for his retreat from the vows, but a responsibility of a different kind: to his own self, to his desire to know himself, to explore the spiritual substratum of his being, which, for him, held a greater significance than the word he had given to Isabel. In the moral dilemma of which value to prioritize, he prioritized his spiritual quest, in which others would stand in his way. Paradoxically, it turned out to be the most responsible action he could have taken. A truly authentic person must choose "the option for what, to what, or to whom he understands himself to be responsible."[50] Isabel found it possible, no matter how far a stretch it was for her, to accept Larry's choice in spite of her love for him, because he did not betray her or meant to hurt her and because she sensed he had greater things to achieve. This is why, perhaps, we may find it easier to believe her judgment of Larry rather than Maugham's.

The last aspect of the state of Larry's psychological maturity that we will touch upon here is his relationship with reality. Did he meet the important prerequisite of mental balance to see reality in an objective way? The same dichotomous view that was employed when his responsibility was considered can be employed here, too. He disregarded most of what average Americans of his age saw as ultimately realistic – money, business, romantic love, family, culture. Larry's reality was of a different kind, for he saw beyond cultural constructs, and into higher, nonmaterialistic, nonconforming truths. So, to the majority, his attitude to objective reality was askew, which is referred to many times in the novel by various characters, but for the spiritually insightful, his view of the world was of a higher order.

Compared to an average person of any era, Larry Darrell does represent a highly mature adult with many characteristics of superb balance on his psychological continuum. The ambiguous traits that he possesses can be viewed in both positive and negative light, but even if seen as flaws, they just make him less of an ideal and more of a human being the reader may identify with. Let us now explore the extent and kind of spiritual maturity that he had achieved.

Larry Darrell's Spirituality

As it frequently happens, particularly in adolescence, a concrete event triggers one's sudden immersion in perennial themes. In Larry's case, that event took place in the war, when his plane got caught in a cross fire, and when his friend Patsy, in order to save Larry's life, shielded him with his plane, and got killed. This experience greatly changed Larry, despite the fact that he was reticent about it. Upon his return to Chicago, everybody noticed his transformation. "He was so normal before the war. One of the nice things about him was his enormous zest for life. […] What can have happened to change him so much?"[51] asked Isabel. What happened was Larry's immediate encounter with death; on top of that, it was the death of a young man, his best friend, who volunteered to die in order to save Larry. In Larry's own words, "I didn't find that easy to get over."[52] The stark contrast between his twenty-two-year-old friend Patsy's vitality, impudence, wildness, genuineness, and the sight of "mangled flesh that looked as if it had never been alive,"[53] or a "marionette […] that the showman had thrown into the discard,"[54] made him sleepless for nights, during which he wondered about evil in the world, about God, about human destiny. Many questions that arose he knew no answers to, and every other concern faded to gray. His life's purpose now was but an attempt to achieve at least some answers to the questions that were besetting him. Others tried to dissuade him, Isabel first of all, fearing that "he's looking for something, but what it is he doesn't know, and perhaps he isn't even sure it's there."[55] Larry wouldn't disagree with her statement, but his urge to unveil deeper truths was stronger than rational counterarguments.

At the start of his quest, Larry had no knowledge of the things he was inquiring into. "I didn't know anyone I could turn to and I wanted to learn, so I began to read at haphazard."[56] Engagement in a kind of autobibliotherapy was the first step that he had made. After he spent weeks and weeks reading psychology, philosophy, and science books in

Chicago libraries, he felt he had exhausted the potentials his country was able to offer, without getting any nearer to the truths that intrigued him, so he left for Paris. There he continued to read, attended lectures at the Sorbonne, and instead of wrapping his quest up and going back to America after two years, as he had planned, he saw "vast lands of the spirit stretching out"[57] before him. The power of his urge to learn about things was overbearing, so he moved further on.

For some years he lingered in Europe, where he acquired most varied experiences, all with an aim of finding alternative routes to the heart of knowledge. Thus he worked as a manual laborer in a mine in Northern France, where his Polish coworker and roommate Kosti, when drunk, talked about ultimate reality and mystical union with God. This made Larry "confused and excited,"[58] and propelled him on in his quest, where the quality of "saintliness"[59] began to shine at the far end of his adventure as an ever-fixed star. In Germany he spent several months in a Christian monastery, living in a barren monastic cell, talking to the fathers and engaging in the regimented religious life of the community. However, he reported that "those good fathers had no answers that satisfied either my head or my heart to the questions that perplexed me."[60] He was nearing the goals he wanted to attain, but his movements were still circumambulatory. What he urged for was to walk straight into the heart of the matter.

As noted earlier, he spent time in several other European countries before moving on to Asia, in which India played a crucial role. Planning to spend only a few days in it, he ended up staying there for several years, and it was there that he concluded his spiritual odyssey and felt ready to return to America. Why was his Indian experience so crucial?

The casual initial encounter with *murtis*, or sacred images of Hindu deities, struck him profoundly and made him feel that "India had something to give that [...] [he] had to have."[61] The exchange between the spiritual heritage of India and Larry's existential quest took place at a subconscious level, stirring Larry's intuition strongly, so he felt he had to take as much time there as he needed to explore this sudden connection.

The Indian subcontinent is huge and culturally varied, so Larry ventured into different environments, getting fascinated with unswerving devotion millions of Indians were expressing in temples, at the shores of the Ganges in Benares, or in the caves of Elephanta around the sacred rock sculptures. The decisive adventure proved to be his stay at an *ashram*, or spiritual retreat, where he took up a *guru* named Shri Ganesha. After two years of spiritual training and maturing, Larry would sometimes leave the community and spend days on his own in a log cabin high up in the mountains. He thus fulfilled the prerequisites for spiritual growth that require solitude, for some of the most intimate spiritual events take place only when no other people are around. After occasional visits to the cabin over a few years, Larry's final solitary sojourn there, which coincided with his birthday, seemed to unveil the hidden truth he had been yearning to plunge into.

What exactly happened to Larry in the mountain woods, at sunrise by the lake, is difficult to ascertain. Maugham's rendition of Larry's experience stirred a lot of negative literary criticism. In any case, on that occasion when Larry's perception of the surging morning light became overwhelming, there were changes at the physiological level making his "heart beating as though at the approach of danger"[62] and his whole body tingle. He also lost track of time. The landscape before his eyes shone in a new light, intensely but brilliantly. The beauty of the sight took on a metaphysical quality, and he felt "a transcendent joy."[63] It was as if he had left his physical body "as pure spirit partook of a loveliness [...] [he] had never conceived."[64] Besides beauty, another sensation fused with it was of "a knowledge more than human"[65] that instantly clarified all his confusions and uncertainties. The intensity of the experience was tremendous and life-altering, but at the same time overbearing, so that Larry thought "if it lasted a moment longer [...][he] should die."[66] When it was gone, he felt "exhausted and trembling"[67] and fell asleep.

Leaving aside criticism whether Maugham's description of Larry's glimpse into higher, unitive knowledge has been authentically rendered or not, what concerns us here is the fact that, having experienced the events described here, Larry felt his aim was attained, his mission concluded, and the inner stability necessary for his return home acquired. Even though the America he was returning to was not a place that encouraged the virtues of "calmness, forbearance, compassion, selflessness and continence"[68] he wanted to practice, he did not feel either discouraged or threatened by it, but with a new spiritual security that he had gained, he felt he might make a positive impact on those Americans who were drawn to the same values that he was living. The goal Larry was striving for seemed to be peace and happiness, and Maugham concludes the novel that his was "a success story."[69]

Larry's spiritual adventure meets all the criteria of religious maturity. In the first place, his search was characterized by rare openness. Instead of joining a religious institution and trying to come to terms with his questions through it, as most frequently is the case in real life, he undertook a journey that took him to unexpected places and made him explore unexpected ideas. The guidelines he followed were dichotomous. On one side, he was certain what he wanted – only those experiences that would genuinely resonate with the yearnings of his soul; on the other, he was not sure where such experiences were to be found, so he was attentively open to anything that might help him come closer to the truths that he sought.

He did not care for spiritual sensationalism, like, for example, "the Rope Trick"[70] or other supernatural feats performed by yogis, for he thought they "hinder[ed] spiritual progress."[71] On the other hand, he did not shrink away from practices such as hypnosis, because it had practical value in that it could be used to help people (he applied it to cure his friend's headaches), and probably because his intuition did not alarm him against it. At the same time, he was unable to be influenced by some *bona fide* spiritual authorities, such as the monks at the Benedictine monastery where he spent several months, because what they conveyed to him did not completely fit into his inner vision. It is quite paradoxical that he did not doubt their genuineness, simultaneously having many doubts about himself, but he still preferred to rely on some profound powers beyond his uncertainties than on the certainty of others, however authentic they were. Due to the adherence to the way of the spirit Larry thought he was suited for "the Middle Ages when faith was a matter of course,"[72] giving little thought to the fact that the historical period he idealized was largely dogmatic and unfriendly to religious openness like Larry's. One of the Benedictine fathers cleared it up for him: "I think it's just as well you weren't born in the Middle Ages. You'd undoubtedly have perished at the stake."[73]

The process of Larry's spiritual maturing was gradual but profound and transformative. Most of the time it took its course beyond Larry's consciousness, as such maturing always does, so that even when he was well advanced on his way he thought he was only groping in the dark. At the end of his stay in the Benedictine monastery, Larry truly felt as a disappointment to the fathers. However, what he was not able to see was perfectly obvious to Father Ensheim, one of the most spiritually open monks he had spent a lot of time with. Refuting Larry's fear of being a disappointment, the Father said to him, "You are a deeply religious man who doesn't believe in God. God will seek you out. You'll come back. Whether here or elsewhere only God can tell."[74]

Larry's distance from full immersion into a faith that would "satisfy both his head and his heart"[75] had been "no greater than the thickness of a cigarette paper"[76] for many years. He spared no time and no effort to make more progress. The religious practices he engaged in were again in accord with his personal standards rather than with the standards of any traditional religion. He disliked petitionary prayers and wondered what kind of god would "bring […] children into the world that he can't or won't provide for."[77] Besides, he deemed it distasteful "to wangle salvation by fulsome flattery"[78] but considered the deeds to the best of one's abilities a much more pleasing form of worship. This idea is directly linked with the psychological virtue of responsibility – Larry did not want to rid himself of it. In the same vein, he challenged the idea of eternal damnation, placing the better part of blame for even the worst crimes in the hands of society. The God he wanted to believe in could not be "an all-wise God who hadn't common sense"[79] and only wanted to make it more difficult for humans to enhance their spirituality by overly testing them, but a benevolent father, "a being enormously better, wiser and greater than man."[80] Larry was ready to renounce most of his materialistic comforts and pleasures, including money and sex, in order to approach the heart of the great mystery permeated with God's goodness. The mature spiritual trait that he featured was the ability to discard dogmas and principles of institutionalized religion that ran counter to logics, conscientiousness, and intuition, but at the same time never to belittle or attack any religious tradition. He was simply trying to find his own way, navigating through the seas and straits of the world's spiritual bounty, finally sailing into the port that did contain what he was searching for. For him, that port was Hinduism.

The oldest of the world's great religions appealed to Larry's spiritual yearnings because it reflected the knowledge that was unconsciously harbored in the deep recesses of his being, and also because it matched his psychological setup. He liked the fact that Hinduism, or at least its Advaita Vedanta[81] branch, did not ask the followers "to take anything on trust"[82] but to "have a passionate craving to know Reality."[83] Within the pragmatic wing of Hindu practices, guided by perfected gurus, Larry experienced spiritual events that irrevocably enlarged his personality and brought a closure to much of his restlessness. One of these events was a meditation by the light of a candle, during which he "saw a long line of figures one behind the other"[84] that apparently represented the bodies of his previous incarnations on earth. Unsure about the length of the experience, and skeptical about the very concept of reincarnation, this event did shift some of his perspectives and contributed to an even greater openness of his religious horizon. The other, even more definitive event was the previously described illuminative experience that he had by the mountain lake at sunrise. Although Larry was not sure if he was "one with the Absolute or if it was an inrush from the subconscious of an affinity with the universal spirit which is latent in all of us,"[85] the experience nevertheless had a strong and lasting impact on his personality.

Which qualities did Larry attain after the long quest and after the ultimately transforming experiences in India? First of all, "the intense sense of peace, joy and assurance"[86] and a freshness of the vision of the world that possessed him during his glimpse into the metaphysical realm remained with him for good. This irreversible subtlety achieved during such "moment[s] of rapture"[87] is one of the signs that the spiritual event in question was not a random psychological or psychopathological incident of the mind, but a genuine contact with the Absolute lore. Larry's experience also meets the principal criteria of a *bona fide* mystical experience as set up by William James (i.e. ineffability, noetic quality, transiency, and passivity). Briefly, the odyssey of the spirit Larry undertook did not fail to bear positive fruit. Upon his eventual return to America, he seems to have gained profound wisdom and weaned himself "from the slavery of selfhood, passion and sense."[88] The ideals of "tranquility, restraint, renunciation, resignation, by steadfastness of mind and by an ardent desire for freedom"[89] and the acceptance of "something [that] is inevitable"[90] cease to be pure ideals and become practical principles that guide his life. Larry at the beginning of the novel is but a bud of hazy spiritual yearnings, while Larry from the final pages of the book is a fully blossomed urban mystic.

Larry's altruism, which was already touched upon in the section where the criteria of his psychological maturity were discussed, may at the same time be taken to represent a criterion of his spiritual maturity. Even though in his youth he broke some promises that involved the happiness of others, he had to do it because any other outcome, in Larry's own words, would "be the betrayal of my soul."[91] In his choice, his soul was the instance of utmost authority, and wronging against it would in no way help others. When he grew somewhat psychologically and spiritually sturdier, he engaged in acts of selfless sacrifice for the benefit of others, which, eventually, turned out futile. What matters, though, is the compassion, the acceptance, the readiness to sacrifice. "When he sacrifices himself man for a moment is greater than God, for how can God, infinite and omnipotent, sacrifice himself? At best he can only sacrifice his only begotten son."[92] This statement from the novel may be theologically problematic for many reasons, but it serves to emphasize sacrifice as one of the fruits of Larry's transformation, regardless of how doomed or even insensible his efforts were.

One more criterion is important to mention, and that is the absence of any form of proselytizing or misusing of God's name. In fact, Larry mentions God only in theological conversations, but in everyday life, he instead uses more open terms for his spiritual standpoints or, better still, puts words aside and lets practical actions speak.

Based on the previous analysis, it does not seem that Larry displays any of the traits of spiritual immaturity. This, however, does not mean that his religiosity deserves no criticism, but as earlier noted, our aim is to evaluate only his attitude to religion, not the nature of his religious beliefs. In more open-minded theological approaches, the nature of one's beliefs is not discussed at all, since it is very personal and unsuited to material proofs. What makes it possible to make conclusions about one's religiosity is not based on what a person believes in, but on how the person's beliefs manifest in the social and the natural environment. "Religion is not about believing in something, it's about doing something!"[93] Larry passes this test with quite a high score.

Still, this chapter would be somewhat incomplete if we did not touch upon some of the problematic aspects of Larry's religiosity. They relate both to his attitude to religion, which is more important to us, and, as previously mentioned, to the way Maugham depicts some of his spiritual experiences.

Where Larry's attitude to religion is concerned, two observations may be made. First, Larry displays some cultural conditioning that runs counter to the unconventionality of his quest. For example, he says that it is not possible for the Westerners to believe in reincarnation "as implicitly as [...] Orientals do."[94] With people like him, "it can only be an opinion."[95] However, on the very same page of the novel, he goes on to describe the inexplicable experience he had while meditating, in which he allegedly saw the bodies his soul had inhabited in the past. He remains somewhat rationally skeptical about the concept of reincarnation even after this occurrence, although the fact that he did have this experience and that he is retelling it rebuts the culturally conditioned doubts that he possessed.

The second, much graver spiritual inconsistency in his generally non-dogmatic approach to religion is the hierarchization of certain paths to perfection and the favoring of them over others. This in the first place refers to his notion that "to attain Reality by knowledge"[96] is superior to "the way of love and the way of works."[97] In other words, he superimposes *jnana yoga* to *bhakti yoga*, *karma yoga* or any other valid path to the divine by saying that "the noblest way, though the hardest, is the way of knowledge, for its instrument is the most precious faculty of man, his reason."[98] For a perfectly mature spiritual person, no way is "the noblest" and no faculty "the most precious." Furthermore, to place reason above other faculties in a spiritual context is additionally problematic, since essential inner events take place at levels far beyond the rational. It would have been acceptable if he had just stated that the way of knowledge is best suited to his personality, for different ways exist because different personality morphologies are better suited to them, but to claim that one path is better than any other one is a stain, however slight, on the profile of Larry's spiritual maturity.

Where actual spiritual practices are concerned, critics ruthlessly debunked descriptions of Larry's mystical experiences. The main criticism refers to their inauthenticity, for Maugham, not one of the best masters of the word, ventured into describing ineffable phenomena without having experienced them. He recounted what he wished to have had happen to him but never had experienced, and so relied heavily on accounts of mystical events given by others. To find the right words to convey the nature of these events is one of the most difficult tasks for those who actually did experience them, and the only language they find remotely adequate is the language of poetry and paradox. Maugham lacked both – actual experience and the poetic gift – but, as noted earlier, these criticisms stand outside the scope of our analysis.

The high level of maturity, along with the less substantial flaws, the inconsistencies, the unconventionality and haziness of Larry's personality, all make him appealing to the reader and a vividly memorable character in English literature. There are more both psychologically and spiritually mature characters in a number of other literary works, like Almustafa in Gibran's *The Prophet*, or a series of gurus in Aldous Huxley's novels

(Dr. Miller, Mr. Propter, Bruno Rontini, etc.), but all of them are somewhat too ethereal and devoid of human quirkiness. This is why Larry Darrell has been chosen to represent the category of the mentioned dual maturity.

Notes

1 Anthony Curtis, *Somerset Maugham*, Windsor: Profile Books, 1982, p. 37.
2 Selina Hastings, *The Secret Lives of Somerset Maugham*, London: John Murray, 2010, pp. 471–472.
3 Richard Cordell, *Somerset Maugham*, London: Heinemann, 1961, p. 131.
4 See: Jeffrey Meyers, *Somerset Maugham, A Life*, New York: Alfred A. Knopf, 2004, p. 260.
5 *Ibid.*, p. 261.
6 Somerset Maugham, *The Razor's Edge*, London: Heinemann, 1964, p. 20.
7 *Ibid.*, p. 19.
8 *Ibid.*, p. 24.
9 *Ibid.*, p. 62.
10 *Ibid.*, p. 137.
11 Larry stated that antagonism "arouses antagonism in you and that disturbs you," *Ibid.*, p. 46.
12 *Ibid.*, p. 143.
13 *Ibid.*
14 *Ibid.*, p. 84.
15 *Ibid.*, p. 31.
16 *Ibid.*, p. 92.
17 *Ibid.*, p. 272.
18 *Ibid.*, p. 29.
19 *Ibid.*, p. 41.
20 *Ibid.*, p. 54.
21 *Ibid.*, p. 268.
22 *Ibid.*, p. 178.
23 *Ibid.*, p. 294.
24 *Ibid.*, p. 303.
25 *Ibid.*, p. 303.
26 *Ibid.*, p. 146.
27 *Ibid.*, p. 175.
28 *Ibid.*, p. 177.
29 *Ibid.*, p. 196.
30 *Ibid.*, p. 261.
31 *Ibid.*, p. 37.
32 *Ibid.*, p. 76.
33 *Ibid.*, p. 2.
34 *Ibid.*, p. 142.
35 *Ibid.*, p. 17.
36 *Ibid.*, p. 140.
37 *Ibid.*, p. 100.
38 *Ibid.*, p. 180.
39 *Ibid.*
40 *Ibid.*, p. 272.
41 *Ibid.*
42 *Ibid.*

43 *Ibid.*, p. 201.
44 *Ibid.*, p. 141.
45 *Ibid.*, p. 173.
46 *Ibid.*, p. 145.
47 *Ibid.*, p. 155.
48 *Ibid.*
49 *Ibid.*
50 Viktor Frankl, *Man's Search for Meaning*, New York: Pocket Books, 1985, p. 132.
51 Somerset Maugham, *The Razor's Edge*, p. 48.
52 *Ibid.*, p. 45.
53 *Ibid.*, p. 243.
54 *Ibid.*
55 *Ibid.*, p. 48.
56 *Ibid.*, p. 243.
57 *Ibid.*, p. 64.
58 *Ibid.*, p. 99.
59 *Ibid.*, p. 148.
60 *Ibid.*, p. 247.
61 *Ibid.*, p. 253.
62 *Ibid.*, p. 266.
63 *Ibid.*
64 *Ibid.*
65 *Ibid.*
66 *Ibid.*
67 *Ibid.*
68 *Ibid.*, p. 271.
69 *Ibid.*, p. 304.
70 *Ibid.*, p. 145.
71 *Ibid.*, p. 146.
72 *Ibid.*, p. 245.
73 *Ibid.*, p. 246.
74 *Ibid.*, p. 247.
75 *Ibid.*, p. 202.
76 *Ibid.*, p. 243.
77 *Ibid.*, p. 245.
78 *Ibid.*, p. 246.
79 *Ibid.*, p. 247.
80 *Ibid.*
81 "a philosophy maintaining that the physical and metaphysical aspects of reality form a seamless unity," Dana Sawyer, *Huston Smith: Wisdomkeeper*, Louisville, KY: Fons Vitae, 2014, p. 40.
82 Somerset Maugham, *The Razor's Edge*, p. 261.
83 *Ibid.*
84 *Ibid.*, p. 257.
85 *Ibid.*, p. 267.
86 *Ibid.*, p. 268.
87 *Ibid.*
88 *Ibid.*, p. 264.
89 *Ibid.*
90 *Ibid.*, p. 271.
91 *Ibid.*, p. 70.
92 *Ibid.*, p. 201.

93 Monique Kester, "Karen Armstrong: Don't do to others you don't want others to do to you," *Speakers Academy Journal*, Rotterdam, 2006, p. 19.
94 Somerset Maugham, *The Razor's Edge*, p. 257.
95 *Ibid.*
96 *Ibid.*, p. 261.
97 *Ibid.*
98 *Ibid.*

4 The Slow-Witted Mystic

Mrs. Dempster and Fool-Saintly Religiosity

Fifth Business (1970), although only the first part of *The Deptford Trilogy* (along with *The Manticore* and *World of Wonders*), is probably the best-known novel by one of Canada's canonical authors, Robertson Davies (1913–1995). "Much of its success arises from its satisfying characterizations"[1] and a "Dickensian richness of character and plot."[2] The reason for including it into this analysis is not the main character Dunstan Ramsay, a retired college headmaster, who recounts the last fifty-five years of his life through a first-person, Jungian narrative of individuation, but a woman who indelibly influenced his spiritual development. Her name was Mary Dempster, and she was foolish in many ways, but, in Ramsay's view, also saintly. He spends "years of passionate questing into mythology and the mysteries of sainthood"[3] in order to investigate whether what lay beyond her psychologically inadequate profile was pure spirituality or not. He is one of the few who believes that it was.

The Story of Mrs. Dempster

Mrs. Dempster, the young wife of one of the local pastors in the imaginary small town of Deptford (based on Thamesville in the province of Ontario), entered Ramsay's life when he was still a preteen boy, on a snowy day in 1908. Playing with another kid in the street, Ramsay ducked a snowball thrown at him. It ended up hitting the young, pregnant wife walking with her husband. She fell, bringing herself to "a series of hysterical crying fits,"[4] and soon afterward gave premature birth to a boy they named Paul. This episode turned out to be crucial for "all the Deptford characters throughout the entire trilogy."[5] Ramsay's mother, being a nearby neighbor, but also considering Mary somewhat simple, went to the Dempsters daily to help the young couple with the baby. Dunstan went with her most of the time. Gradually, he switched his attachment from his mother, whom he started experiencing as inadequately warm and flexible, to Mrs. Dempster, who was turned into "an idealized maternal figure."[6] Ramsay's fascination with the woman who is socially "rejected as unfit even to be a parson's wife"[7] grew stronger and stronger after she performed three feats that made him think of her as of "a miracle-working saint."[8] Later in life, when Mary's son ran away from home, when her husband died in 1918, and when her mental illness aggravated to the point of having to end up in a psychiatric institution, Ramsay was the only person who visited her and helped arrange her funeral when she passed away. Even "the undertaker mistakes him for her son."[9] As noted earlier, the course of his life and his obsession with saints was greatly influenced by the ways of Mary Dempster. Let us see what the three miraculous acts that she allegedly performed were. The entire novel is roughly constructed around them, and its "six parts divide rather neatly. In each of the first three, a 'miracle' of Mary Dempster's is recorded. In each of the last three, Dunstan moves closer to discovering the place his fool saint occupies in his life."[10]

What Dunstan Ramsay sees as Mary's first miracle in fact "outrages the villagers"[11] of Deptford. One night she goes missing, and the whole village sets out in search of her. They finally glare their flashlights onto a scene of her "copulating in the town's gravel pit with a tramp."[12] She seems undisturbed by being discovered in such a compromising situation, and her husband, though "crushed by Mary's public humiliation,"[13] still "takes her courteously by the arm and gently walks home with her."[14] What actually happened is that a tramp intended to rape her, but instead of resisting or getting paralyzed by fear, "the pitiful woman pities him, is gentle with him,"[15] and transforms "personal violation to negotiated contract."[16] The implications of this act, and the reasons why Ramsay saw it as a feat of saintliness, will be discussed later in the chapter.

Soon after the pit incident, Mary's husband tied her to a long rope inside the house, which she now hardly ever left, so as not to bring more disgrace upon herself and her family. Dunstan was, of course, forbidden to see her, but he still found furtive ways of getting into the Dempsters' house and talking to Mary. On an occasion when his parents were out at a fair, Dunstan "seeks her aid when he believes his brother has died, and she performs her second miracle."[17] Willie Ramsay had been ill for a long time, and that evening, when Dunstan was alone with him, he went "white and cold and stiff."[18] The first person Dunstan turned for help was "that woman, who was an insane degenerate."[19] When she arrived, she looked at the patient "solemnly but not sadly, then she knelt by the bed and took his hands in hers and prayed. [...] After a while she raised her head and called him. 'Willie,' she said in a low, infinitely kind, and indeed almost a cheerful tone. [...] She shook his hands gently, as if rousing a sleeper. [...] Willie sighed and moved his legs a little."[20] He had come back to life. For Dunstan, this event "is, and always will be, Mrs. Dempster's second miracle."[21]

The third miracle took place at the World War I battlefield of Passchendaele in Belgium, where Ramsay found himself after voluntarily enlisting in the army. He made the choice of becoming a soldier after his mother had given him an ultimatum of choosing between her or Mrs. Dempster. She could not bear the thought of him communicating with both of them at the same time. In the midst of the battle, Ramsay is violently wounded within the walls of a bombed church. "Before he loses consciousness, he sees a vision of a Madonna with the face of Mrs. Dempster."[22] The fact that he managed to survive such violent trauma convinces him that Mary "'miraculously' saved[...] his life"[23] and ascribes the act as her third miracle.

Why was Mrs. Dempster perceived socially in such diametrically opposite ways by the majority on one side and by Dunstan Ramsay on the other? Was she a lunatic or a saint? Or both? Definitive conclusions are impossible due to the shiftiness and the fluidity of the categories embodied in her, so let us attempt to outline her psychological and her spiritual portraits, which some are able to reconcile, and some are not.

Mrs. Dempster's Personality Traits

The aforementioned inconsistency in the evaluation of Mary Dempster's personality is evident even in the critical texts and reviews of the novel. Some authors call her a "supposed madwoman"[24] with a "curious way of comprehending things,"[25] some use the word "dotty,"[26] and to others she is an "apparent madwoman."[27] The way she is described in the novel does leave room for such ambiguities.

Before the pit incident, Mrs. Dempster was seen as benevolently silly and an inadequate housewife. She would "laugh so much when nobody else could see anything to laugh at,"[28] and "did a little cleaning and some inept cooking, and laughed like a girl at her failures."[29] When she gave birth to her little son Paul, she loved and cherished him, breastfeeding him in such a way that "all the neighbors had to admit that she did it well,"[30] albeit a little too unabashedly for the small town taste, with "everything showing, even though her husband was present."[31] Paul did receive the emotional warmth and support from his mother, but "he was in his appearance a pitifully neglected child."[32] This is another example of her tendency to disregard the tangible and the rational, but be fully immersed in the below-the-surface qualities. In the same vein, it would bring her great joy to go around the village giving things away, even though her gifts were inadequate, either worthless ("bunches of wilted rhubarb, or some rank lettuce, or other stuff from her garden, which was so ill tended"[33]) or extravagant ("she gave an ornamental vase to a woman who had taken her a few bakings of bread; the vase was part of the furnishings of the parsonage"[34]). Despite the disapproval such acts of hers received in Deptford, some still saw the value beyond them and their inspirational potential: "The pity is that more people with more to give don't feel the same way."[35] She would also "spend a whole morning wondering from house to house,"[36] not knowing "where she was going next, and sometimes she would visit one house three times in a morning, to the annoyance of a busy woman who was washing or getting a meal for her husband and sons."[37] Briefly, it is not difficult to figure out why her unwillingness to "subscribe to the Deptford wives' mandatory code of conduct"[38] disseminated "the opinion [...] that nothing would ever make a preacher's wife out of that one."[39]

The gravel pit event turned the benign, silly Mrs. Dempster into a dangerous lunatic. First of all, what exasperated the villagers was the fact that upon finding her in such a compromising act, "Mrs. Dempster [wa]s the only calm, self-possessed person there."[40] She showed no signs of embarrassment, and acted as if she knew what she was doing, and that there was nothing wrong in it. "It is an incredible deviation from the reaction we might expect from a woman so flagrantly taken in adultery, humiliated before her neighbors."[41] In order to clarify her calmness, more light should be shed on the event from the perspective of the tramp.

Many years after the incident, Ramsay came across a Christian volunteer and charity worker named Joe Surgeoner, who turned out to have been the infamous Deptford tramp. Surgeoner then recounted what had happened that night, and the effect the event had on his life. He met this young woman wondering on her own, which was strange, because she was clean and did not look like a female tramp. He "threatened her and asked for money,"[42] but since she didn't have any, he "started to push her down and grab at her clothes."[43] Instead of displaying fear, "she said, 'Why are you so rough?'"[44] which made the tramp cry. Then, she held his head "to her breast and talked nicely"[45] to him, which made him cry even more. However, he still wanted her, and it seemed to him "as if only that would put [...] [him] right,"[46] so that is what he told her. Her response perplexed him greatly: "You may if you promise not to be rough!"[47]

Looking back on the event, Surgeoner said that it "was glory come into [...][his] life."[48] He realized things were not completely hopeless, as his pessimistic homeless lifestyle had suggested, but that there was redeeming potential in the world. In his case, this potential was embodied in the unknown young woman who was neither hysterical nor paralyzed by fear at his attempt of rape, but profoundly human and compassionate, though in a bizarre and socially outrageous way. The life-changing effect Mary Dempster's act had on Surgeoner convinced him that God "worked through that woman,"[49] that she was "a blessed saint,"[50] and that her "complete and utter sacrifice"[51] for him "was a miracle."[52]

When her husband asked why she did it, Mary "looked him honestly in the face and gave the answer that became famous in Deptford: 'He was very civil, 'Masa. And he wanted it so badly!'"[53] Degrading her honesty to a most profane level, men would make lewd jokes about her, kids would ask her son: "Hey, Paul, does your Ma wear any pants?"[54] while women were disgusted because "Mrs. Dempster has not been raped, as a decent woman would have been – no, she had yielded because a man wanted her."[55] Nobody, save for Ramsay, and of course Surgeoner, had the psychological and spiritual sensitivity to see beyond the culturally and socially imposed concept of her "supposedly profane action."[56]

What was it that actually lay at the core of her controversial act of compassion? She intuitively responded to a violently desperate urge of a rejected human being by accepting him; taking his needs into account; and sacrificing her own safety, decency, tastes, and social standing for him. In other words, the nonverbal message of her compliance was that he was worthy of being listened to, gratified, sacrificed for, "that he still was a human being, not an animal."[57] The act stirred diametrically opposite reactions – on one side, the "God fearing" villagers were horrified, and on the other, Surgeoner was reborn. Mary herself displayed no great excitement in either of these ways. She was unable to rationalize her actions and at least try to defend herself, because she lacked the mental capacity to do so, while abounding in spiritual intuition. Feeling no need to emphasize her good deeds, she probably thought her reasons would be obvious to everybody. In the light of saving a fellow human's destiny, what significance does a casual carnal act have? What really mattered was that somebody was taken out of "Hell and [...] the worst of fire"[58] into, in Surgeoner's own words, "a clear, pure pool where I could wash and be clean."[59] If "Deptford's gravel pit [i]s an allegory of hell,"[60] then "Mary's descent can be seen as akin to the apocryphal descent in some Orthodox traditions of the mother of God into Hell, where harrowing and salvation take place."[61] Joe Surgeoner saw it in that light; Dunstan Ramsay did, too.

Amasa Dempster was racked by humiliation, shame, helplessness, and grief, but even though his wife was ruining his career and his life, he still cherished feelings of tenderness and compassion for her. By not chastising or punishing her brutally for the ludicrous act, as a huge majority of husbands of the era would have, he joined Ramsay's and Surgeoner's non-accusing alliance. Still, he had to protect what was left of his dignity by keeping "her tied to a long rope inside the house, so that she could move freely through it but not get out."[62] By doing this, he also protected their child and her own self from further dishonor. Thus encaged, "she began to look very strange indeed, and if she was not mad before, people said, she was mad now."[63] The local priest diagnosed her with "a degeneration of the brain, which was probably progressive."[64] The withdrawal of freedom (which she had so relished), not social detestation (for she did not develop an understanding of how others perceived her), contributed to further deterioration of her mind. However, she still was the only person Ramsay could think of to turn to for help when his brother apparently died, and she was still well enough to perform another act which figures in the novel as her second miracle.

An incident that irrevocably decomposed Mary Dempster's fragile state of mind, and that would hang over her as the heaviest shadow until her last breath, was the disappearance of her ten-year-old son Paul, who chose to run away with a circus show rather than be mercilessly teased by other kids about his crazy, "hoor"[65] mother. "Mary Dempster took it very bad and went clean off her head. Used to yell out the window at kids going to school, 'Have you seen my son Paul?'"[66] This happened a little after her husband had died. When she finally realized that Paul had gone for good, the local doctor "had to give her very strong morphine."[67] One of the villagers said, "I've never seen such grief."[68] Unable to fare on her own, an aunt who lived near Toronto took her in. It would be many years before Ramsay saw Mrs. Dempster again, for he had gone to war prior to these events and was told about them upon his return to Deptford.

However, the previous statement that Ramsay did not see Mary Dempster while he was in war might not be entirely true. He did claim to have seen her face in "a statue of the Virgin and Child"[69] just before he lost consciousness in a bombed church on the Belgian battlefield. Also, he claimed she was "a visitor to [...][his] long coma."[70] The fact that he eventually did wake up he ascribed to Mrs. Dempster's third miraculous intervention. She instigated the "transformation of the hell of Passchendaele into a visionary redemption,"[71] as well as Ramsay's obsession with "the study of saints, the ultimate goal of which [wa]s to have Mary Dempster canonized."[72]

Once he saw her again many years later, she was a very different person from the one Ramsay remembered. She appeared "an unremarkable woman really, except for the great sweetness of expression; her dress was simple, and I suppose the aunt chose it, for it was a good deal longer than the fashion of the time and had a homemade air."[73] She also had no recollection of Ramsay. However, when he spoke about Paul, "the aunt had to intervene, and take her away,"[74] because every mention of him still "roused painful associations."[75] The aunt added that "when she thinks of him, it is awful to hear her cry and carry on."[76] The pain of a mother who lost her child was alive and unrelenting in her mentally unsettled but emotionally magnified life.

Although Paul was lost to Mary, Ramsay did meet him under extraordinary circumstances and under a different name – he was now the world-famous magician Magnus Eisengrim. When they spoke about Paul's mother, Ramsay was taken aback at how cold and disinterested Paul was. Some of his childhood traumas he had run away from were still weighing heavily on him, and he did not seem either ready or willing to cast them aside. It was not only "the cruelty of people who thought her kind of madness was funny"[77] that he had to deal with, but also something that affected him in a viciously personal way: his own father imposed the guilt on Paul for the responsibility of "robbing her of her sanity."[78] One of the established psychological truths is that children easily absorb the guilt implemented in them even though they were not in a position to earn it, that the guilty conscience remains in their system in later life, and, usually subconsciously, sabotages their well-being. This was why Paul, unable to accept his past in a more mature way, did not want to have anything to do with his mother, not even send his greetings. "So far as I am concerned, it is over, and if she dies mad, who will not say that she is better dead?"[79]

When the aunt died, Ramsay "visits Mrs. Dempster, and finally has her placed in an asylum, as the sad, best thing he can do to help."[80] After a while, her overall condition improved. "She could look after herself, talked helpfully and amusingly to other patients, and was of use in taking some of the people who were more confused than herself for walks."[81] For the first time after the Deptford days, her expression would at times regain sweetness and humorous perceptiveness.[82] The medication and therapy she was receiving probably dulled the pain of old losses and gave some structure to her days, so that a higher degree of self-satisfaction and the altruistic streak in her were able to resurface to some extent. She did not display any certain signs of suffering, while the pathological symptoms she did show were predominantly of cognitive nature: "She had no ordered notion of the world about her, and in particular she had no sense of time. Amasa Dempster she sometimes recalled as if he were somebody in a book she had once read inattentively."[83] Unlike her husband, her son was very much alive to her, but she thought of him as of a child. "Paul, to her, was still […] a lost boy – lost a distance of time ago that was both great and small – and to be recovered just as he had run away."[84] In fact, she did not think he had run away but was "enticed by evil people […] to rob a mother of her child."[85] This paranoid idea of conspiracy fitted better into her system than the truth that he had run away from her. On the one hand, the defense she employed protected her self-dignity, however shredded, but on the other, due to her faulty social perception, she was unaware of Paul's public humiliation and genuinely saw no reason for his escapade.

Ramsay visited her on a weekly basis, his visits being the highlights of her sequestered life. Like most institutionalized patients, despite her remission, or because of it, she yearned to leave the hospital. "She was always waiting for me on Saturday afternoon with her hat on. I knew what the hat meant; she hoped that this time I would take her away."[86]

The delicateness of her functionality easily gave way to decomposition as soon as the painful topic was brought up again. Ramsay had been away on a trip during which he met Paul. When he returned to Canada and visited Mrs. Dempster, he was in two minds whether to mention this to her or not. "How could I tell her that I had news of Paul if I […] would neither bring her child to her or take her to him?"[87] Still, wishing "to provide her with comfort and security,"[88] Ramsay told an unlikely lie, that Paul sent his love. "She was so excited, and so unlike herself, that I was shaken and even said that Paul was maintaining her in the hospital, which God knows was untrue."[89] Ramsay's fear of mentioning the lost child seemed unsubstantiated for only a few moments while her excitement was in full swing. However, what ensued was far graver than Ramsay could have predicted. The natural next step Mary wanted to take was to be taken to her son. Realizing that was not the plan, her paranoid thought process fabricated the situation in which "the hospital was an elaborately designed prison where she was held to keep her from her son! She knew well enough who was her jailor."[90] Of course, it was Dunstan Ramsay, "who pretended to be a friend, [but] was a snake-in-the-grass, an enemy, an undoubted agent of those dark forces who had torn Paul from her."[91] The anger she felt, however, was unparalleled to "grief and desolation"[92] that overtook her again.

Not only did Mrs. Dempster fall apart mentally and emotionally after the described incident, her body started failing her, too. She became weaker, got diabetes; her kidneys and heart were malfunctioning. Even though the doctors did not think her life was endangered, Ramsay knew that she was "breaking up."[93] He could not talk to her, only sometimes "looked at her through a little spy-hole in the door."[94] A phone call from the hospital that Mary Dempster had a heart attack and would very likely have another came as no surprise to Ramsay. He hurried to her deathbed. In an unexpected return of mental clarity and memory before her final hour, she recognized Ramsay as if she had seen him for the first time after Deptford, and said: "I thought he was a boy."[95] Half an hour later she was dead, "a small, elderly woman ready for burial."[96] Unrelentingly haunted by the idea that she was a saint, Ramsay "bent over the head of Mary Dempster and sniffed for th[e] true odor of sanctity."[97] All he could smell, however, was "a perfume [...] that had obviously come out of a bottle."[98]

The question crucial for this chapter, and one of the most striking questions in the novel itself, has been iterated several times: madness, saintliness, or both? That there was a great deal of madness in her life, using the word in a non-euphemistical manner, is a proven fact. What intrigues is whether her madness could have been paired with saintliness. Ramsay made it his life mission to confirm his belief that it was.

The psychopathological diagnosis that could be ascribed to Mary Dempster is not one of a personality disorder. Broadly speaking, degrees of personality distortions are to be found within the whole population, but that was not the core of Mrs. Dempster's mental illness. She was not predominantly antisocial, avoidant, obsessive-compulsive, dependent, histrionic, narcissistic, schizoid, schizotypal, borderline, masochistic, sadistic, depressive, negativistic, or even paranoid, despite the fact that she became prone to paranoid ideation. Prior to developing psychiatric ailments and psychotic episodes, her major shortcomings were of cognitive nature, particularly in the social domain. There can be no mention of even a semblance of psychological maturity in her life. However, this definitive statement may be somewhat problematic, if not from a strictly scientific perspective, then at least from the perspective of general human experience, because strict delineation between the psychological and the spiritual is nonexistent in real life. Even though the comment on the state of her mental health cannot be seriously challenged, the underlying richness of her spiritual life cannot but assuage the finality of that comment. Why did Ramsay, along with a few others, believe that she had an extraordinary depth of spiritual understanding bordering saintliness? This question has been partially answered in the previous outline of the part of the plot that is of our concern, but let us take a closer look at the characteristics of her spirituality as seen through Ramsay's eyes.

Mrs. Dempster's Spirituality

A rather long paragraph in the novel encapsulates the spiritual virtues of the twenty-six-year-old Mrs. Dempster, as trapped in the unenviable situation after the gravel pit episode. Despite the unfavorable circumstances, she showed no anguish, but had "a breadth of outlook and a clarity of vision that were strange and wonderful."[99] She was calm, content, devoid of "fear, of apprehension, of assumption that whatever happened was inevitably going to lead to some worse state of affairs."[100] Davies plays with ambiguity here, as he does throughout the novel, not only where Mary Dempster is concerned. Her peace and inner satisfaction could be either expression of foolish ignorance of causes and consequences, or a brahmanical, unattached acceptance of the things she cannot change. Once she told Ramsay, "There's just one thing to remember; whatever happens, it does no good to be afraid."[101] Her words, substantiated by her actions, "astonished and enriched"[102] him.

Her laughter was also interpreted dichotomously. To the Deptfordians, it was "the uncomprehending giggling[...] of a fool";[103] to Ramsay, it was laughing at the things people took too seriously, like her husband did religion ("he was likely to drop on his knees at any time and pray with a fervor that seemed indecent"[104]). She also found eccentric religious practices such as spiritism quite amusing, sensing their potential inauthenticity. As Davies put it somewhat imprecisely, "she was wholly religious,"[105] not in a philosophical sense, but in the sense of living "by a light that arose from within."[106] She had no concern of how others saw her, for she had an inner confirmation that what she was doing and how she was was in line with deeper, unfathomable, life-affirming sources. "She knew she was in disgrace with the world, but did not feel disgraced; she knew she was jeered at, but felt no humiliation."[107] Innocence and authenticity governed her behavior, not austere social norms. She would "hoist[...] up her skirt to run, which was a girlish thing no grown woman ever have done."[108] The freedom that arose from her spiritual assuredness fascinated Ramsay on one hand, and made her a target of the villagers on the other, particularly the subconsciously envious women, to whom such freedoms were denied. "Her youth, femininity, and madness,"[109] her "emotional, highly sensitive girlish nature"[110] advocated against her in the clerical circles, too. Accepted by few, and rejected by many, she trudged on to wherever life was taking her.

Mrs. Dempster's peculiar ways do not contain any of the indicators of crooked spirituality. Not a trace of fundamentalism, bigotry, egotism, xenophobia, authoritarianism, or literalism is to be found in her. Due to the psychological impairments and bizarre socialization, her religiosity might superficially be associated with attributes such as childish, magical, unreflective, oversimplified, and alike, but upon closer analysis it can be seen that her personal deficiencies did not mix into her spirituality. Rather than just childish, she was meta-childish; rather than just unreflective, she was meta-unreflective. The two inevitably enmeshed levels of personhood, the psychological and the spiritual, were in her case somehow kept apart so that the deficits of the mind would not mar the domain of the soul. When she slid into dependency, slow-wittedness and even psychosis, she never exploited religious imagery or language, and never involved religion as either the cause or the crutches of her plight. In a supra-rationally, lucid way, it seems as if there was an embedded knowledge in her of what is what.

If we were to list the characteristics of spiritual maturity, most of them would apply to Mary Dempster. Her ostracizing acts, primarily the way she related to the tramp in the Deptford gravel pit, were prompted by compassion, acceptance, tolerance, and finally the willingness to self-sacrifice. The way she handed out things, either valueless or inappropriately valuable, testifies to her detachment from materialism, while the calmness with which she handled home arrest after the pit incident testifies to her philosophical detachment, albeit in an unphilosophical manner. The only situation where her emotional detachment did collapse was the disappearance of her child. Taking into account the unphilosophical nature of her mind, a different kind of reaction from her would have been questionable not only in the maternal, but also in the spiritual context. Furthermore, she possessed a kind of certainty in the inner powers. As long as she was still more or less accountable, she derived from them the strength to go on. Even though godly powers seemed to sustain her, she never went around talking about God, knowing that actions spoke, not words.

The set of criteria of spiritual maturity that are less about intuitive qualities and more about the intellect, such as an all-encompassing philosophy of life, the ability of four-tiered interpretation or of a shift of perspectives, are quite hazy where Mrs. Dempster is concerned. She lacked the intellectual potential to endorse them, and on top of that was burdened by psychological and emotional challenges that slid her toward disintegration. Hence, it would be bold to posit that her spiritual profile included elements such as enlargement of personality or sophisticated inner change. When her reason got clouded, even moral integrity, let alone the responsibleness of her choices, was unavoidably compromised. Still, lacking the instruments to maintain the aforesaid qualities, her heroism lies in the fact that she did not misuse spirituality to mask her anguish or madness. Besides, being advanced on the spiritual level, despite the deterioration at the psychological one, might be redeeming in the context of saintliness, since the spiritual level, as proposed in the introductory chapters, is hierarchically higher (or deeper) than the psychological level, and thus in a way overarches it. "A higher dimension, by definition, is a more inclusive one. The lower dimension is included in the higher one; it is subsumed in it and encompassed by it."[111] This does not mean that the levels or dimensions are interchangeable, just that they differ ontologically and hierarchically.

Inquiring a range of people of faith directly or indirectly about Mrs. Dempster's spirituality, over the years Ramsay received a whole spectrum of different answers. Protestant ministers in Deptford were unanimously clear, calling her "a moral idiot"[112] and naming Ramsay's ideas about her saintliness blasphemous. The Catholic priest also dismissed her alleged sanctity, making rationalizations about the three miracles – in the first one, Surgeoner became "as extreme in his zeal as he was in his sin,"[113] which was always a dubious matter for Father Regan; the affair of raising Willie from death was also inconclusive because the local doctor said the boy had never died in the first place; and the vision that Ramsay saw at the battlefield took place while Ramsay was "out of [...][his] head."[114] All the good deeds and love that fool saints possess "comes to nothing – to worse than nothing, because it is virtue tainted with madness"[115] and because they lack one of the crucial Virtues – Prudence. "Father Regan dogmatically warns him against pursuing a 'fool-saint.'"[116] Even though holy madmen, banished by official religion, sometimes acquire popular following, Mary Dempster was not considered more than a lunatic even by the common people. Upon his return from the war, Ramsay learned the village news by the local barber. When he asked whether Mary died from flu like so many others, the barber responded: "Oh no, she didn't get the flu. The kind is always spared when better folks have to go."[117]

The closest Ramsay came to a confirmation of Mrs. Dempster's spiritual grace was in Europe, during his conversations with Padre Blazon, an old Jesuit, himself a little eccentric, belonging to the circle of Bollandists, who are traditionally involved in the scholarly study of Christian saints. Taking time to mull over what Ramsay had told him, Blazon's conclusion was as follows: "She would never got past the Bollandists, but she must have been an extraordinary person, a great lover of God, and trusting greatly in His love for her."[118] However, more important for Padre Blazon than the matter of whether she qualified to be a saint or not was the fact that "she endured a hard fate, did the best she could, and kept it up until at last her madness was too powerful for her. Heroism in God's cause is the mark of the saint."[119]

Ramsay and Surgeoner were the ones with the most extreme take on Mary Dempster's saintliness, for they believed that she was one. However, Padre Blazon knowingly told Ramsay that the world's confirmation of it played no crucial role. "If you think her a saint, she is a saint to you."[120] End of story. The matters of spirituality are too subtle to be absolutely agreed on, even among the religious. This grain of relativism thrown in by the wise Jesuit was further enhanced by asking Ramsay the question of who this woman was in his personal life. Relating to the third miracle, he said that "lots of men have visions of their mothers in time of danger."[121] Knowing what we know of Ramsay's detachment from his own mother and attachment to Mary Dempster, his urge to prove she was a saint might have abided "in psychological truth, not in objective truth."[122] The whole matter thus became even more confounding and inconclusive. However, paradoxical shiftiness beyond the rationalistic surface constitutes the very nature of spirituality, as expounded by mystics over times and cultures. Controversies about idiosyncratic seekers of God always come in abundance.

Placing the ambiguous business of Mary Dempster's saintliness in one of the major foci of the novel, Robertson Davies presents his ideas on religion as of something quite different from what traditional faith institutions teach and preach. He rather sees it as a myth that "abound[s] in parapsychological phenomena,"[123] combining spirituality, ethics, art, magic, and psychology. Instead of the exoteric, he delights in the esoteric. Some critics even called *Fifth Business* "a modern myth."[124] He sees across the confines of denominational conventionality and looks into "larger notions of faith and belief"[125] that address "the miraculous and the mysterious in life"[126] and feed "a hungry part of the spirit."[127] Davies strips one's true religiosity to its sphinx-like essence that is generally in collision with the dominant social mores, and for which "institutions are insignificant."[128] To him, religion is "psychologically rather than literally true."[129] Constructed on such a premise, *Fifth Business* represents a fruitful source for the exploration of the theme of spiritual and psychological maturity. It also contains much more material on this matter that, however, exceeds the scope of this book.

Some seek the roots of the Christian sub-tradition of fool saintliness "with St. Paul who first used the expression 'a fool for Christ's sake' and referred to the idea of divine folly."[130] However, it seems that the cradle of what is known as this tradition today comes from "the often unacknowledged Russian Orthodox foundations"[131] of *iurodstvo*, with its multiple hagiographical records of nonorthodox, mostly ascetic saint-foolishness, which "flourished from the Middle Ages up to the eighteenth century."[132] It probably started with the Byzantine ascetic Symeon Salos, or Symeon the Holy Fool in the sixth century AD who introduced "a new way of conveying spiritual teachings"[133] in an eccentric, almost tantric way. The occidental counterparts have existed "both in Western Catholicism and in the Protestant denominations,"[134] while more puritanical Christian strands do not look favorably on "mixing religious worship with foolishness and playful blasphemy [and] rejected the tradition of folly for Christ's sake as degenerate and degrading to Christian integrity and enlightened human reason."[135] The concept of deconstructing and perverting the rationally established religious molds does not sit well with hard-core Christians. Holy fools' "generally outrageous behavior does not at all conform to our cherished ideas of religiosity, morality, and sanctity."[136] The unanimous rejection of Mrs. Dempster by all the Deptford clerics, then, comes as no surprise.

Similar to the mystics belonging to different religions, whose accounts of mystical experiences coincide with each other to a great extent, fool saints are also to be found within (and simultaneously without) various religious traditions, guided by similar anti-standard principles. In the Islamic tradition, fool saints usually thrived within Sufism, whereas the orthodox communities not only looked unfavorably upon them, but undertook outright persecutions. In his descriptions of unorthodox modern-day devotees in India, William Dalrymple mentions a Muslim woman named Lal Peri who was "the sort of deeply eccentric ascetic that both the Eastern Christians and Sufis have traditionally celebrated as Holy Fools. She was an illiterate, simple and trusting woman, who saw the divine and miraculous everywhere."[137] The same source also mentions the traditional *'Urs* ceremonies, or death anniversaries performed at the tombs of various Sufi saints in South Asia, which represent "a compendium of everything which Islamic puritans most disapprove of: loud Sufi music and love poetry [...], men [...] dancing with women, hashish [...] being smoked, huge numbers [...] venerating the tomb of a dead man and [...] routing their petitions through the saint, rather than directly to God in the mosque."[138]

Hinduism, a religion known for the acceptance of most varied paths toward the divinity, has had a long tradition of *sadhus* and *tantrics* who, seen through Western eyes, definitely classify as fool saints, due to their complete rejection of conventions. Even the famous Bengali saint Chaitanya Mahaprabhu (1486–1534), who to this day has a large number of worldwide followers, and who is considered to be a manifestation of Krishna himself, has been called "the Madman of Madmen."[139] The term *tantra* mentioned several times earlier represents one of the many Hindu principles for achieving *moksha*, or liberation. It cherishes "the idea of reaching God through opposing convention, ignoring social mores and breaking taboos."[140] In practice, the opposition to convention may include living in cremation grounds, involving in elaborate sexual acts, sacrificing of animals, drinking wine from skulls found at a graveyard, and myriad more. The controlling element must be *bhakti*, or devotional love, for if that one is missing, *tantra* on its own would not be just a wild abandon, but "very dangerous."[141]

Where Buddhism is concerned, tantric practices have been accepted there as well, cherished for the great part in Nepal, Tibet, and Bhutan. It is often referred to as *Vajrayana*, the lesser-known of the Buddhist paths to the Truth (the major ones being *Theravada* and *Mahayana*). To Western ears, probably the most famous name of a Buddhist fool saint is Chögyam Trungpa (1939–1987), a highly controversial figure, or "a great lion of *dharma*,"[142] who even held seminars on "crazy wisdom" and wrote a book with the same title. Tibet has its own line of the so-called "holy madmen of Tibet" who were recorded to have worn "outfit[s] fashioned from human remains"[143] or composed "verses not to the Buddha, but to an old man's impotent member."[144] Certain authors also see Zen practices, which juggle the confounding anecdotes of the absurd, as approximating madness.

As with mental illness, every case of fool saintliness is idiosyncratic and a category in itself. Whether all fool saints had mental shortcomings like Mrs. Dempster is difficult to establish and would require a completely new research. Suffice it to hypothesize that in these cases, the psychic and the noetic levels did get enmeshed and interpenetrated, but which of them is the overpowering force needs to be determined for every individual case. What can be ascertained, though, is that what lies at the heart of their spirituality, behavior, philosophy, and general outlook of the world is a grotesque paradox, unpalatable on the surface, but in many cases marked with ultimate profundity and lucid spiritual clarity. The widely open field of saint-foolish paradox seems to include the features of eccentricity, passivity, subversion, and various other individual peculiarities.

Mrs. Dempster meets the criterion of passivity, for she does not purposefully walk around looking for wonders and initiating miraculous acts. She was somewhat like St. Andrew the Fool, "a slave of Scythian origin"[145] from around the sixth century, who took "no initiative"[146] and had "something passive"[147] about himself. This holds true for any other historical personality classified as a fool saint. Robertson Davies is also explicit in the novel that holy madmen "are more usually passive."[148]

Mrs. Dempster's eccentricities, although shocking to the prudish Deptfordians, are bland in comparison to the lifestyles of historical fool saints. Despite the incomparably smaller scale of Mrs. Dempster's outrageousness, parallels between her and actual holy madmen may still be drawn. While St. Andrew "grabbed food shamelessly, drank sewage"[149] and Symeon Salos "exposed himself to sexual temptation [...] and [...] relieved himself openly,"[150] Mrs. Dempster was just unabashed when discovered in the midst of an intercourse with a tramp. She had her fair share of "unlettered simplicity, public self-humiliation, [...] childish naiveté which often borders on pure ignorance and/or insanity,"[151] was prone to "talk[ing] nonsense,"[152] and definitely held "a denigrated, outsider status"[153] which disallowed her to "communicate with this world successfully."[154] Hidden under such rough surface, only a few managed to see through to her noetic sublimity.

Is there a spiritual rationale behind such a phenomenon as foolish saintliness, and what is the relationship between the psychic and the noetic planes of existence in fool saints? Having suggested that holy foolishness might be "the incarnate opposite of holy wisdom,"[155] the question that might be posed next is whether this foolishness is a conscious choice, a repudiation of "the vainglorious wisdom of the world,"[156] a psychological necessity, due to the frailty of the mental makeup as in the case of Mrs. Dempster, or being overwhelming with "too much insight into the divine."[157] The answers to these questions must be sought for each fool saint individually, but it might be that all of the above holds true for every one of them, in different variations and proportions. The bottom line might be: "If the wisdom of the world is but a folly to God, [...] God's own foolishness is the one true, divine wisdom."[158]

The question of whether Mrs. Dempster is a fool or a saint has been reiterated throughout this chapter multiple times, and the conclusion cannot but leave it open-ended. The ambiguity of matters allows for different interpretations of the character of Mary Dempster. The fictional narrator, Dunstan Ramsay, stays true to his conviction that a more than human saintliness abided within her simple personality. He believes that "sometimes the mad and sightless can understand things better, and more clearly, than the sane and the sighted."[159] In accordance with this belief, he had an epitaph inscribed upon Mrs. Dempster's tomb:

Requiescat in pace
MARY DEMPSTER
1888–1959
Here is the patience
And faith of the saints.

Notes

1 Ellen D. Warwick, "The Transformation of Robertson Davies," *The Canadian Novel Here and Now: A Critical Anthology*, Vol. 1, ed. John Moss, Toronto, ON: New Canada Publications, 1983, p. 68.

2 Edward Quinn, *History in Literature: A Reader's Guide to 20th Century History and the Literature It Inspired*, New York: Facts on File, 2004, p. 263.

3 Gordon Roper, "Robertson Davies' *Fifth Business* and 'That Old Fantastical Devil of Dark Corners, C. G. Jung,'" *The Canadian Novel Here and Now:*

A Critical Anthology, Vol. 1, ed. John Moss, Toronto, ON: New Canada Publications, 1983, p. 61.

4 Robertson Davies, *Fifth Business*, London: Penguin, 2001, Kindle edition, e-book.

5 Rosmarin Heidenreich, *The Postwar Novel in Canada: Narrative Patterns and Reader Response*, Waterloo, ON: Wilfrid Laurier University Press, 1989, p. 64.

6 Ellen D. Warwick, *op. cit.*, p. 70.

7 Sue Sorensen, *The Collar: Reading Christian Ministry in Fiction, Television, and Film*, Eugene, OR: Cascade Books, 2014, p. 259.

8 Russel M. Brown and Donna A. Bennet, "Magnus Eisengrim: The Shadow of the Trickster in the Novels of Robertson Davies," *Jungian Literary Criticism*, ed. Richard P. Sugg, Evanston, IL: Northwestern University Press, 1992, p. 289.

9 Ellen D. Warwick, *op. cit.*, p. 70.

10 *Ibid.*, p. 71.

11 Gordon Roper, *op. cit.*, p. 62.

12 Sue Sorensen, *op. cit.*, p. 258.

13 Victor J. Lanes, *Aspects of Robertson Davies' Novels*, New York: Peter Lang Publishing, 2009, p. 123.

14 Sue Sorensen, *op. cit.*, p. 258.

15 Victor J. Lanes, *op. cit.*, p. 121.

16 *Ibid.*, p. 122.

17 Gordon Roper, *op. cit.*, p. 62.

18 Robertson Davies, *op. cit.*

19 *Ibid.*

20 *Ibid.*

21 *Ibid.*

22 Gordon Roper, *op. cit.*, p. 62.

23 Ellen D. Warwick, *op. cit.*, p. 70.

24 Sue Sorensen, *op. cit.*, p. 257.

25 Victor J. Lanes, *op. cit.*, p. 122.

26 Robert A. Palmer, *A Literary Cavalcade II*, self-published, 2013, p. 7.

27 William Closson James, *Locations of the Sacred: Essays on Religion, Literature, and Canadian Culture*, Waterloo, ON: Wilifred Laurier University Press, 1998, p. 51.

28 Robertson Davies, *op. cit.*

29 *Ibid.*

30 *Ibid.*

31 *Ibid.*

32 *Ibid.*

33 *Ibid.*

34 *Ibid.*

35 *Ibid.*

36 *Ibid.*

37 *Ibid.*

38 Victor J. Lanes, *op. cit.*, p. 122.

39 Robertson Davies, *op. cit.*

40 Victor J. Lanes, *op. cit.*, p. 121.

41 *Ibid.*, p. 122.

42 Robertson Davies, *op. cit.*

43 *Ibid.*

44 *Ibid.*

45 *Ibid.*
46 *Ibid.*
47 *Ibid.*
48 *Ibid.*
49 *Ibid.*
50 *Ibid.*
51 Sue Sorensen, *op. cit.*, p. 258.
52 Robertson Davies, *op. cit.*
53 *Ibid.*
54 *Ibid.*
55 *Ibid.*
56 Sue Sorensen, *op. cit.*, p. 258.
57 Victor J. Lanes, *op. cit.*, p. 122.
58 Robertson Davies, *op. cit.*
59 *Ibid.*
60 Sue Sorensen, *op. cit.*, p. 258.
61 *Ibid.*
62 Robertson Davies, *op. cit.*
63 *Ibid.*
64 *Ibid.*
65 *Ibid.*
66 *Ibid.*
67 *Ibid.*
68 *Ibid.*
69 *Ibid.*
70 *Ibid.*
71 Edward Quinn, *op. cit.*, p. 263.
72 Rosmarin Heidenreich, *op. cit.*, p. 65.
73 Robertson Davies, *op. cit.*
74 *Ibid.*
75 *Ibid.*
76 *Ibid.*
77 *Ibid.*
78 *Ibid.*
79 *Ibid.*
80 Gordon Roper, *op. cit.*, p. 62.
81 Robertson Davies, *op. cit.*
82 See: *Ibid.*
83 *Ibid.*
84 *Ibid.*
85 *Ibid.*
86 *Ibid.*
87 *Ibid.*
88 *Ibid.*
89 *Ibid.*
90 *Ibid.*
91 *Ibid.*
92 *Ibid.*
93 *Ibid.*
94 *Ibid.*
95 *Ibid.*
96 *Ibid.*
97 *Ibid.*

98 *Ibid.*
99 *Ibid.*
100 *Ibid.*
101 *Ibid.*
102 *Ibid.*
103 *Ibid.*
104 *Ibid.*
105 *Ibid.*
106 *Ibid.*
107 *Ibid.*
108 *Ibid.*
109 Sue Sorensen, *op. cit.*, p. 259.
110 Rosmarin Heidenreich, *op. cit.*, p. 67.
111 Viktor Frankl, *Man's Search for Ultimate Meaning*, p. 16.
112 Robertson Davies, *op. cit.*
113 *Ibid.*
114 *Ibid.*
115 *Ibid.*
116 Gordon Roper, *op. cit.*, p. 61.
117 Robertson Davies, *op. cit.*
118 *Ibid.*
119 *Ibid.*
120 *Ibid.*
121 *Ibid.*
122 *Ibid.*
123 Rosmarin Heidenreich, *op. cit.*, p. 70.
124 Gordon Roper, *op. cit.*, p. 60.
125 Sue Sorensen, *op. cit.*, p. 257.
126 Edward Quinn, *op. cit.*, p. 263.
127 Robertson Davies, *op. cit.*
128 Stephen Bonnycastle, quoted in: Sue Sorensen, *op. cit.*, p. 259.
129 Robertson Davies, *op. cit.*
130 Dana Heller, "Holy Fools, Secular Saints, and Illiterate Saviors in American Literature and Popular Culture," *CLCWeb: Comparative Literature and Culture*, 2003, Vol. 5, No. 3, http://dx.doi.org/10.7771/1481-4374.1193.
131 *Ibid.*
132 *Ibid.*
133 Priscilla Hunt, "Holy Foolishness as a Key to Russian Culture," *Holy Foolishness in Russia: New Perspectives*, eds. Priscilla Hunt and Svitlana Kobets, Bloomington, IN: Slavica Publications, 2001, p. 1.
134 Dana Heller, *op. cit.*
135 *Ibid.*
136 Georg Feuerstein, *Holy Madness: The Shock Tactics and Radical Teachings of Crazy-Wise Adepts, Holy Fools, and Rascal Gurus*, New York: Paragon House, 1991, p. xx.
137 William Dalrymple, *Nine Lives: In Search of the Sacred in Modern India*, London: Bloomsbury, 2009, p. 121.
138 *Ibid.*, p. 115.
139 *Ibid.*, p. 248.
140 *Ibid.*, p. 215.
141 *Ibid.*
142 Sherab Chödzin, "Foreword," Chögyam Rinpoche, *Crazy Wisdom*, ed. Sherab Chödzin, Boston, MA: Shambala, 2001, p. ix.

143 David M. DiValerio, *The Holy Madmen of Tibet*, New York: Oxford University Press, 2015, p. 1.
144 *Ibid.*
145 Lennart Rydén, "Introduction," *The Life of St. Andrew the Fool*, ed. Lennart Rydén, Uppsala: Acta Universitatis Upsaliensis, Studia Byzantina Upsalensia, 1995, Vol. 4, No. 1, p. 32.
146 *Ibid.*
147 *Ibid.*
148 Robertson Davies, *op. cit.*
149 Lennart Rydén, *op. cit.*, p. 35.
150 *Ibid.*
151 Dana Heller, *op. cit.*
152 Lennart Rydén, *op. cit.*, p. 35.
153 Dana Heller, *op. cit.*
154 *Ibid.*
155 Lennart Rydén, *op. cit.*, p. 34.
156 Dana Heller, *op. cit.*
157 Lennart Rydén, *op. cit.*, p. 34.
158 Dana Heller, *op. cit.*
159 William Dalrymple, *op. cit.*, p. 254.

Part III

Portraits of Religious Pathology

5 Hustling Man of the Cloth[1]

Elmer Gantry and Narcissistic Religiosity

America's first Nobel laureate in literature, Sinclair Lewis, brought enormous resentment upon himself after the publication of his 1927 novel *Elmer Gantry*. The clerical circles as well as the wider public, still under strong church influence back in the late 1920s, were abhorred, while respective local governments banned the selling of the novel in several cities in the USA, Scotland, and Ireland. The US Post Office Department even banned the circulation of any catalogs that listed the book.[2] The formal grounds to demonize *Elmer Gantry* were the sexual adventures of the eponymous preacher character, and his use of inappropriate language (such as "damn" or "hell"). The true reason, however, was Lewis's exposition of hypocrisy of some members of the clergy, "the shenanigans and deceitful scheming of pompous preachers,"[3] which was (and still is in many societies) a sore spot to discuss, but also a motive incessantly present in literary texts. Besides being banned and publicly castigated, the author also received threats of physical violence and was called Satan's cohort. Still, the novel was the number one bestselling book in 1927.

Elmer Gantry is an unsympathetic character that some even call "one of the great beasts of all literature."[4] He is a young college athlete at the beginning of the novel, who ends up becoming a religious leader for all the wrong reasons. Critics have lavishly disparaged him, calling him "a quintessential scoundrel, charlatan, and womanizer, an extravagant faker, [...] an opportunist with few scruples and morals,"[5] an "operator immemorial, egocentric and ruthless,"[6] a "crassly amoral preacher,"[7] "a flamboyant man who had a passion for publicity that equaled the most carnal Hollywood icon."[8] In the urban jargon, he has become a symbol of hypocrisy and was turned into "the 'Elmer Gantry' syndrome of misconduct by religious leaders."[9]

The adjectives that reverberate around Gantry's aura include manipulative, egocentric, false, hedonistic, greedy, and vain. He undoubtedly deserves all the indignation and infamy that he received – his conduct caused the downfall and even death of people around him. However, a question may be asked: who, in their right mind, would behave in such atrocious ways? Do people like Gantry not lack some basic prerequisites of psychological sanity, even though they keep functioning in the world, and even though they fail to experience subjective suffering and pain for the way they are? Sinclair Lewis, however, did not approach his character from a psychological perspective, since psychology was still a rather young science at the time, and since his aim was first of all to write a satire of the American standards of his era. He was not only criticizing people like Gantry, whom he drew upon real life characters, but also "the inhumanity of the religious environment within which [they] exist."[10] Still, his depiction of Gantry can be dovetailed almost too neatly into the modern idea of the narcissistic personality disorder, despite the fact that the first comprehensive scientific study on personality disorders came out fifteen years after Lewis's book (Hervey Cleckley's *The Mask of Sanity*, 1941), with only short papers by Freud and a few other psychologists discussing the topic before 1927. Lewis, however, had profound and implicit psychological knowledge.

Generally on Narcissistic Personality Disorder

What is it that turns a person into a pathological narcissist? What characterizes such people in general? How do they treat others? What are their values? What is their religion like? Answers to all of these questions may be sought through a psycho-religious analysis of the literary character of Elmer Gantry.

The psychologist Len Sperry states that "the optimal criterion for [narcissistic personality] disorder is a '[...] grandiose sense of self-importance.'"[11] It means that if this particular characteristic is evident in an individual, they are very likely to be narcissistic, either within the more normal range on the continuum of personality, or across the pathological lines. The "normal range" refers to the narcissistic personality style, which is acceptable due to its relative flexibility, while the latter refers to the narcissistic personality disorder, characterized by extreme rigidity and intensity. At the very beginning of the novel, Lewis gives a nutshell summary of Elmer's personality: "Elmer assumed that he was the center of the universe and that the rest of the system was valuable only as it afforded him help and pleasure. He wanted everything."[12] The quote fully meets Sperry's "optimal criterion."

The roots of psychological disorders are rarely organic, though some are more connected with certain biological and biochemical disbalances than others. Where narcissistic personality disorder is concerned, "the role of biogenic factors is unclear."[13] Whether or not there are some organic causes has not yet been established with any certainty. As frequently is the case with psychological disorders, the etiology is largely grounded on psychogenic factors, the large bulk of which lies in the attitudes of the parents/caregivers in a person's childhood. Although the relationship between family atmosphere and the development of psychological pathology is at best correlational, unsubstantiated by hard evidence, it still represents one of the major factors in interpreting the genesis of mental illness.

What kind of parental treatment might cause children to develop narcissistic defenses against what they experience as too difficult to bear? Across the decades, psychologists have suggested opposite parenting styles as detrimental in this respect. They can be "either highly permissive or highly authoritarian."[14]

On what seems to be the permissive side, parents overly dote on their children, referring "to the baby as 'his royal highness.'"[15] They overvalue the child, "gloss over and forget all his shortcomings."[16] Noncontingent praise is lavishly given, due to which "narcissists fail to develop the motivation and skills ordinarily necessary to elicit these rewards."[17] Such caretakers do not provide "optimal frustrating experiences"[18] that children sometimes need in order to get a more realistic image of themselves. Instead, the children expectedly learn how to always choose the easier way out. They are taught that it is possible to get something for nothing, which is not a lesson toward a constructive life, nor toward self-knowledge, since it does not provoke them to reach within for potentials hidden in the depths of personality, but leaves them wallowing in superficial ease that might be acceptable in their family settings, but not in the real world they need to go out into as soon as they are of an appropriate age.

On the authoritarian end of the spectrum, future narcissists might receive anything from utter neglect to constant pampering. In the latter case, however, pampering comes at a high price, for it can be accompanied with criticism, absence of warmth, humiliation, rigid expectations, and spitefulness. Children's potential talents are singled out as the only qualities on which parental attitudes depend – if cherished and put on public display, parents will be nice to them; if disregarded, parents' essential coldness comes blatantly to the surface. Children understand they are but trophies that make their parents look superior in the eyes of others, and that only the behaviors that contribute toward this end will be reinforced. The genuine child's personality is deemed irrelevant and the normal narcissistic needs of infancy are unmet, which gives rise to a corruption of these needs into their pathological counterparts in adulthood. The ambiguity of such relationships might even be more toxic than the harshness of outright neglect.

Parents may impose the narcissistic schema on their children either by "flattery, indulgence, and favoritism [...or] rejection, limitations, exclusion, or deficits,"[19] but what they fail to give in any of these unwholesome variants is what children need most – the substratum for healthy development based on unconditional love, respect, responsibility, honesty, and joy. Unable to get what they quintessentially need, freight with "a loss of self-respect,"[20] children unconsciously develop psychological immunity systems which allow them to cope with the situations. Narcissism is but one of such alternative routes of development.

Which exact mechanisms are at play in the narcissistic structuring of personality is not clear. What is clear, though, is the child's urge to survive adversity. Probably due to some inborn psychological and temperamental traits, some of them survive "by forcing or manipulating others to do what they needed and wanted."[21] At the same time, they alienate themselves from their feelings, because feelings are experienced as too painful. Some suggest that "thin-skinned or hypersensitive"[22] children are at risk of becoming narcissists, due to the relative intensity of their emotions. Growing up, they fail to integrate some of the core elements of their personalities which cause emotional pain, and continue to develop only certain aspects of their personal potentials, keeping others locked up in unapproachable cellars. Although locked away, the unintegrated facets of personality perform their surreptitious tasks and provoke much anxiety and rage in this person, but narcissists never try to establish contact with them. Instead, they apply the learned patterns of escapism. All the libidinal energy is invested in the shell of the personality, the image, the ego, while the self is left undeveloped and gaping. In Otto Kernberg's opinion, the superficial image is then uncritically merged with the ideal self, which "leads to conceptions of grandiosity and omnipotence."[23] The seven miles of maturation are being completely skipped.

Elmer Gantry's Early Development

Does Elmer Gantry's childhood narrative fit into any of the aforementioned developmental challenges? Although the novel does not dwell on Elmer's life before college and gives only scant biographical data of his childhood, a keen observer might be able to pick enough information to start inquiring into and forming a solid picture of the shortcomings of his early days. He had no siblings, and psychology proposes that the development of narcissistic personality disorder is "particularly likely with only children."[24] Furthermore, his mother was a widow, which represents an additional risk of strengthened control and worry. But these facts are only "technicalities" that do not necessarily have significant negative effects on children when parenthood is conducted in a well-balanced way.

Elmer Gantry's mother, though, could in no way be accounted for being well-balanced in any way. "She was a small woman, energetic, nagging but kindly […] and she had unusual courage."[25] The description so far does not reveal any unwholesome traits. However, glimpses into her instable personal and parental style are available in the phrase that she was "once given to passionate caresses and now to passionate prayer,"[26] besides being "drained by early widowhood and drudgery."[27] Elmer was genuinely afraid of her even "though she came only to his shoulder, such was her bustling vigor, her swift shrewdness of tongue, such the gallantry of her long care for him."[28]

Mrs. Gantry is an example of a controlling parent who does not allow their children any private space. She applied herself to instilling her own values in her son, the traditionalistic, corny values of a God-fearing life, without once hesitating to question them or give him the possibility of choice. The detrimental methods she used, which might well have been unconscious, were those of emotional blackmail and threat. She would be "weeping when he failed to study his Sunday School lesson,"[29] but also "waiting to snatch at his soul if he showed weakening."[30] Instead of supporting him to evolve naturally, she projected ready-made pictures of his future life, which envisioned "Elmer with a famous church; with a cottage in Colorado for the summer; married to a dear pious little woman; with half a dozen children; and herself invited to join them for the summer; all of them kneeling in family prayers, led by Elmer."[31]

The relationship between mother and son was essentially an unhealthy one. Considering the fact that she found "her only emotions in the hymns and the Bible,"[32] it can be doubted whether she had any genuine feelings for Elmer, apart from when he was an obedient, religious son. He tried "affectionately to live out his mother's plan of life for him"[33] and, despite feeling "demoted to childhood, as he always was in his mother's presence,"[34] his "only authentic affection was for his mother."[35] On the other hand, he secretly engaged in all the forbidden pleasures, such as fighting, gambling, drinking, and seduction. Mrs. Gantry sensed that things were not right below the surface, and despite him doing formally whatever she expected of him, such as going to bed at nine-thirty, helping with the house chores, and accompanying her to church, at night he could hear "her sobbing as she knelt by her high-swelling, white-counterpaned, old-fashioned bed."[36]

Unaware that his mother's relationship with him was not one of genuine acceptance, and unaware that she did not nourish his authentic person but the image of him she had created in her head, Elmer danced as she played – on the surface he gave her what she wanted, but privately he did what *he* wanted. Since the most important person in his life disregarded his genuine self, and denied him of warm motherly love, by the same token, he placed little value on his own self. The deep anguish and frustration found vent in gratification of base urges and greed, while the authentic self remained in a state of atrophy. Thus a Dorian Grayish rift between his outward and inward personalities gradually ripened and finally bore an abundance of toxic fruit.

Elmer Gantry and Narcissistic Personality Disorder

The sentence quoted earlier on Elmer being the center of the universe ticks the most important criterion box for the narcissistic personality disorder – a bearing of grandiosity and exaggerated self-importance. People like him "draw their sense of security and satisfaction from being above the crowd – stronger, brighter, more beautiful, wealthier, less fallible."[37] Even though narcissists are not normally lacking in intelligence (they are "sharp and alert; their thinking is clear and logical"[38]), their self-image is "naïve, unexamined, but tenaciously held."[39] It shields them from the implicit sense of essentially being a failure, the acceptance of which would push them down into severe depression.

Elmer's academic intelligence was not overly sharp, but the fact that he managed to manipulate people and attain all the set goals indicates that he was not dull either. His intelligence was narrowed down to the practicalities he wanted to achieve, and did not branch out onto higher levels. He sees himself as "the most popular man in college,"[40] and even though the truth was that he excelled in athletic prowess and had some kind of personal charisma, other students were "a bit afraid, a bit uncomfortable, and more than a bit resentful"[41] of him. Like most narcissists, if measured, he would have had "a low score on [...] social introversion,"[42] which means that he was not aware of the ways others perceived him, due to the narcissistic defense grid that coarsened his social sensitivity. The sense of being superior was not tapering off as he was advancing into adulthood, but rather intensifying. Every occasion was interpreted as Elmerocentric. Among others, particularly those he perceived as socially lower, he "felt large and sophisticated and prosperous [...] like a city broker visiting a farmer cousin."[43] Traveling abroad made him "a lot more satisfied when being an American."[44] Playing a hero during a disaster at sea, "he dragged in a woman who had already safely touched bottom. He had rescued at least thirty people who had already rescued themselves."[45] Even his watch was reminiscent of its owner: "large, thick, shiny, with a near-gold case."[46]

Another of the unmistakable narcissistic qualities includes fantasies of success. Again, they are not based on reality, since "achievement here is not a process or a personal growth experience,"[47] but a wishful visualization of the narcissists' greatness disconnected from all organic contexts. This characteristic is in line with their tendency "to focus on images and themes rather than on facts and issues."[48] Expectedly, "Elmer swallowed ideas whole; he was a maelstrom of prejudices."[49] The wishful fantasies he engages in testify to the extent of his sense of grandiosity. They range from "when I get to be a bishop,"[50] through inviting his mother "to the White House and lunch with me the PRESIDENT,"[51] to becoming "the dictator of the world"[52] and greater than the greatest historical personalities. "Not even Napoleon or Alexander had been able to dictate what a whole nation should wear and eat and say and think. That, Elmer Gantry was about to do."[53] All the while, he guises his personal appetites under the alleged fight for morality, which makes him even more grotesque. The novel ends on a note of Elmer praying for "a crusade for complete morality and the domination of the Christian church through all the land. [...] We shall yet make these United States a moral nation!"[54] Although Sinclair Lewis's intention was first of all satirical, he presented a textbook example of a person with the narcissistic disorder so accurately drawn and so much in accordance with the latest psychiatric criteria that it sounds astounding to contemporary ears.

A feature inevitably linked with the sense of grandiosity, self-importance, and unrealistic success is the narcissistic feeling of specialness. People like Elmer Gantry see themselves as unique, understood only by "other special or high-status people."[55] Whatever talent they have "is amplified and reconstructed as objective evidence of his or her exceptional stature."[56] The idea that "only someone special can go unpunished"[57] probably lies at the root of this self-belief, knowing how obsessively narcissists try to shun responsibilities. In any case, Elmer shares this sense of being the chosen one. Although "to elect any one as class-president twice was taboo [...] at the beginning of Senior year, Elmer announced that he desired to be president again."[58] He sees no reason why rules could not be bent where he was concerned. In the religious context, which is discussed a little later, he had a feeling that "maybe the Lord has some great use for me."[59] When he became a member of a club of the wealthy, he "felt ennobled by belonging to the same club with a Rolls-Royce."[60] Excellence, whether material, social, intellectual, or spiritual, was what he sought as his natural environment. Although he did not have what it takes to belong to the greatest, he forced his way there, compensating for the buried feeling of inferiority.

The most important side of things for narcissists is the outward appearance, since it is a rare quality that helps them infiltrate into the circles they long to belong to. They are thus prone to invest overly in the constant impeccability of their image, whether behavior or looks are concerned. The façade is maintained carefully, and communication with others is staged in a "socially facile, pleasant, and endearing"[61] manner. Many people get perceptually manipulated by this, which is the narcissist's aim. Gantry's followers were almost ecstatic "as they felt the warmth of his handshake, as they heard the amiable bim-bom of his voice, saw his manly eyes, untroubled by doubts or scruples,"[62] and were delighted to recognize "him as a future captain of the hosts of the Almighty."[63] However, careful observers may detect betraying signs of pathology – the insincerity in his voice ("spoken language is normally suffused with 'tone,' embedded in an expressiveness which transcends the verbal"[64]), the unnaturalness of his facial expressions ("the fixed smile"[65]), the lack of aliveness in his eyes ("their eyes are dull; no light shines through them"[66]).

Thanks to natural good looks and an athletic figure, Elmer Gantry brought his façade to perfection. "He shaved, he touched up his bluff handsomeness with lilac water and talcum, he did his nails, sitting in athletic underwear, awaiting his new suit, sent down for pressing."[67] Such metrosexual attitude might not be a rarity any longer, but ninety years ago it was much more telling than it would be today. When his material circumstances became graver, he still managed to possess "a beautiful new morning coat, three excellent lounge suits, patent leather shoes, a noble derby, a flourishing top hat, but he had only two suits of underclothes, both ragged."[68]

His public behavior was also in discord with his genuine intentions. "Though he occasionally kicked the dog in the country, he was clamorously affectionate with it in town."[69] Being essentially indolent in the library, "he did like to rush about, meet people, make a show of accomplishment."[70] Everything about him was about the show. Unlike a great number of bigots, he would even conceal his thorough racial and anti-Semitic hatred and cover it up with superficial civic tolerance, since it added to his positive image. The idea that he privately entertained was "to keep all foreigners, Jews, Catholics, and negroes in their place, which was no place at all, and let the country be led by native Protestants, like Elmer Gantry."[71] Sensing, however, that the social climate was not favorable for such stances, "it seemed to him more truly American, also a lot safer, to avoid the problem."[72]

All the flawed ideas about their own selves are reflected in the narcissists' dealings with other people. Just as compassion is one of the most important tests of healthy religiosity, empathy and morality largely indicate the state of one's psychological well-being. People with narcissistic personality disorder are not able to form lasting, committed, loving relationships. Needing an audience to applaud them, they always require company, but at the end of the day, they are utterly alone, since people do not warm to them due to the narcissists' own lack of warmth and sincerity. People hanging out with narcissists are usually flawed themselves, as they "often possess masochistic traits or at least a near-pathological measure of self-doubt."[73] Such personal shortcomings make them blind for anything but the outer success of the egocentrics, which they admire.

Instead of friends, narcissists need loyal admirers who never criticize them. Their ego is fed by the "admiration and the acclaim of the crowd."[74] The extent to which they can take flattery is unpalatable to a decent person. At the slightest hint of criticism, though, they go completely berserk and vindictive. There is an "intense, hidden aggression" ready to be "vented against anyone who withholds a steady supply of compliments."[75] Does this aggression originate from the unexpressed and unacceptable rage toward parents who perhaps overly criticized, or withheld warmth, or expected perfection from the child? Psychologists would agree that things probably do follow such a script.

The manipulative, scheming Elmer was pathologically impervious to outer influences that might have swayed him from his egoistic ways. However, praise and admiration would turn him into a blinded cub. The criminally minded secretary Hettie, who seduced Elmer and almost completely destroyed him, did not need too much cunning to take

Elmer where she wanted to. Apart from the attractive looks and brazen advances, the only thing she had to do was to utter such babble as: "Dearest ittle honeykins bunnykins, I adore you, I haven't got another doggoned thing to say but I say that six hundred million trillion times. Elmer!"[76] He was readily cajoled, and all his defenses would drop. At the pulpit, the holiest feeling that he experienced was the excitement of standing "before thousands and stir them by telling them about divine love."[77] It plunged him into a fantasy in which he saw himself "as a white-browed and star-eyed young evangel, wearing a new frock coat, standing up in a pulpit and causing hundreds of beautiful women to weep with conviction and rush down to clasp his hand."[78] When people did come up to him after the sermon to express their admiration, he would wring "their hands with a boyish gratitude beautiful to see."[79] He would thus, unknowingly, show others the softest side in him, and had he not been so detrimental to the people around him, he could almost have been genuinely pitied for the chronic and the acute urge to be unconditionally loved.

Narcissists hardly give anything to others for the sheer joy of giving, but only out of calculation that something more significant will be given back to them. On the other hand, they take whatever they can – admiration, material values, time. Furthermore, they feel entitled to receive "favorable treatment or automatic compliance"[80] from everyone, and turn against all those unwilling to succumb to their egoistic requests. They do not realize that others are doing them favors, but believe "that what others do for them is only what they deserve and what they are entitled to."[81] Elmer Gantry was no exception in regard to this criterion of pathological narcissism, too. "He was merely astonished when he found that you did not understand his importance and did not want to hand over anything he might desire."[82] Piece by piece, his narcissism gets rounded up in a perfect prototype of this particular personality disorder.

Apart from the individuals they perceive as superior, or in other words those they may benefit from one way or another, and to which they are sickly condescending, narcissists "show a degree of arrogance that verges on contempt for the common humanity."[83] In his college class, he disliked every single student, finding them "too rustic or too pious, too inquisitive [...] or simply too dull."[84] The girls he hung out with were "unworthy of his generous attention."[85] Later, when he got ordained, Elmer bought off some workers to officially join his church for certain practical reasons of his. However, he "could not consider the converts human."[86] These attitudes place him within the "pure" variant of the narcissistic personality disorder, called "elitist" by Theodore Millon or "phallic-narcissistic" by Wilhelm Reich. Interestingly enough, Elmer fits into three out of four common variants of this disorder. Besides being elitist, he is also unprincipled and amorous (more on this later). The only subtype that skips him is that of a compensatory narcissist that combines the traits of negativistic and avoidant personality disorders with the narcissistic foundation.

Being exploitative is second nature to narcissists. Erich Fromm called them people of the "exploitative orientation."[87] Swindling, forcing, seducing, and manipulating others is the only way familiar to them to achieve a goal. They do this unblinkingly, unperturbed by ethical concerns. Other people are but means on their ascent to an aim. Having crossed out their own true selves, narcissists are unable to relate to the selves of others. They treat them as inhumanely as they do their own authentic person. The only difference here is that they indulge themselves and harm others in their self-indulgence.

In childhood he had "hung cats."[88] Cruelty to animals, along with bedwetting and arson, all represent fairly indicative early signs of psychopathy. In college, "Elmer forced himself into the managership in Junior year by threatening not to play football if he were not elected."[89] In relationships with women, he would seduce them by sweet-talking and false promises and then abandon them, which was not only emotionally hurtful to the girls involved with him, but also socially, considering the mores of the early twentieth century. This places him within the category of the amorous narcissist, in which narcissistic and histrionic features interlace. Such people are "often defined by the game of erotic seduction they play with objects of their affection."[90]

His fishy dealings also included copying from theologians and philosophers and integrating their ideas into his own sermons. While doing so, he hoped "nobody there tonight has ever read Ingersoll. [...] Besides, I'll kind of change it around."[91] When he was finally awarded the honorary doctorate from the local university, which he coveted passionately, he accepted it saying he did not care about receiving such a degree, "but I do know it might please my congregation."[92] In the society, his hypocrisy was at large, while his unmasked exploitative nature was at wide display only in his home, where he tyrannized his wife and children. "Sundays were to his nervous family a hell of keeping out of his way."[93]

The subcategory termed "unprincipled narcissism" is a mixture of the narcissistic and the antisocial personality characteristics. Such people enjoy "gaining the trust of others and then outwitting or swindling them."[94] Elmer's weapon in these dealings, devoid of the tiniest drop of ethics, was his beaming, false religiosity. Before using others for his purposes, he first "turned on his spiritual faucet and worked at being charming."[95] Since church was his institution, he abused it for personal gain, without a single authentic spiritual bone in his whole body. What is surprising is not so much his criminal ways to climb the social ladder, but the hordes of followers tricked by his deceptions. The conformist laxity dulls people's sense of distinction between genuine and sham. A similar situation is more of a historical rule than an exception at the political, corporate, cultural, and other scenes where the powerful flex their manipulating muscles. Delighted by the strength of the loud, the crowds surrender to them, lulled by the consolation that their safety lies in going with the flow. Such fake sense of security is imposed on them by the manipulators who require absolute consent, so that they can feed their starving egos and to be able to carry out their grandiose plans. Little do the followers care that "the association between narcissism and abuse of power by grandiose charismatic types within organizations is well known."[96]

The sore spot that is at the root of all narcissistic behavior is probably the unfulfilled yearning for love. The play around emotions is the key to understanding people like Gantry. This play is intricate, paradoxical, stunting, yet simple. Denied unconditional warmth in childhood, narcissists kill all shards of emotion in them, because "the ego's safety lies in a deadened body."[97] The compensation for this cardinal lack comes in the form of hedonism, since "this very deadness creates a hunger for sensation."[98]

After being withheld love at an early age, when it was needed probably more than anything else, save food, some children equate love with pain. Ridding themselves of pain, they rid themselves of love, and develop such personality structures in which love is omitted from the circulation of forces that energize the person. Thus abandoned in the underground dungeons of personality, love is fettered and rotting away. To revisit it is too painful for narcissists, so they let it decay. However, it is not only love that is being forsaken – the same solitary confinement that secludes love also secludes the person's genuine self. The common notion that egocentrics only love themselves is thus essentially false. They cannot love themselves because they do not have themselves. What they love is the imaginary construct they have of themselves, an image that is a barren recipient of love, for it cannot reflect it back or give another person anything valuable in return.

The emotional self-paralysis renders narcissists unable to love others, to commit themselves, to form genuine relationships. Intimacy implies sharing and "an exposure of the self"[99] – for them an impossible mission. Unable to relate to their own emotions, narcissists see others in the exact same way. "When we deny our feelings, we deny that others feel."[100] This very trait of having no empathy is what makes them as unpopular as they are, and as difficult to empathize with.

Narcissists are prone to mask the absence of warmth by shows of affection and nurturance. They can be very "skilful in pretending a love for women or simulating parental devotion to their children."[101] Sometimes they even engage in altruistic activities, but only if it brings some external reward. Intellectually they know what love is, and try to incorporate it within their superficial way of functioning. Though they might want love, they are unable to find it in another person. What they find in others are objects they might use or avoid for their own pleasure or benefit. Sex is love's main substitute. Still, narcissists are not utterly devoid of feelings, since that would render them inhuman. The feelings are only shut away from the person, with occasional breakthroughs into narcissistic realities. What breaks through, though, are mostly moments "of casual fondness [...] always strictly limited in degree."[102] The tepidity of their emotionality is greatly outweighed by the intensity of negative emotions, such as rage, envy, or dissatisfaction. The meager spectrum of their emotions usually ranges between "an irrational rage and a maudlin sentimentality."[103]

Elmer Gantry's emotional life was as desolate as that of any narcissist. He engaged in the standard patterns of behavior, unfeelingly hurting colleagues, girls, family, and opponents. The woman he chose to marry, Cleo, did not suspect that on their very wedding day, his main thought was: "Oh, good God, I've gone and tied myself up."[104] Instead, the face he presented to her "was very manly, gentlemanly in fact; he concealed his distaste for her and entertained her."[105] Two months after the wedding, he managed to become "indifferent enough to stop hating her."[106] This indifference, however, meant making her life miserable at all times, and gloating when his parades of righteousness made her cry. "He had satisfaction in hearing her sob that night."[107] When he fell for the swindling secretary Hettie, Elmer unabashedly cultivated the following wishful idea: "O God, why can't Cleo die, so I can marry Hettie."[108]

Having children is not a reason enough for narcissists to warm up. Elmer treated his own boy and girl lovelessly, too. They "were afraid of him, even when he boisterously decided to enact the Kind Parent for one evening and to ride them pickaback, whether or no they wanted to be ridden pickaback."[109] At meals, he would glare "at the children if they stirred in their chairs,"[110] and on Sundays, if they were louder than permitted, he would chide them mercilessly, instilling perverse guilt into them for "committing an unexampled sin by causing him to fall into bad tempers unbecoming a Man of God."[111]

Elmer thought he loved his mother, but he only feared and wanted to love her, as she was unlovable. The first person who came close to the sanctified position his mother had held was Sharon Falconer, a charismatic female preacher with her own share of personality distortions (discussed in a later chapter). Bedazzled by her flamboyance, as Dr. Faustus was upon summoning "the face that launch'd a thousand ships,"[112] Elmer came as close as possible to what is considered love for another being. Without going into a detailed analysis of the true nature of that love, it has to be admitted that he was ready to surrender to Sharon and that he could "for once love so much that he did not insist on loving."[113] Still, due to essential immaturity of both these lovers, their romance could not have developed in any meaningful direction. Such uncharacteristic emotional episodes only show that Elmer did have emotions somewhere deep within, but that he was not able to develop the capacity to love to any significant degree. Most of the time, though, when he wanted to appear emotional, he would "look as though he were wounded clear to the heart [...] He folded his hands in front of his beautiful morning coat, and looked noble, slightly milky and melancholy of eye... But he was not milky. He was staring hard enough."[114]

What appears as a "fragile paper house of egotism"[115] from one point of view is from another hard, crookedly ossified skeleton of narcissistic psychological functioning. It is as if "ropes of sand," to use George Herbert's metaphor, tied up the whole personality tightly. Even though the psychopathic scaffolding seems cast in iron, and in practice it more often than not proves impervious to even a slight change, the whole narcissistic, as well as any other disordered personality structure, is in fact a ramshackle machinery that requires constant maintenance. Narcissists go along the rather established routines. The principle of utmost importance for them is keeping their emotions at bay. They get into the habit of denying and blocking them all the time, particularly emotions such as "sadness and fear. They are singled out because their expression makes the person feel vulnerable."[116] Instead, they put on an act of power, which does contain strength, but does not serve the advertised function. It serves narcissists only as a protection against humiliation, weakness, unloveability, and builds up their image, but does nothing to modify the self. Reality checks do not apply to narcissists. They rather change reality rationalizing it into the way it fits them, redoing the past, "put[ting] a subtle spin on events, convincing both themselves and others that they were right all along."[117] Their own principles are stronger than the principles of common decency. "Rationales need not be defended as absolute, for they can always be reconfigured for new purposes as they arise [...] Morality and values are simply a constraint on the subject's unbounded desire for omnipotence."[118] Rigidity characteristic of all personality disorders is the glue of pathological narcissism, too. In this case, it is the heightened perfectionistic drive and a tendency to see things dichotomously as either all-good or all-bad.

What is it, then, that lies behind the mask? How do narcissists feel when the curtains fall and when they find themselves alone on the dark stage? Most likely, they feel empty, alone, unable to tap into the pool of inner meaning, since they have cut all channels into it. Hiding from the self they find intolerable, they "deny[...] the self and end[...] in a loss of the self."[119] The only remaining choice is to play a preconceived role, for no authentic identity is ever established. Hence, they "often fit stereotypic sexual roles,"[120] in accordance with their rigid dichotomous worldviews. In case their muscled up balance is disturbed, they see themselves, again dichotomously, as utter failures, and become depressed, which they manage to keep at bay as long as their defenses are rejecting the unfavorable facts. Since the maintenance of defenses requires large amounts of psychic energy, narcissists are given to substance abuse to bolster them up, but are at the same time overly sensitive to insults, or whatever it is that they experience as insults. Their uncontrollable, intense rages and acting-out episodes betray the vulnerability of their feverishly perpetuated constructions of psychological functioning. The fact that narcissists are frequent victims of posttraumatic stress disorder also shows the unreality of their emotionlessness, for "traumatic events generally puncture the bubble of [...] narcissistic fantasies."[121] In brief, people like Elmer Gantry lead lives marked by "affective childhood frustrations that breeds in the adult person a 'nostalgia' for denied love," lives in which values and humanness are relativized by the pathological needs of a false identity eventually "leading to involuntary self-destructiveness."[122] Narcissists are not categorized as psychotic, but the fact that they live out of touch with their feelings makes them insensitive to reality – the main criterion of one's mental health. "Since feelings are a basic reality of a human life, to be out of touch with one's feelings is a sign of insanity."[123]

Save for the equally flawed followers who were blinded by Elmer Gantry's pomposity, all those with at least a shred of psychological maturity easily saw through his falsehood. One of the college students remarked about Elmer: "He'll never hold any office again, not if I can help it!"[124] Elmer, on the other side, was narcissistically unaware "that he was unpopular. He reasoned that men who seemed chilly to him were envious and afraid, and that gave him a feeling of greatness."[125] Later in life, when he was on a ship to Europe, he approached an elderly couple and offered them his ministerial wisdom. Walking away from them, he complacently thought, "Well, I've given those poor old birds some cheerfulness to go on with."[126] The effect of his address on the couple was, however, diametrically different. The lady indignantly told her husband, "Fabian, if that swine ever speaks to me again, I shall jump overboard! He's almost the most offensive object I have ever encountered!"[127]

Gantry's bubble was impenetrable, even after the experiences that should have at least made him reconsider his ways. Escaping a very realistic downfall by the skin of his teeth, having fallen for the charms of Hettie who wanted to destroy him, he promised that he would never be unfaithful to his wife again. "I've learned my lesson. I'll never look at a girl again."[128] As soon as he gave this promise to himself, "he turned to include the choir, and for the first time he saw that there was a new singer, a girl with charming ankles and lively eyes, with whom he would certainly have to become well acquainted."[129] The foolhardiness with which he refused to learn lessons and change inwardly speaks of the highly advanced level of his disorder.

Elmer Gantry's Religiosity

Having gone into all the personality shortcomings of Elmer Gantry as one of the most perfect literary narcissists, what kind of religiosity could have been maintained under such brutally callous mental grid? It is a fact that he was a rather successful preacher and that his ministry at times provided him with more than a decent income. However, it takes no great wisdom to conclude that his religion was counterfeit, just like most of the things about him were. He could easily have been an atheist, but due to some random developmental factors, he had an attitude of respect for religion even before he became ordained. Let us examine the nature of the religious connection in his life.

Elmer's mother was religious, and since he held her in an Oedipally high esteem, he also took over the values that were inseparable from her. Besides, fearing Mrs. Gantry, he also came to fear God and the church. "He was afraid of it. It connoted his boyhood."[130] That was not an exceptionally unusual childhood view of God, particularly in the American Christian environment where "God was always creeping about to catch small boys in their secret thoughts."[131] The narcissistic way of overcoming fear is by putting on the mask of power. Accordingly, Elmer was also fascinated by "a black-bearded David standing against raw red cliffs – a figure heroic and summoning to ambition, to power, to domination!"[132] His later career in the church was but a perpetuation of "a dream on childish omnipotence, never outgrown."[133]

As a college student, Elmer was not ready to fulfill his mother's wishes of becoming a preacher, as he would grumble: "Oh, gee, Ma, I don't know. Trouble is, fellow don't make much money preaching. Gee, there's no hurry. Don't have to decide yet."[134] Even later, when he did get into church business, in moments of sincerity, he would regret: "Oh, Lordy, Lordy, Lordy, I wish I had a good job selling real estate!"[135] The value orientation of his life was anything but spiritual. Still, he fell into the religious trap he was primed into, first of all by his mother, backed up by school authorities, fellow student-zealots, and clergymen. They all staged a church ceremony at which Elmer was to be tested whether he'd receive the divine call or not. "It was up to God. A fellow had to have a call before he felt his vocation for the ministry [...] Their task now was to get Elmer into a real state of grace."[136] In the end, it wasn't up to God any more, at all.

The outcome was as expected, for it was not too difficult to manipulate Elmer into "receiving" the call. It took a medley of his mother's emotional blackmail ("Won't you make your old mother happy?"[137]), the fear for his soul ("how terribly dangerous it is to put off the hour of salvation"[138]), the college dean's presentation of future prospects ("banquets [...] heroic struggle against vice [...] finest ladies [...] cheaper professional training"[139]), and the factor definitely decisive for a narcissist – to be adored ("To move people – Golly! [...] To be addressing somebody or something [...] and being applauded"[140]). He finally gave in, exclaiming, "I'd never been willing to kneel down and confess myself a miserable sinner. But I'm kneeling now, and, oh, the blessedness of humility!"[141]

However, all the while he "wasn't [...] kneeling at all; he was standing up, very tall and broad."[142] What he expressed as the blessedness of humility "sounded like his announcements of an ability to lick anybody in any given saloon."[143] The nail in the coffin of the irreversibleness of the moment of "transformation" was stricken again by the great conductor, his mother: "You've made your old mother so happy! All my life I've sorrowed, I've waited, I've prayed and now I shan't ever sorrow again! Oh, you will stay true?"[144]

Elmer's reasons for accepting the religious vocation were emotional, psychological, material, and thus completely insubstantial in an authentic religious sense. Even faking it for years did not make him any more sensitive about matters of the soul. The way he preached his religion was not only hypocritical, since it came from the wrong platform, but also harmful, misleading believers into dark alleys of corruption.

Most of his practices illustrate the aspects of immature religiosity described in the first part of this book. One of his fundamentals is literalism, which goes along with the acceptance of ready-made religious formulae not arrived at through inner processing. The Bible is to be believed in literally, from cover to cover; otherwise, it is degraded to "a Bible full of holes."[145] Preaching is not to be founded on illusion, but on "good hard scientific FACTS – the proven facts of the Bible."[146] The "truth" preached by his branch of the Baptist Church was that there was no salvation unless the believer has had a "baptism by immersion."[147] The poor soul was lost "if he'd just been baptized by sprinkling or pouring."[148] In the same vein, another branch of the Baptist Church taught that "slavery was the will of God,"[149] again "proved by the Bible, irrefutably."[150] Gantry's literalism is so paramount that it overshadows all ethics and renders it irrelevant. "If you don't believe in the virgin birth and the resurrection, atonement, and immersion, than it don't make no difference about your so-called good works and charity and all that, because you're doomed and bound to go straight to hell."[151] This is one of the sad truths that applies to fundamentalists the world around, and it distorts religion into its complete opposite.

Such an approach in which religion is understood as a word by word enactment of scripture tolerates no doubts – for what would remain if the cornerstones of this kind of religion were removed, and what kind of position would the followers find themselves in but an agony of being clueless and completely lost. This is why doubts are to Elmer "contemptible, quibbling, atheistic, smart-aleck,"[152] all the more so since in rare moments of honesty he was also prone to question his beliefs, "now colder with doubt than with the prairie wind, now winning back some of the exaltation of his spiritual adventure!"[153] Although he could have dealt with his own occasional uncertainties, he would not let others allow even a tiniest hint of them, for they represented threats to the religious edifice he and his kin were erecting. Expectedly, criticism was experienced not merely as a threat, but as an outright attack. This is what Elmer had to say about Robert Ingersoll's agnosticism: "That rotten old atheist [...] Fellow that couldn't believe in the Bible, least he could do was not to disturb the faith of others."[154]

The practice of the falsely religious is frequently to demonize the members of all other religious, racial, class groups, or briefly anyone who does not unquestioningly adhere to all the accepted rules and truths of the particular religious organization. In the novel, a spiritual adviser is telling Elmer about "the evil spell of Buddhism and a lot of these heathen religions."[155] A diligent learner, or more precisely a natural, Elmer permitted his congregation "to hate all Catholics, all persons who failed to believe in hell and immersion, and all rich mortgage-holders."[156] Failing to be inclusive (which was the characteristic of the faith of all the founders of religions), attitudes like Elmer's are dangerous for humanistic and democratic progress, not to mention the corrupting effect they have on people's spirituality. Unfortunately, similar ideas are held by too many people to this day, in most world's religions, the globe around. Religious intolerance, a *contradictio in adjecto*, is as alive today as it has been in the past, largely perpetuated by religiously (and inevitably psychologically) flawed religious leaders.

Elmer Gantry's kind of religious distortion had an unmistakably narcissistic flavor. The "parent sin"[157] of *hubris*, or "lack of humility,"[158] is a trademark of this character's psychological and religious functioning. The most annoying position for him was to be among a crowd "unnoticed and unadmired, as though he were an ordinary layman."[159] Unaware, or more likely unwilling to care that he was actually walking in the footsteps of the one who showed "the first disobedience" to God, Gantry never even came close to facing the Narcissus within him.

His self-grandiosity as a religious figure made him dream about "affect[ing] the whole world"[160] and inclined to "mothering the world, whether the world liked it or not."[161] At the same time, he pined for the title of Doctor of Divinity and for mystical experiences that would single him out as the one "exempt from the ordinary rules of conduct that portray the way Jesus lived."[162] Bearing in mind his overall demeanor and ideological world, he could hardly have experienced a touch of mysticism, for he remained unchanged throughout his life, while mystical experiences do leave an indelible change in one's character. It may only have been either pretenses, tokens of specialness, or tepid emotionalisms that he confused for, or, more precisely, wanted to believe to be mystical experiences. With narcissists, such pretenses and emotionalisms are "another form of escapism,"[163] means of securing "religious superiority [...] to judge and deprecate others,"[164] and "hypomanic states of exaltation"[165] rather than genuine encounters with higher dimensions.

Narcissists endorse God as a replacement for a loving and protective parent that they never had. In case they were in the focus of their parents' essentially unloving attention, they will feel special in God's eyes, too, but will probably be unable to love him. Whatever they do, God must tolerate and continue to love and care for them, "so that they can retain their own psychological equilibrium."[166] Used to exploit others, they also exploit the divinity, and in their "prayer claim that God will do exactly as they ask."[167] When they feel God is betraying them, or when they see no more benefit from their religious engagement, they do not find it difficult to abandon religion altogether. If narcissists had "an awareness of grace and a [...] capacity for gratitude,"[168] their religious struggle would have been more existential, and their (im)moral reasoning not so uncomplicated. However, what marks them is a "poignant spiritual deficit,"[169] which makes it difficult to speak of genuine narcissistic religiosity. Elmer Gantry took up religion as an instrument of reaching through to his mother. The novel does not follow him to a point of abandoning religion (for ceasing to be lucrative), but such an epilogue would not be too difficult to envisage.

Elmer Gantry's religious fakeness is on open display to any astute observer. When a Professor asked him where he had got some fine ideas and metaphors from, he responded: "Oh, [...] I can't hardly call them mine, Professor. I guess I just got them by praying."[170] The first half of the statement is true, the latter fake, for he plagiarized the ideas, as he was prone to. Saying that he got them by praying singled him out as spiritually special. In truth, he had a bunch of phrases "for immediate and skilled use,"[171] none of which was of his own creation. When asked what he felt while singing in church, he said: "Why, I was thinking how happy we'll all be when we are purified and at rest in Beulah Land,"[172] while in fact he was daydreaming about a new seduction he was about to attempt. The falsity of his psychological life only got extended to his religious life, and instead of gaining depth from spirituality, he imposed the worst kind of shallowness on to it.

All the coarseness of his interpersonal dealings is reflected in his ecclesiastical performance, too. Manipulation was a constant way of achieving goals. At a certain point in his preaching enterprise with Sharon Falconer, they desperately needed repenting sinners who would come forward during the service show. In order to secure them, he found some homeless men in a mission and promised them "five dollars apiece"[173] if their act proved convincing. He certainly was not picky about the means to attain the pseudo-religious goals. In order to secure a large congregation, "it don't hurt one bit to scare 'em into being righteous with the good old-fashioned Hell."[174] The poetry of religion was junk to him. Charity was also a nonexistent element in his gospel. When a big guy kept interrupting Gantry's meeting and asking provocative questions, he "yanked that yahoo out of his seat and threw him out on his ear, and say, the whole crowd [...] did give him the ha-ha! You bet."[175]

Dazed by charismatic figures like Gantry, the followers easily swallow the claptrap wrapped in a religious packaging. The only authentic religious contribution Gantry ever had to offer was a ditty going: "Hallelujah, Praise God, hal, hal, hal! / All together, I feel better / Hal, hal, hal / For salvation of the nation – Aaaaam-MEN!"[176] He proudly released it as the first piece in a whole genre he called "Hallelujah Yell." Trivializing religious experience, he went on to include entertaining numbers during services, started radio broadcasts, and talked about things he had no clue of such as "soul breathing,"[177] because they sounded enlightening. In essence, he struggled to understand the basic concepts of religion. During a spell while he was kicked out of church, he went about as a "New Thought" proponent, but esoteric, occult, mystical ideas did not sit well with him. He did "accomplish [...] seven pages of the *Bhagavad-Gita*,"[178] but despite it remaining completely in the obscurity of oriental lore to him, he still went about basing his pseudo-spiritual speeches on the lines of Hinduism's Bible.

Not everybody is fooled by narcissistic acts, though it still cannot be said that the majority sees through their insincerity. There always were individuals around Gantry who figured out the place he was coming from, but they never formed a critical mass so as to expose him to the wider audiences. If they became too dangerous a threat, Gantry had his ruthless ways of eliminating them. He was "an atheist in sheep's clothing"[179] and some preachers said that "those of us that are halfway decent suffer from being classed with Gantry."[180] However, he took no heed, as long as he knew that his manipulations would keep the masses of conformist followers within his spell. Sinclair Lewis gives another illustration of the lesson the humanity is slow at learning, that "'the self-absorbed' leader in churches, in politics, in medicine, and in international affairs is likely to project his or her narcissism onto a large screen of public adulation."[181] This is not to say that narcissists should be discriminated against, but only thwarted from getting their hands on social positions with a powerful influence on larger groups of people, such as religious leadership most certainly is.

"Know thyself," an immemorial instruction given in the Vedas, inscribed on the Temple of Apollo at Delphi, offered by Shakespeare through Polonius' mouth ("This above all: to thine own self be true"[182]), fell short on Elmer Gantry's ears. The misfortune with any pathological narcissist runs along similar lines – they are people who do not know a tiny little bit about themselves, and who blindly run away from facing their hearts. Living in a world of puffed up fantasy, they might become aware "that their entire life has been an inauthentic sham"[183] only when it is rather late to make amends with their own selves and with others they had inevitably wronged. The general belief that narcissists love themselves is a misconception, for they don't know what love is. The emotionalism they are prone to is not to be confused with love. Not knowing themselves, not knowing others through love, are they able to compensate for these shortcomings through faith, in case they are religious? Although it is difficult to judge on any one's personal relationship with God, the acts and affects of a narcissist do not reveal any genuine spirituality.

Talking about Elmer Gantry's spirituality is a paradox. Religion comes from the noetic core of being, while Elmer had no contact with that core, barred from his conscious person by the rigid psychopathological shield of an egoist. Even though he had no religion to speak of, but only mimicked the clichéd behavior of a man of God, engaging in all kinds of under the counter dealings all the while, he was recognized in society as a spiritual leader.

Burt Lancaster won an Academy Award for his role of Gantry on the big screen back in 1960. Over half a century later, Gantry-like preachers are still at large, disseminating narcissistic toxins. A comparison is sometimes made to the influential, now deceased evangelist "Jerry Fallwell as a modern-day Elmer Gantry."[184] Kevin Roose, who spent a year as a disguise student at Liberty, Falwell's Christian University, and published a book on his experiences there, states that the world of evangelism, and especially of televangelism, is "filled to the brim with hucksters and charlatans and Elmer Gantry-type swindlers."[185] Even though some psychologists claim that narcissistic personality disorder is endemic to the USA and "does not occur with frequency in other nations,"[186] I have personally encountered narcissists in other settings, too. Narcissistic religious leaders are easily to be found globally, had a solid methodology for identifying them been invented, and had an interest in religious psychopathology been more alive.

Notes

1 Christine Rosen, *Preaching Eugenics: Religious Leaders and the American Eugenics Movement*, Oxford: Oxford University Press, 2004, p. 5.
2 See: Wayne Wiegand, "Collecting Contested Titles: The Experience of Five Small Public Libraries in the Rural Midwest, 1893-1956," *Libraries and Culture*, Vol. 30, No. 3, Summer 2005, pp. 368–384.
3 Michael G. Moriarty, *The Perfect Ten: The Blessings of Following God's Commandments in a Postmodern Way*, Grand Rapids: Zondervan, 1999, p. 79.
4 Mark Schorer, "Sinclair Lewis," *Seven Modern American Novelists, An Introduction*, ed. William Van O'Connor, Minneapolis: The University of Minnesota Press, 1964, p. 60.
5 Down B. Sova, *Banned Books: Literature Suppressed on Social Grounds*, New York: Facts on File, 2006, p. 124.
6 James Lea, "Sinclair Lewis and the Implied America," *American Fiction between the Wars*, ed. Harold Bloom, New York: Chelsea House, 2005, p. 85.
7 William Vance Trollinger Jr., *God's Empire: William Bell Riley and Midwestern Fundamentalism*, Madison: The University of Wisconsin Press, 1990, p. 3.
8 Michael G. Moriarty, *op. cit.*, p. 78.
9 Kenneth E. Aupperle and Deane Van Pham, "An Expanded Investigation into the Relationship of Corporate Social Responsibility and Financial

Performance," *Employee Responsibilities and Rights Journal*, Vol. 2, No. 4, New York: Springer, 1989, p. 263.
10 Mark Schorer, *op. cit.*, p. 60.
11 Len Sperry, *Handbook of Diagnosis and treatment of DSM-IV-TR Personality Disorders*, New York: Brunner-Rouledge, 2005, p. 149.
12 Sinclair Lewis, *Elmer Gantry*, A Project Gutenberg of Australia eBook, 0300851, May 2003.
13 Len Sperry, *Handbook of Diagnosis and treatment of DSM-IV-TR Personality Disorders*, p. 152.
14 Theodore Millon, *op. cit.*, p. 359.
15 Alexander Lowen, *op. cit.*, p. 13.
16 Sigmund Freud, "On Narcissism: An Introduction," ed. Philip Rieff, New York: A Touchstone Book, 2008, p. 58.
17 Theodore Millon, *op. cit.*, p. 358.
18 Lucia Imbesi, paraphrased by Len Sperry, *Handbook of Diagnosis and treatment of DSM-IV-TR Personality Disorders*, p. 152.
19 Len Sperry, *Handbook of Diagnosis and treatment of DSM-IV-TR Personality Disorders*, p. 153.
20 Alexander Lowen, *op. cit.*, p. 216.
21 Wayne E. Oates, *Behind the Masks: Personality Disorders in Religious Behaviour*, Louisville, KY: The Westminster Press, 1987, p. 52.
22 Len Sperry, *Handbook of Diagnosis and treatment of DSM-IV-TR Personality Disorders*, p. 148.
23 Theodore Millon, *op. cit.*, p. 347.
24 Len Sperry, *Handbook of Diagnosis and treatment of DSM-IV-TR Personality Disorders*, p. 153.
25 Sinclair Lewis, *Elmer Gantry*
26 *Ibid.*
27 *Ibid.*
28 *Ibid.*
29 *Ibid.*
30 *Ibid.*
31 *Ibid.*
32 *Ibid.*
33 *Ibid.*
34 *Ibid.*
35 *Ibid.*
36 *Ibid.*
37 Wayne E. Oates, *op. cit.*, p. 43.
38 Alexander Lowen, *op. cit.*, p. 128.
39 Wayne E. Oates, *op. cit.*, p. 43.
40 Sinclair Lewis, *Elmer Gantry.*
41 *Ibid.*
42 Len Sperry, *Handbook of Diagnosis and treatment of DSM-IV-TR Personality Disorders*, p. 156.
43 Sinclair Lewis, *Elmer Gantry.*
44 *Ibid.*
45 *Ibid.*
46 *Ibid.*
47 Theodore Millon, *op. cit.*, p. 356.
48 Len Sperry, *Handbook of Diagnosis and treatment of DSM-IV-TR Personality Disorders*, p. 148.
49 Sinclair Lewis, *Elmer Gantry.*
50 *Ibid.*

51 *Ibid.*
52 *Ibid.*
53 *Ibid.*
54 *Ibid.*
55 Theodore Millon, *op. cit.*, p. 332.
56 *Ibid.*, p. 357.
57 *Ibid.*, p. 350.
58 Sinclair Lewis, *Elmer Gantry.*
59 *Ibid.*
60 *Ibid.*
61 Len Sperry, *Handbook of Diagnosis and Treatment of DSM-IV-TR Personality Disorders*, p. 148.
62 Sinclair Lewis, *Elmer Gantry.*
63 *Ibid.*
64 Oliver Sacks, *The Man Who Mistook His Wife for a Hat*, New York: Harper & Row, 1987, p. 81.
65 Alexander Lowen, *op. cit.*, p. 128.
66 *Ibid.*
67 Sinclair Lewis, *Elmer Gantry.*
68 *Ibid.*
69 *Ibid.*
70 *Ibid.*
71 *Ibid.*
72 *Ibid.*
73 Theodore Millon, *op. cit.*, p. 350.
74 Alexander Lowen, *op. cit.*, p. 45.
75 Theodore Millon, *op. cit.*, p. 348.
76 Sinclair Lewis, *Elmer Gantry.*
77 *Ibid.*
78 *Ibid.*
79 *Ibid.*
80 Theodore Millon, *op. cit.*, p. 332.
81 Wayne E. Oates, *op. cit.*, p. 45.
82 Sinclair Lewis, *Elmer Gantry.*
83 Alexander Lowen, *op. cit.*, p. 22.
84 Sinclair Lewis, *Elmer Gantry.*
85 *Ibid.*
86 *Ibid.*
87 Erich Fromm, *Man for Himself: An Inquiry into the Psychology of Ethics*, New York: Rinehart & Co, 1947, p. 64.
88 *Ibid.*
89 *Ibid.*
90 Theodore Millon, *op. cit.*, p. 364.
91 Sinclair Lewis, *Elmer Gantry.*
92 *Ibid.*
93 *Ibid.*
94 Theodore Millon, *op. cit.*, p. 337.
95 Sinclair Lewis, *Elmer Gantry.*
96 Theodore Millon, *op. cit.*, p. 355.
97 Alexander Lowen, *op. cit.*, p. 177.
98 *Ibid.*
99 *Ibid.*, p. 123.
100 *Ibid.*, p. 49.

101 Harvey Cleckley, *The Mask of Sanity*, Augusta, GA: Emily Cleckley, private printing, 1988, p. 347.
102 *Ibid.*
103 Alexander Lowen, *op. cit.*, p. 62.
104 Sinclair Lewis, *Elmer Gantry.*
105 *Ibid.*
106 *Ibid.*
107 *Ibid.*
108 *Ibid.*
109 *Ibid.*
110 *Ibid.*
111 *Ibid.*
112 Christopher Marlowe, *The Tragical History of Dr. Faustus*, www.gutenberg.org/files/779/779-h/779-h.htm, e-text, accessed at 9 August 2017.
113 Sinclair Lewis, *Elmer Gantry.*
114 *Ibid.*
115 Wayne E. Oates, *op. cit.*, p. 46.
116 Alexander Lowen, *op. cit.*, p. 75.
117 Theodore Millon, *op. cit.*, p. 345.
118 *Ibid.*
119 Alexander Lowen, *op. cit.*, p. 123.
120 Len Sperry, *Handbook of Diagnosis and Treatment of DSM-IV-TR Personality Disorders*, p. 156.
121 Theodore Millon, *op. cit.*, p. 363.
122 *Ibid.*, p. 342.
123 Alexander Lowen, *op. cit.*, p. 4.
124 Sinclair Lewis, *Elmer Gantry.*
125 *Ibid.*
126 *Ibid.*
127 *Ibid.*
128 *Ibid.*
129 *Ibid.*
130 *Ibid.*
131 *Ibid.*
132 *Ibid.*
133 "san o decijoj svemoci, nikada prevazidjen," Giacomo Dacquino, *op. cit.*, p. 139.
134 Sinclair Lewis, *Elmer Gantry.*
135 *Ibid.*
136 *Ibid.*
137 *Ibid.*
138 *Ibid.*
139 *Ibid.*
140 *Ibid.*
141 *Ibid.*
142 *Ibid.*
143 *Ibid.*
144 *Ibid.*
145 *Ibid.*
146 *Ibid.*
147 *Ibid.*
148 *Ibid.*
149 *Ibid.*

150 *Ibid.*
151 *Ibid.*
152 *Ibid.*
153 *Ibid.*
154 *Ibid.*
155 *Ibid.*
156 *Ibid.*
157 Wayne E. Oates, *op. cit.*, p. 43.
158 Theodore Millon, *op. cit.*, p. 342.
159 Sinclair Lewis, *Elmer Gantry.*
160 *Ibid.*
161 *Ibid.*
162 Wayne E. Oates, *op. cit.*, p. 49.
163 Alexander Lowen, *op. cit.*, p. 224.
164 "religioznom superiornoscu [...] da bi osudio i potcenio druge," Giacomo Dacquino, *op. cit.*, p. 140.
165 "hipomanicka stanja egzaltacije," Snezana Milenkovic, *op. cit.*, p. 118.
166 "kako bi zadrzali sopstveni psihicki ekvilibrijum," Giacomo Dacquino, *op. cit.*, p. 139.
167 Wayne E. Oates, *op. cit.*, p. 47.
168 *Ibid.*, p. 45.
169 *Ibid.*
170 Sinclair Lewis, *Elmer Gantry.*
171 *Ibid.*
172 *Ibid.*
173 *Ibid.*
174 *Ibid.*
175 *Ibid.*
176 *Ibid.*
177 *Ibid.*
178 *Ibid.*
179 *Ibid.*
180 *Ibid.*
181 Wayne E. Oates, *op. cit.*, p. 45.
182 William Shakespeare, *Hamlet*, http://shakespeare.mit.edu/hamlet/full.html, e-text, accessed at 30 July 2014.
183 Theodore Millon, *op. cit.*, p. 364.
184 Fein Bruce, "Hustler Magazine v. Falwell: A Mislitigated and Misreasoned Case," *Willam and Mary Law Review*, Vol. 30, No. 4, Williamsburg, VA: 1989, p. 905.
185 Kevin Roose, *The Unlikely Disciple: A Sinner's Semester at America's Holiest University*, New York: Grand Central Publishing, Kindle e-book, 2009.
186 Theodore Millon, *op. cit.*, p. 333.

6 A Demon Next to an Angel

Father Joseph and Masochistic Religiosity

The phrase *grey eminence* is commonly used to denote a "behind the scenes" person of great influence at high levels of decision-making, but it is not a widely known fact that in 1941, Aldous Huxley (1894–1963) published a book with the same title. At the heart of this book is the enigma of the historical character of Father Joseph, who was, put very simply, both a saint and a devil. Several days after his death, a desecrating note by "an anonymous practical joker"[1] appeared on his grave, saying: "Passer-by, is it not a strange thing that a demon should be next to an angel?"[2] What made Father Joseph contain and epitomize the extremes of the spiritually most sublime and most diabolical is the question Huxley tries to deal with in this book.

The subtitle of *Grey Eminence* defines it as "a study in religion and politics." As much as the main character is a riddle, the very genre of the book is riddling, too. Huxley ambiguously and generically calls it a study, although the opening chapter reads like a most exquisite example of a historical novel. However, "the novelist gives place to the historian, who in turn yields to the philosopher."[3] In a private letter, Huxley later categorized this discursive novel as a "speculative and philosophical biography of a most extraordinary person."[4] Such loosely determined gender form best suited his ambition to look into the paradox of the aforementioned historical personality of Father Joseph, though not only for sheer curiosity. Huxley's motives ran deeper than that, spurred by "the impulse to cultivate space for human potentialities."[5] By exposing the case study of how profound spirituality can go awfully awry, he wanted to warn his readership of the signs of malevolent pathology lurking behind the mask of superficially perfect religiosity.

Aside from the essayistic outings into historical episodes and religio-philosophical digressions, the focus of the book is on the life and deeds of Father Joseph. He was a Capuchin monk of aristocratic descent who lived in France in the sixteenth and seventeenth centuries. Besides having mystical experiences from an early age and practicing an uncompromising ascetic lifestyle, the monk was also an influential politician and close collaborator of King Louis' XIII Chief Minister Cardinal Richelieu, known for his authoritarian attitudes and Machiavellian employs to maintain power and secure strong royalist centralism in France. Father Joseph's involvement in mysticism on one side and in high politics on the other represents a paradox that Huxley tried to explain from a religious and political standpoint. Here we will try to shift the attention to the psychological perspective, which is largely neglected in the book, even though its pages abound in raw psychological material. However, let us first briefly sketch out the most important biographical facts of Father Joseph's life.

A Brief Biography of Father Joseph

François Leclerc du Tremblay, as was his birth name, was born on 4 November 1577 into a Calvinist family of lawyers and landed nobility. His inherited title would have been Baron de Maffliers had he not formally rejected secular life. He also had two younger siblings, a brother and a sister (who was "brought up in the Catholic religion, so that she might enter a convent and so spare [... the parents] the expense of dowry"[6]). While François was still a schoolboy, his father died, which left him profoundly stricken with grief. Even at the young age of ten, this family death provoked in him a strong sense of the precariousness and the vanity of the world.

He had entered boarding school in Paris when he was eight. In fact, he himself asked to be sent there, "on the ground that he was being spoiled by his mother,"[7] whom he loved dearly. In school, he met Pierre de Berulle, who later became a cardinal and "the most influential member of the French School of mysticism."[8] The two boys were drawn to each other and "discuss[ed] the deepest problems of metaphysics and religion."[9] On the other hand, he was "as mercilessly beaten, bullied and ill-fed as little boys were in most of the boarding schools of the period."[10] When life in Paris became dangerous in 1585 due to the French Wars of Religion, François moved to le Tremblay near Versailles, and continued education there under a private tutor.

Upon reaching adolescence, François experienced the standard infatuation of calf love, "his first and final excruciation of the heart."[11] Instead of embracing the thrill, he was "troubled with the sense of guilt"[12] and decided to shut away from these intense feelings. Tried as he did, "before the week was out, he was as much the slave of his passion as he had ever been."[13] However, the pangs of conscience did return, and he renewed his vows to stay away from love just as he had decided to leave home when he was eight in order to stay away from the love of his mother. In both cases, the idea was to remove the obstacles from his path to a religious life.

What additionally heated up his religious fervor was finding an old book in the streets, thrown away by some passing soldiers. It was "a Christianized biography of Gautama Buddha,"[14] which reaffirmed his desire to devote himself entirely to a religious calling. In the meantime, he did go through his schooling process, but "was only waiting for the right moment, the final and unmistakable call."[15] The fact that he was a gifted horseman, went on a grand tour to Italy, took "his degree in gentlemanliness in less than one year,"[16] spent a year at court where he left an excellent impression, continued his education as a young man at the school of the Louvre where he learned diplomacy and many other skills, partook in the siege of Amiens, visited England accompanying the French ambassador – none of these considerable worldly successes deterred him from pursuing a monastic life.

His determination to join a religious order involved a lot of drama. He secretly left home in order to become a Carthusian, a member of a Christian sect who "lived immured and in almost perpetual silence"[17] and usually never saw their families again. Before joining this order, he still wanted to obtain his mother's consent, but she withheld it. She had already searched for a proper girl he would marry and expected him to take up family duties. After intense negotiations, during which he fell physically ill, they reached a compromise – he was to join the slightly more liberal Capuchins, which would enable her to continue seeing him from time to time. She is said to have converted to piety herself after these events.

Father Joseph became ordained and set off on a lifelong involvement in performing religious duties: founding monasteries, reforming existing ones, converting Protestants, establishing Catholic missions, dreaming about the crusades. Simultaneously, he was also equally drawn to another passion – the life of high politics. Besides his natural inclination, it was also the historical circumstances and some encounters, most notably the one with Cardinal Richelieu, that made him get enmeshed in political decision-making at the highest level.

His political activities included audiences with the Pope in the hope of securing support for the new crusades, negotiations with the Protestants and anti-royalists amid the civil war, organizing and running Richelieu's secret police, writing of political propaganda, and encouraging Richelieu to persist in the siege of La Rochelle, where 20,000 people perished in most inhumane ways. He did everything to prolong the Thirty Years' War against Germany, despite the fact that cannibalism, along with many other atrocities, was spreading in Europe as a direct consequence of the war. Father Joseph did it all unblinkingly, for the greater glory of France, which he considered "to be the instrument of divine providence [and which] he was able, with a good conscience and without suspecting that he was committing idolatry, to worship though she were God."[18]

Due to the austere life that Father Joseph was leading from an early age, he was prone to occasional health problems. Also, as a result of straining his eyes over numberless volumes of books, he developed "progressive defect of vision which advanced throughout his life until, at the end, he was nearly blind."[19] The illness which eventually proved fatal were two strokes in 1638, the first of which left him partially paralyzed, while to the second he succumbed at the age of 62. A priest who was asked to preach the funeral sermon for Father Joseph responded "that he could not, with a good conscience, praise a man who had been the instrument of the Cardinal's passions, and who was hated by the whole of France."[20]

This roughly outlines the life of the person after whom the phrase "grey eminence," in circulation until the present day, has been coined.

Several strands, inextricably interwoven, characterize Father Joseph's personality and his overall presence in the world. In *Grey Eminence*, Huxley tried to trace out his religious and political involvements. Here the focus will be on the development and consequences of Father Joseph's psychological and spiritual maturity, while political, historical, and theological matters may randomly be touched upon only for the sake of highlighting some aspects of the mentioned psycho-spiritual analysis.

Father Joseph's Psychological Development

Starting the psychological analysis from scant notes about François' early childhood, it can be said that he greatly differed from average norms characteristic of early developmental stages. The emotional life of pre-school children, though "highly differentiated, [...] elaborate and complex,"[21] is inconstant and "can change as rapidly as they switch from one activity to another."[22] They "experience many, but still not all, of the adult's emotional repertoire."[23] In the case of young François, however, what characterized his behavior was some kind of extreme constancy. His first understanding of the world was more precocious, but also more removed from the standard, than is usual at the generally mutable pre-school stage of development. Even at such a young age, he expressed a "dual nature"[24] that was to become a hallmark of his adult personality. This duality of the "strange and very remarkable little boy"[25] abided in his simultaneous introversion and activeness. Socially, he was "isolated even in company [and] lived in nobody could discover what private world of his own."[26] He could relax only "in situations where other people were not immediately and personally involved."[27] This introversion included extraordinary brightness, which was, at the same time, in line with his activeness – not only physical, but also intellectual – "he could be ardently enthusiastic about things and ideas."[28] It seems that the stage for what Father Joseph would become later in life was set very early on.

Emotionally, under the detached surface, the boy was a boiling pot of "violent impulses, gusts of consuming passions not only of love, but of hatred and anger too."[29] This is quite normal for children at that age, as is a passionate love for one's parents, which he shared, along with a strong attachment to "the home, to the family servants, to the dogs and horses, the pigeons and the tame ducks, the falcons."[30] What was not usual was his "iron wall of self-control, of voluntary reserve."[31] Unlike most children, he lacked spontaneity and "shrunk from what he felt to be indecency of expressed emotional intimacy with other human beings."[32] Identifying and expressing emotions is a developmental challenge for children aged three to five, but in the throes of this confusion, they give vent to emotional upheavals within. François blocked all such vents, by courtesy of his intellectual precocity, which probably gave rise to a hypertrophied superego. Why was his young mind convinced that it was indecent to express feelings? Instead of enjoying the rollercoaster of childhood emotions, this "little Spartan"[33] suppressed them sternly and mercilessly, "undertook all kinds of supererogatory self-mortification"[34] and "consistently refused to accept for himself any mitigation."[35] This stands at the root of the schism that is to be taken to an extreme in his later life.

Another area in which his precocity was obvious was religion. It is not uncommon for children to cherish magical beliefs in God and "successfully think about agents that are not visible,"[36] but François's experience was extraordinarily advanced. At a tender age of four, he was told the story of Christ on the Cross by the servants, which he then related to his parents when "brought down to the dinner table."[37] He mentioned in minute detail "the scourging, the crown of thorns."[38] Otherwise emotionally restrained, on this occasion, "as he describes the crucifixion, his voice trembles and, at once, he breaks down into irrepressible sobbing."[39] From that day on, "the image of Calvary [...] of what wicked men had done to Jesus"[40] haunted him throughout his life and was in his imagination "more vivid than what he actually saw at his feet."[41]

Can a connection be established between the state of his young psyche and the unordinary intensity of such religious feelings? It would be reductionistic to explain this religious flare-up solely as a compensation for his otherwise suppressed emotions. However, some kind of complex connection is most certainly there. What is suppressed into the unconscious finds oblique ways to get out. All the natural feelings he was denying for some unclear reason found a return highway in the story of the crucifixion. For some reason, also unclear, his young mind approved of religious emotions, through which many others found their vent, too. While recounting the events of Calvary, "pity and love and adoration suffused his whole being."[42] Still, it was not only "a sensible warmth"[43] that he was experiencing – and at this point we are perhaps approaching the crucial fact of Father Joseph's overall inner life – this warmth "was at the same time a kind of pain."[44]

The way he embraced pain and sought it wherever he could, but also the way in which this ruthless autosadism was detrimental to great masses of people who were affected by Father Joseph's exploits, represents the cornerstone of his life story. The pain he relished was related to some internalized guilt that never abandoned him. The way he explained it – namely that he himself "had helped to hew the cross and forge the nails, to plait the scourge and the crowns of thorns, to whet the spear and dig the sepulchre"[45] – was naïve, even within the context of the doctrine of original sin. His guilt sprang up from a different source, but he either did not know it or did not want to know it. As it seems, there is no way of guessing what it might have been either, since relevant nature/nurture facts from his early childhood life are unavailable today.

It is a fact that the principles of displeasure and pain were guiding his daily life from the day the early childhood experience of "seeing" and feeling Jesus' suffering took place. This is obvious in the way he lived his life and the choices he made. Children do not turn away from pleasure, and do not reject the bond with the (allegedly) loving parents; adolescents do not turn their backs on the first stirrings of romantic and sexual love. Still, François abandoned everything that he enjoyed (except for God, pain, and later politics, all of which he overindulged in). Being an excellent horseman, as soon as he joined the order of the Capuchins, he said goodbye to this activity that had given him great pleasure. Taking the vows of poverty implied that no monk could use or handle money, or own any possession. They had to beg for what they needed, be "permanently dirty and in tatters,"[46] while following "a rigid discipline,"[47] fasts, and severe penances. His unfulfilled desire to join the Carthusian order, which was an "imitation of primitive Egyptian monasticism"[48] and involved "the final and absolute sacrifice of self,"[49] points to the extent of his desire to completely abnegate himself. All of this was done on behalf of performing God's will, as was everything else he did throughout his life. However, with a mental substratum like his, which rigidly adhered to pain and unknowingly backlashed in hurting others, his spirituality was not strong enough to annihilate the drawbacks of his flawed personality.

While still a novice in the monastery, he took his self-sacrificing to an ever higher level than required, as if the prescribed norms were not harsh enough. At times such displays were discouraged even in the monastic environment. However, he was "hungry for a life of confinement, and enforced inactivity – hungry for it precisely because he knew it would be the most difficult of all for him to bear."[50] Instead of gaining spiritual refinement as a result of such worldly deprivations, there is an impression that he indulged in them for their own sake. "That Spartan taste of his for the uncomfortable and the strenuous continually manifested itself, sometimes in oddest ways."[51] He would "worship standing, bare-footed on the flagstones"[52] or stand on one leg when sleepiness sometimes overtook him. Needless to say, all this was cloaked in the pretext of religion.

The book opens with the unforgettable scene of a Capuchin friar in his midlife, with a face "gaunt with self-inflicted hardship,"[53] walking across the face of Europe to meet with the Pope in Rome. His barefoot legs are "muddy to the knees"[54] while he walks "at a day's hottest hour [...][in] a furnace of the air."[55] In the second half of the book, when Father Joseph is involved in a concrete military situation, he refuses to take up quarters in the house occupied by Cardinal Richelieu, but chooses instead "a deserted summer-house standing beside a broad ditch."[56] When "the tides were high, the ditch overflowed, ankle deep, into the friar's bedroom"[57] and most of the time it was "damp and windy"[58] inside. The whole picture is rounded up with his diet of stale bread and dishwater, the sheetless bed, "the hair shirt he had worn all day beneath his stained and ragged habit,"[59] the unhealed wounds on his back and shoulders from penitential scourgings, which always made "the first contact with the mattress [...] acutely painful."[60] One particularly bizarre example shows his willingness to take up tortuous medical treatments of the day and apply them himself. As his blindness was progressing, he submitted to a procedure "which consisted in periodically cauterizing the back of his head with a hot iron,"[61] that was allegedly good for the failing eyesight.

Even though the religious order he belonged to did require austerity, his excess of self-punishment was crossing the boundaries of purposeful strictness. The results of such attitude toward himself were visible not only on his physical appearance, but also behind the nearby walls of the sieged La Rochelle, where cases of uttermost human horror and tragedy were taking place.

The religious activities and feelings of Father Joseph always converged toward the single sanctum of pain and suffering. First of all, he was "guardian and spiritual director of a new reformed order of nuns, the Calvarians, whose principal devotion was to be directed to the suffering mother at the foot of the cross."[62] Later on, when he was put in charge of missions, "he rejoiced at the thought of all that it might be granted to him to do and suffer in this missionary service."[63] There was an undeniable "obsessive, hallucinatory preoccupation with the sufferings of Calvary which had haunted his mind from earliest childhood."[64] He made one of the most common mistakes in religion, i.e. to equate God with a concept not only inferior to the notion of what God should be, but to an infinitely lesser, sometimes even petty construct. For him, God was France, and, essentially, God was pain. This is why in all of his expressions of religious rapture, an element of pain is inevitably there: "happiness of [...] of adoration intense to the point of physical pain,"[65] "rapture and devotion of compassion, love and pain,"[66] "nothing but the shining rapture of love and suffering."[67] The nature of his mystical experiences may be dubious, but what is certain is that "there were times when he could hardly speak of the sufferings of Christ without falling into a rapture."[68] Moreover, "mentioning the crucifixion he was so much moved that his senses left him, he fell down in a faint and remained for some time afterwards in a state almost of catalepsy."[69] Some unsimulated religio-emotional events did occur in his being, but what is questionable is whether those events were spiritually pure, or rather tinged with psychopathological instigation.

After listing so much evidence of the pain principle as crucial in Father Joseph's life, a legitimate question may be posed of whether he meets the clinical criteria of the masochistic personality disorder.

Father Joseph and the Masochistic Personality Disorder

The clinical category of masochistic personality disorder is quite ambiguous. It was included in an appendix of the revised edition of *DSM*-III-R from 1987, but excluded from the two later editions. Whether psychiatry considers it as a separate personality disorder or not, "it continues to enjoy widespread currency among clinicians."[70] In any case, "masochistic phenomena are found in individuals across the diagnostic spectrum."[71] The criteria for the disorder expounded in *DSM*-III-R are used here to help us make assumptions about the nature and the degree of Father Joseph's masochism.

The psychological construct of masochism includes the generally well-known characteristic of seeking and enjoying pain. However, the masochistic pattern involves further defeating principles, such as pathological self-sacrificing, embracing suffering, shunning pride, love, warmth, and kindness, rejecting help, choosing "people and situations that lead to disappointment, failure, or mistreatment."[72] As all of this runs counter to the instinctual pleasure principle and contradicts the "broad, fundamental features of the self,"[73] masochism represents 'the most perplexing'[74] human phenomenon, "one of psychology's greatest puzzles."[75] Even Huxley uses a similar phrase for Father Joseph, describing his life "as the strangest of psychological riddles."[76]

As seen previously, the hero of *Grey Eminence* did actively seek pain and suffering, mostly under a religious pretext, and he also did overdo all the acts of self-sacrifice. Thus, he already fulfills two of the criteria for this personality disorder. Let us now consider whether other aspects of masochistic pathology apply to him, too.

It has already been noted that he shirked from love: leaving his mother in childhood, forcing himself to stay away from the girl he feel in love with in adolescence. This first passion, as strong as it was, represented for him an "enemy of high ambition"[77] and left him heavily "troubled with the sense of guilt."[78] Was his urge to devote himself entirely to religion the only reason for which, at such tender age, he managed to block the proverbially intense emotions and desires of the first love, or was it rather that the need for punishment by denying himself what was dearest to him overpowered everything else? The reason to suspect that the latter was more likely the motivation behind his behavior was the attitude he took to the female gender later in life, developing "a real horror of women in general and of the love of the sexes."[79] For him, "the only satisfactory woman was a cloistered woman, and the only tolerable way to enjoy female company was through the wicket of a confessional or the bars of a convent parlour. Otherwise, 'they should only be visited like wild beasts, whom one is content to see without approaching.'"[80] Huxley astutely notes that "the intensity of Father Joseph's aversion was proportionate, no doubt, to the intensity of his early passion and the amount and violence of the force he had to use against himself in order to master it."[81] This reveals the fact that, instead of tolerantly accepting women as at least part of the human race, Father Joseph projected his frustration onto the whole sex, as a compensatory revenge for the love he had deprived himself of.

The masochistic criteria of "discard[ing] genuinely caring persons"[82] and rejecting "legitimate sources of nurturance"[83] have thus been met. Furthermore, Father Joseph seems to possess another trait that Millon unambiguously classifies as masochistic – being "subtly attracted to those who are insensitive or even sadistic."[84] The closest relationship that Father Joseph formed in his life was the one with Cardinal Richelieu, who was an epitome of "the utterly incompatible combination of the churchman and the statesman."[85] Could they have formed a functional and warm human relationship, taking into account Richelieu's constant hunger and vigilance "for an opportunity to snatch the smallest morsel of [...] political power?"[86] The Cardinal was also known to have an inclination "to cover his actions with the prestige of religion and high morality."[87] Was this kind of religious and political alliance worth the sacrifice of genuine emotions that Father Joseph had to make (supposing he was capable of them)? Or was it just a symbiotic impulse of a disordered personality structure being drawn to its complementary counterpart?

It has to be noted that Father Joseph was not prideful or arrogant; the mask of humility that he wore was incompatible with either pride or arrogance. First of all, his ascetic appearance dissociates him from the deadly sin of hubris. He also consciously and actively fought against boastfulness in any shape or form, keeping "perpetually on his guard against [...] lapses into pride and vanity."[88] Even when punishing his subordinates for breaches of the monastic rules, he did it with "gentleness and humility,"[89] somehow managing to remain personally uninvolved, "except as the channel through which a force, recognizably divine, was flowing."[90] On the other hand however, and based on a similar principle of personal noninvolvement, he renounced private ambitions, but was, vicariously and under a religious umbrella, "able to go on indulging the passions connected with ambition,"[91] such as "malice, domination and glory, while retaining the conviction that he was doing the will of God."[92] Superficially, it was not about him, but essentially it so was.

Power or fame did not interest him in their crude forms. "As a politician, he worked without show or noise, keeping himself deliberately in the background: as a writer, he courted anonymity in print and was content for the most part to leave his productions unpublished."[93] After the victory at La Rochelle, he declined the offered position of a bishop, displaying "no personal satisfaction at his triumph."[94] If he was to be baited to participate in a political enterprise, the "glittering tin minnows"[95] of money and power were of no interest to him – subtler awards were required; first and foremost, the idea that what was being planned was for the glory of God and a greater Good. Briefly, as will be shown when we move to the discussion of Father Joseph's religiosity, what was at the core of his existential acting in the world was "the final and absolute sacrifice of self."[96] Or, at least, that's what he wanted to believe. On the other hand, when at Ratisbon he learned that his contemporaries, with good reason, thought negatively of him, instead of bursting the bubble image he created for himself, he made defensive rationalizations and "demanded an apology"[97] for the insults. Such attitude does not genuinely support the position of humility and self-sacrifice he promoted at every step.

All this testifies to the fact that Father Joseph, at least on the surface, and in line with the clinical description of a classical masochist, governed all his activities "specifically to avoid a sense of pride,"[98] championing "an unpresuming and self-effacing manner."[99] What lay beneath, however, was not humility of the pure at heart, but a toxicity of a much more sinister kind.

There are a few traits in a typical masochistic script that Father Joseph did not follow. One is the rejection of "the attempts of others to help,"[100] another the "need to fail."[101] Overall, instead of deliberately putting obstacles in his own way, as a classical masochist would do, he was too ambitious and too active to completely fit in that mold.

The way he first got in touch with Richelieu shows that he did seek help when deemed necessary. In order to accomplish some of his early religious tasks, he "turned for assistance and advice to the bishop of the neighbouring see of Lucon, [...] Armand Jean du Plessis de Richelieu."[102] In other instances, too, not only would he not shirk from support, but actively sought it. This is inevitably linked with the breach of the other masochistic criterion – the embracement of failure. In Father Joseph's case, failure was completely unacceptable, even at enormous cost. This fact was thinly veiled by him disowning personal contributions to various feats he was engaged in, but this does not make an essential difference; it just makes things more pathologically complex.

Would a failure-oriented person cherish such zeal for a new Crusade, a zeal that called for "a sea of other people's blood?"[103] On several occasions, when even Richelieu showed signs of weakening, "the friar revived his courage and, by sheer strength of will, carried him forward, through all difficulties, to the desired goal."[104] Father Joseph's political activism included such ambitious endeavors as the "great work of national unification";[105] and where winning a war was concerned, he "use[d] of all the resources at his disposal, both human and divine."[106] Even in his last days, while giving a lecture, he had "a sudden paroxysm of retching and vomiting [... but] went on with his discourse."[107] There was nothing to stand in the way of his persistence.

Apart from the need to experience physical discomfort and pain, Father Joseph's biography is also filled with examples of undaunted activeness: he would present himself to political subjects "without waiting for instructions from his superiors,"[108] and would hurry over mountains, with open wounds on his feet, "at the rate of fifteen leagues a day, across the face of Europe"[109] in order to meet the Pope and win him over for the project of a new Crusade. The successes he strove for were allegedly not intended for his personal glorification, but for a greater good. The means he employed thereby were crudely inhumane. His skewed ideals took on a shape of a dubious God and the centralized kingdom of France. But however selflessly he gave of himself, he "failed to see that vicarious ambition is as much of an obstacle to [mystical] union as personal ambition."[110]

The textbooks and manuals declare that if a person meets at least five of the criteria of a personality disorder, he or she can be diagnosed with it. Hence, despite the fact that Father Joseph had some pronounced anti-masochistic traits, he still met many of the requirements that allow us to label him a masochistic personality.

Before turning to the influence of his masochism on the religiosity he professed, let us briefly dwell on a more detailed analysis of what lay at the root of his masochism.

First of all, Father Joseph thought that the cloak of religion he was desperately hiding under was big enough to cover up all of his deficits. Many saw through his deceptions; he himself opted for voluntary blindness. The dealings he was engaging in essentially reeked of dishonesty, duplicity, ruthlessness, and lack of empathy. Was he, as an outstandingly intelligent introvert, aware of the nature of his actions? And if the truth at least sometimes did penetrate his mind, what was he doing to neutralize the inevitably arising cognitive dissonance? Let us describe his intrapersonal style and his political involvements as an illustration of the underlying principles of his overall functioning before answering these questions.

It seems that dishonesty was one of the leading guidelines in a large portion of Father Joseph's social interaction. The examples that bolster this statement are, unfortunately, too numerous. He did not shy away from using religious manipulation in order to put forth his own political agenda. Thus, to the Huguenots leader Condé, who fell ill during negotiations, Father Joseph expounded the dangers his soul would be exposed to if he died "leaving his country a prey to civil war."[111] On another occasion, he told the very Queen of France, Marie de Medici, "that God would damn her everlastingly"[112] if she conducted certain political actions. Like an encapsulation of a most corrupt politician, he employed a wide gamut of forms of persuasion, going from damnations to more mundane "offer[s] of gifts from the royal exchquer, pensions, honours, positions in the administration."[113] In matters of war, "he was for ever propounding the most brilliant schemes,"[114] and also resorted to writing leaflets of false political propaganda. His passion "to be well informed, preferably by secret and exclusive channels"[115] was so strong that he would "prowl[...] about the town in disguise, spying for the Cardinal, or giving bribes and instructions to agents so secret and so sinister that they could not be interviewed except by night, at street corners or in the back rooms of disreputable taverns."[116] Being dishonest himself meant that he disbelieved others, too, particularly "foreigners *et dona ferentes*."[117]

The flip side of the coin of dishonesty is the inevitableness of duplicity. In Father Joseph's case, duplicity was largely present, too. The very nickname Huxley calls him by, Ezechiely Tenebroso-Cavernoso, epitomizes the paradox that "human beings find no difficulty at all in entertaining, successively or even at the same moment, convictions which are totally incompatible with one another."[118] In other words, one side of his character was of "the enthusiast, the visionary, the Franciscan evangelist and mystic,"[119] while the other revealed "the man who never gave himself away, the poker-faced diplomatist, the endlessly resourceful politician."[120] His negotiating style reflected this trait, as he applied different methods crafted with guile, rich in expression, encompassing a wide scale of opposing tones. He would reason, cajole, "permit[...] himself an outburst of blunt frankness [...] Then, all of a sudden, the tone would change again, and he was once more the visionary friar, licensed by his habit to denounce wrong-doing even in the highest place, to give warning even to princes of its fatal consequences in this world and the next."[121] So his interaction, either in political negotiations or in ecclesiastical dealings, contained the expertise needed for success, but lacked only one quality that comes from the noetic depths of our being – spontaneity.

It is quite astounding that someone as religiously far advanced as Father Joseph was completely lacking in empathy. He lived in the allegedly "higher" religious domains in which there was no room for ordinary human reality. In order to reconcile these two disconnected realms, the subjective world he inhabited was based on "his own voluntary ignorance."[122] Regarding the outcome of his actions, he was "quite indifferent to the appalling sufferings for which his policy was responsible."[123] Huxley even compares his detachment to the one displayed by Arjuna at the battlefield of Kurukshetra, although qualitatively they were different kinds of spiritual indifference, expressed under different circumstances. Father Joseph seems to have had a life mission of bringing innumerous human sacrifices to the altar of his morbid god. How otherwise to understand the uninterrupted line of atrocities that resulted from his engagements on many different levels? In the poems that he was composing, which were "the only emotional indulgence he permitted himself,"[124] he openly illustrated this propensity – "to quench the fires of my ardour, I must drown me in a sea of blood."[125]

It would take too long to list all of the horrors Father Joseph caused directly or indirectly. Briefly, he did everything to prolong the wars in which people turned to cannibalism because they "were slowly starving. The horses, the cats, the dogs – all had been killed and devoured; even the supply of rats was running low."[126] When some Protestants deserted cities under siege in order to save their lives, they would be promptly hanged, despite promises that they would be spared. "In France, the huge sums required to finance the foreign policy of Father Joseph and his master, the Cardinal, were being extorted, sou by sou, from those least able to pay."[127] He was rightly called "one of the forgers [...] of our disastrous destiny"[128] who was constantly involved in "criminal follies of high statesmanship [...] satanic struggle for power in a world [...]the orgies of violence and cunning."[129] If one is known by the fruits of their actions, "the devil must [have] be[en] in this friar's body."[130]

Was the friar aware of the way others perceived him? It seems that he learned about being hated only late in life, to his great surprise, and he required an apology. He did have his admirers and followers, King Louis XIII being one of those who "respected the Capuchin's political judgment and was impressed by his burning eloquence."[131] The determination and power of such single-minded people never fail to fascinate individuals or even masses that lack the ability to notice crucial deficiencies beneath the mask of power. Still, Father Joseph was also widely hated by many, "generally and cordially detested,"[132] and "enjoyed the worst possible reputation among the rank and file of the Catholic laity and clergy."[133] This "ardent nationalist"[134] was considered "a renegade, an enemy of God and man,"[135] an "absurd, clerical White Knight, full of crack-brained notions which were made to seem even more ridiculous than they actually were by his habit of guaranteeing them as divine revelations."[136] Returning to the questions posed in a previous paragraph, let us consider the possibility that Father Joseph was aware of the reasons for being hated, and the way he dealt with those insights.

The situation about how aware of his actions he was is not clean-cut. There were moments when he would question their propriety, but most of the time "he was really convinced that the policies pursued [...] were [...] in accordance with God's will."[137] Such ambiguous positions are not impossible in real life, for we are able to convince ourselves that what we are doing is right, at the same time hiding deep down the true knowledge that we, for some reason, cannot accept. This knowledge does surface occasionally, and at such moments, Father Joseph tried "actively to annihilate his political actions"[138] by prayer or fasting or whatever other method of religious austerity he employed, but never once was he tempted to reconsider what he was doing. He resorted to classical defense mechanisms such as rationalization. "Calumny was what the servants of Christ had been taught to expect – yes, and even rejoice in; for to be tried by calumny was a sign, if one were following the way of perfection, that God considered one ripe for the hardest lessons. To suffer slander without resentment or bitterness was possible only to souls that had lost themselves in God."[139] As previously noted, his major justification was of a metaphysical kind, and he believed "that what seemed bad from a merely human viewpoint might really and actually be good."[140]

The true nature of things, however, resurfaced more frequently as he was growing older and weaker. At a certain point, he became fully aware that most of the time he had deluded himself, that his activities were "unannihilatable,"[141] and that he, in fact, discarded his own enormous spiritual potential. This frustration and the realization that he essentially misused his time made him dejected and bitter. Eventually, he came to see himself not any different from "the pagans and the Turks,"[142] whom he hated so much and deemed ultimately inferior. In the end, he deeply regretted ever having entered politics, but it was too late to change anything at that point. Like Marlowe's Faustus, he offered to burn his books only after midnight had struck.

But Father Joseph is more complex and more disordered than the previous paragraph might suggest. Despite the regrets he started to feel in old age, the part of him "that craved for action"[143] in fact never left him. Until there was a breath of life in him, "from his bed, he continued to write memoranda on policy and to direct the secret service."[144] When he became unable to write or dictate, he had the chronicles of the crusades read to him aloud. Instead of the messages of forgiveness or repentance, the things that he opted for to hear in his last earthly moments were "these strange tales of heroism and brutality, of devotion and greed, of single-mindedness and the most cynical double-dealing."[145] Remaining true to the contradictions that were his biographical trademark from early childhood until his very last moments, Father Joseph exemplifies a *corruptio optimi est pessima* case of a person with enormous potential who, due to mental deficiencies, never goes through an inner transformation toward integration, and not only squanders the vast inner potential, but uses it to the detriment of the self and, much worse, of many others.

Father Joseph's Religiosity

If we were now to discuss Father Joseph's religious sentiment, a question may be posed whether or not it was completely counterfeit throughout his lifetime. Huxley thinks that it was not. The instances of access to pure spirituality took place in the young days when his contemplations were "profound to the verge of trance."[146] Struck by the story of Calvary, and experiencing an early grief due to his father's death, he had a "precocious conviction that ours is a fallen world."[147] Amid secular worries and temptations, he would feel "a sense of the presence of God – a sense which gave him such extraordinary joy, that [...] he almost fainted."[148] Expressed in language that smacks of masochism, his heart was "penetrated [...] with the wound of [... God's] piercing design,"[149] marking it with a "tender hurt."[150]

When love, whether for family members or for a girl, started clouding his religiosity, he resolutely rooted love out. When politics started doing the same thing, he embraced it wholeheartedly. As a consequence, "the old facility of communication between his soul and its God and Saviour was lost."[151] With years passing by and death coming near, he was "becoming ever more acutely conscious of the failure."[152] The game of hide-and-seek with the divinity was over. Once "an aspirant to sanctity,"[153] he was now completely lost to the unitive life of a mystic. "He had the dreadful certainty that God had moved away from him."[154] The final hours on the deathbed were his last chance to repent, which, allegedly, he did in a sincere way. "With an immense effort of will, Father Joseph lifted his right hand and feebly struck it several times against his breast."[155] In tears, he was repeating the phrase "render an account"[156] over and over again. It would be interesting to guess, in the fashion of medieval morality plays, whether this repentance had an effect on the destiny of his soul or not. Such an idea could have been entertained had Huxley written an account of Father Joseph's posthumous experiences, as he had done with Eustace Barnack in *Time Must Have a Stop* (1944). In this case, however, it is entirely up to the readers to come up with their own scenarios.

One of the basic concepts of both psychology and religion – the self – was heavily contested in Father Joseph's existential experience. The interplay between spiritual excellence (the desire to put God above the self) on one hand, and the pathology of self-relating on the other, is showcasing the complexity of the nature of his psycho-religious makeup. One thing is obvious – he consistently tried to "be annihilated into passive nothingness,"[157] which, in some religions, such as Buddhism, is the utmost aim. This is one of the reasons the Christianized biography of Buddha that he read as a youth resounded with him so deeply. To die for the world and the self in order to set the scene for God to emerge in one's life is a theological ideal that runs not only in Buddhism, but in most other religious traditions, too. However, the way it gets transplanted onto a masochistic backdrop mostly just reinforces the deep-rooted personal pathology.

Father Joseph's urge for self-abnegation was exceeding the limits of spiritual propriety simply because it was extreme. Being intelligent and spiritually well-informed, he was supposed to know that it was not an act to be pursued violently. Instead, the idea was to "somehow operate without effort; or rather he must permit himself to be operated, passively, by the divine will."[158] Still, in practice it looked more like another military siege. His desire to kill the self sided more with "the key to the essential nature of masochism – the denial of self"[159] and "the aggressive drive"[160] against the self than with the requirements of spiritual advancement. It was aimed, "like any political tyranny, at the extinction of individuality."[161] The psychological reason behind masochistic self-hate, usually subconscious, is "a heavy burden of oppressive guilt"[162] that can be placated only by "symbolic self-flagellation,"[163] or, in Father Joseph's case, even actual, physical scourging of the flesh. The intricacies of the relationship between guilt and self are too complex to be further explicated here, let it suffice to just point out to their acute presence in this case study.

The proofs that Father Joseph's annihilation of the self was not wholesome or divinely inspired, but that an "intimate connection between narcissism and masochism"[164] was at play, are numerous. One who genuinely aspires to sanctity does not "burn[...] with the holy ambition to become a saint,"[165] like he did. Huxley concludes that "enough of the Old Adam remained in him to succumb to those extremely subtle temptations prepared by his attendant Satan."[166]

The way he approached his individual being with an aim to siege and conquer it characterizes his approach to religion, too. He saw spiritual advancement exclusively as a violent struggle to root out "a sleepless hostility to God one carried about in the depths of one's own mind and body."[167] Being puritanically obsessed with human "resourcefulness in the art of sinning"[168] (at the same time repressing his own serious sins), he set out on a war against the idols he considered false.

It is redundant to say that the only acceptable religious path for him was Catholicism, or even more narrowed down – French Catholicism. "As for himself, kind Providence had decreed that he should be born a Catholic."[169] In a provocative manner, he enjoyed setting up Capuchin convents in Calvinist cities, to spite and covert the sinning lot. Upon a visit to England, he found the English "pleasant, friendly people"[170] who were, alas, "all heretics, and therefore all irrevocably doomed. The whole nation was doomed."[171] Nonacceptance of other religious traditions is that one most crudely obvious sign of religious immaturity.

Approaching religious activism as a battlefield war in which he sacrificed his own comfort to the extreme, completely neglecting compassion toward himself or anyone else, reveals that the essence of his self-sacrifice was not benevolent, but laden with unwholesomeness. This masochistic unwholesomeness springs from unresolved psychological and emotional problems, primarily the feelings of guilt, and frequently lashes out in a sadistic manner, which Father Joseph's callousness was a proof of.

Many psychologists agree that "the concept always refers to sadomasochism."[172] The masochists' "ostensibly altruistic acts create grounds for inducing guilt in others."[173] Instead of inspiring divine love as an advanced spiritual figure, Father Joseph acted more like the masochistic "self-sacrificing vampires whose kindness bleeds their victims dry."[174]

Some instances of his religious rigidity and abhorrence of other religious traditions have already been mentioned. French Catholicism was the only true path for him. Upon entering the convent "the infidels were a constant subject of conversation and even of prayer,"[175] and his political activism relied on the idea that "Huguenots must be broken."[176] The attitude toward non-Christian religions was even more extreme. In *The Turciad*, his religious epic, the tension between Christianity and Islam in the Near and Middle East is highly politicized. Christ hates the fact that Muslims have overtaken the Holy City "and urges the heavenly powers to do something about it."[177] Even the Virgin "would be glad to participate in a Crusade."[178] As for Mohammed, he is depicted outright as Satan's student. In a cave near Mecca, in which "a chimney goes down directly into hell,"[179] Mohammed was "instructed in the arts of mischief by Lucifer."[180] The outcome of this lecturing was the Quran, which propagated the conquest of the Holy Land.

Such crude depiction of a rivaling religion may have been less shocking in Father Joseph's age and time, but even in the centuries before him there had been voices clearly denoting religious tolerance and egalitarianism. One of the examples may be the late-fourteenth-century English cleric William Langland (1332–1386) who wrote the following lines in his poem *Piers Plowman*: "For cristene and vncristene – clameþ it vchone,"[181] roughly translating as the equal right of either Christians or non-Christians to claim the truth.

Father Joseph's propensity for religious exclusivity was unmistakably in line with his political views, for which it is too generous to be described as just conservative. He was "one of the earliest and clearest advocates of totalitarian power politics; he embodies the totalitarian spirit."[182] Huxley notes that such an outcome (totalitarianism, idolatrous religions, deifications of the nation, the party, the local political boss[183]) is inevitable whenever "the *ksatriyas* do what only the theocentric *brahmin* has a right to do,"[184] and *vice versa*. Obviously, Father Joseph "is an eminent example of this [...] confusion of the castes."[185]

The two realms that Father Joseph tried to serve simultaneously do not go hand in hand. Huxley "deplores the evil mingling of spiritual and material values."[186] The Capuchin might have had the desire to transform the world, but eventually he was "being transformed by the world."[187] Politics corrupted his spirituality, and spirituality rendered his politics disastrous. It seems that in both of these domains, a typical neurotic "shift[...] from the essentials to the periphery"[188] took place, whereby losing the gravity of essential values led centripetally toward many detrimental outcomes.

The two major secular idols Father Joseph worshiped were France ("one of the chosen instruments of Providence"[189]) and the Crusades. In his mind to fight for these ideals was the perfection of his overall religious endeavor, which Huxley calls "spiritual patriotism."[190] In real life, however, this fight incited wars and unprecedented suffering of the innocent.

Driven by insatiable ambitions, he used all the spiritual resources for the crude needs of politics and wars, as if spirituality was just a means to achieve some more concrete, higher ends. The nuns in his monasteries were turned into "powerful praying machines, capable, if put into high gear and worked for twenty-four hours a day, seven days a week, of precipitating, so to speak, out of the ether, very considerable quantities of the divine favour."[191] Besides, "he made use of visions and revelations – sometimes his own, more often those of the Calvarian nuns under his charge – as significant factual data, to be taken into account in framing policies and conducting military campaigns."[192] In his dreams, he sees Christ who explains "why a holy war is so urgently necessary,"[193] while "the Virgin invests him with the insignia of the Christian Militia."[194] Huxley concludes that "if these were the fruits of mental prayer and the unitive life,"[195] it is much healthier and benevolent to be a *bon vivant* who either does not believe in God, or performs only sporadic and perfunctory religious duties.

Father Joseph's involvement with religion was neither sporadic nor perfunctory. It was characterized by genuineness that he could not have faked when he was "grief-stricken by the story of his Saviour's death"[196] as a young child. Later in life he tried to maintain the authenticity of his religious orientation, in the first place by manifold acts of self-sacrifice, humility, readiness to put God, or whatever he thought God was, before anything else. While preaching sermons, people would "groan aloud in fear of hell, weep for their offences, raise supplicating hands towards the mercy seat,"[197] which meant that he had the charismatic power to strum the deepest strings of the human soul. Surprisingly, he also did not believe in forced religion – as soon as Huguenots became politically obedient they would "be allowed to worship as they pleased,"[198] and made to convert only based on their own free will. Another spiritually mature feature came about by the end of his life, and that was the instance when he became more aware that his spirituality had deteriorated and that he was, essentially, cut off from the noetic core of his spiritual being. However, the aforementioned examples of religious achievements were too feeble compared to the amount of religious morbidity he displayed over the long years of his clerico-political career.

Many of the toxic aspects of his religiosity have been mentioned earlier. The *Turciad* is a direct expression of his xenophobia and narrow-mindedness. Instead of meekness and warmth that proverbially go along with saintliness, Father Joseph's practice of religion was marked by superstition, controversy, exhortation, and "greed for merely mundane information."[199] At times, he was no subtler a manipulator than Elmer Gantry, for they both used the construct of hell to "do excellent service."[200] Probably worst of all was his indifference to the pain inflicted on others, and particularly an overall lack of compassion, which many religious scholars (today most notably Karen Armstrong) deem to be the crucial tenet of religiosity without which no other quality matters much. It is wholly perverse and off target to think that the sufferings "of ordinary human beings are so infinitesimal as to be practically negligible"[201] compared to Christ's Passion, which was an idea underlying Father Joseph's theology.

The visions he had of the afterlife were almost completely materialistic, which might be due to a lack of mysticism in his spirituality. Overall, and despite the fact that he strove for highest spiritual advancements, his religiosity is largely nonmystical: the language he uses is too "violently emotional"[202] to be in line with the writings of the mystics; he was overzealous (the mystics warn that "the hunger and thirst after God may become an obstacle"[203]); there was too much occultism and human ambition in his strivings; the trancelike states he would experience were "signs, possibly of divine grace, but certainly of human weakness, and probably also of inadequate training."[204] Besides, his blind and dogmatic adherence to the Catholic Church was too rigid to allow him to explore areas of empirical mysticism. The mystery that remains after him was some kind of an "anomalous nature of Father Joseph's spiritual life, one side of it centered in God, the other in all too human cravings."[205]

In *Grey Eminence*, Huxley tries partly to pin the causes of such a state of affairs down to the nature of the particular brand of mysticism Father Joseph was practicing. He calls it a "personalistic pseudo-mysticism"[206] which was too anthropocentric and too Christocentric. Besides, the spiritual masters he was following "never discussed the relationship between political action on the one hand and, on the other, the unitive life, the doing of the will of God," [207] which might have given him a license for his political involvements. Even today, there are some opinions that "a person can be a monstrous plotter, yet his 'self-understanding,' his existential religious experiences, can be impeccably 'authentic.'"[208] However, it is rather obvious that there was a serious flaw in Father Joseph's religiosity, and it is too naïve to believe that he was not aware of the implications of his political actions and their interference with his spirituality simply because his spiritual teachers did not discuss this segment of life. Where was his conscience hiding? How could he have stomached all the horrors he initiated? After all, the branch of religion one follows is, at the core, quite immaterial, for true believers always transcend the inevitable restrictions of their particular traditions. Just like it is impossible to say that any psychotherapeutic technique renders better results than any other (it always comes down to the therapist), it is equally inadequate to blame the type of religion Father Joseph was following for the way he was. The main fault was residing in the pathology at the psychic level of his personality.

Eventually, Father Joseph remains an example of "powerful spiritual energies fatally channelled in the wrong direction."[209] The account he had to render to his maker was probably among the graver ones in human history. "It's terrifying to see what sincere believers will do because they think they know."[210] Aspiring to become a saint, he took a path that led to hell within himself, inevitably pushing others into that hell, too. Karen Horney sees the root of this in the ravaging force of self-hate, which she names "perhaps the greatest tragedy of the human mind."[211] So, the quality of saintliness he desired so much escaped him, since it goes hand in hand with innocence, and "innocence is defined in dictionaries as freedom from guilt or sin, especially through lack of knowledge; purity of heart; blamelessness; guilelessness; artlessness; simplicity, etc."[212] Based on this definition, it may be concluded that there was nothing either innocent or saintly about Father Joseph.

Notes

1 Aldous Huxley, *Grey Eminence*, London: Chatto & Windus, 1949, p. 262.
2 *Ibid.*, p. 271.
3 C. V. Wedgewood, "The Mystic and the World," *Aldous Huxley, The Critical Heritage*, ed. Donald Watt, London, New York: Routledge, 2005, p. 335.
4 *Letters by Aldous Huxley*, ed. Grover Smith, London: Chatto & Windus, 1969, p. 460.
5 Brian Smith, Elements and Causes: Deducing the Present from the Past in Aldous Huxley's *Grey Eminence*," *Aldous Huxley Annual*, eds. Bernfried Nugel, Jerome Meckier Vol. 12/13, Münster: Lit Verlag, 2013, p. 85.
6 Aldous Huxley, *Grey Eminence*, p. 16.
7 *Ibid.*, p. 20.
8 *Ibid.*
9 *Ibid.*
10 *Ibid.*
11 *Ibid.*, p. 23.
12 *Ibid.*
13 *Ibid.*, p. 25.
14 *Ibid.*, p. 26.
15 *Ibid.*, p. 28.
16 *Ibid.*, p. 27.
17 *Ibid.*, p. 38.
18 *Ibid.*, p. 119.
19 *Ibid.*, p. 85.
20 *Ibid.*, p. 262.
21 Michael Lewis, *The Rise of Consciousness and the Development of Emotional Life*, New York, London: The Guilford Press, 2014, p. 31.

22 Carol Seefedt, Barbara A. Wasik, *Early Education*, Upper Saddle River, NJ: Pearson/Merrill/Prentice Hall, 2006, p. 54.
23 Jerome Kagan, *The Human Spark: The Science of Human Development*, New York: Basic Books, 2013, p. 216.
24 Lilly Zähner, *Demon and Saint in the Novels of Aldous Huxley*, Bern: Francke Verlag, 1975, p. 91.
25 Aldous Huxley, *Grey Eminence*, p. 17.
26 *Ibid.*
27 *Ibid.*, p. 18.
28 *Ibid.*
29 *Ibid.*
30 *Ibid.*, pp. 17–18.
31 *Ibid.*, p. 18.
32 *Ibid.*
33 *Ibid.*, p. 20.
34 *Ibid.*
35 *Ibid.*
36 Justin L. Barrett, *Born Believers: The Science of Children's Religious Belief*, New York: Free Press, 2012, p. 44.
37 Aldous Huxley, *Grey Eminence*, p. 18.
38 *Ibid.*, p. 19.
39 *Ibid.*
40 *Ibid.*, p. 7.
41 *Ibid.*
42 *Ibid.*
43 *Ibid.*
44 *Ibid.*
45 *Ibid.*
46 *Ibid.*, p. 41.
47 *Ibid.*
48 *Ibid.*, p. 37.
49 *Ibid.*, p. 38.
50 *Ibid.*
51 *Ibid.*, p. 83.
52 *Ibid.*
53 *Ibid.*, p. 2.
54 *Ibid.*, p. 1.
55 *Ibid.*, p. 269.
56 *Ibid.*, p. 149.
57 *Ibid.*
58 *Ibid.*
59 *Ibid.*, p. 195.
60 *Ibid.*
61 *Ibid.*
62 *Ibid.*, p. 19.
63 *Ibid.*, p. 97.
64 *Ibid.*, p. 199.
65 *Ibid.*, p. 9.
66 *Ibid.*, p. 10.
67 *Ibid.*
68 *Ibid.*, p. 95.
69 *Ibid.*, p. 96.
70 Theodore Millon, *op. cit.*, p. 522.

71 Deanna Holtzman and Nancy Kulish, "Introduction: The Suffering of Sisyphus," *The Clinical Problem of Masochism*, ed. Deanna Holtzman and Nancy Kulish, Lanham, MD: Jason Aronson, 2012, p. 1.
72 Theodore Millon, *op. cit.*, p. 521.
73 Ray F. Baumeister, *Masochism and the Self*, New York, London: Psychology Press, 1989, p. 6.
74 *Ibid.*
75 Ray F. Baumeister, *op. cit.*, p. 1.
76 Aldous Huxley, *Grey Eminence*, p. 15.
77 *Ibid.*, p. 23.
78 *Ibid.*
79 *Ibid.*, p. 26.
80 *Ibid.*
81 *Ibid.*
82 Theodore Millon, *op. cit.*, p. 520.
83 *Ibid.*, p. 523.
84 *Ibid.*, p. 520.
85 William Robson, *The Life of Cardinal Richelieu*, London: George Routledge, 1854, p. 3.
86 Aldous Huxley, *Grey Eminence*, p. 101.
87 *Ibid.*, p. 175.
88 *Ibid.*, p. 108.
89 *Ibid.*, p. 141.
90 *Ibid.*
91 *Ibid.*, p. 135.
92 *Ibid.*
93 *Ibid.*, p. 133.
94 *Ibid.*, p. 88.
95 *Ibid.*, p. 131.
96 *Ibid.*, p. 38.
97 *Ibid.*, p. 174.
98 Theodore Millon, *op. cit.*, p. 520.
99 *Ibid.*, p. 528.
100 *Ibid.*, p. 521.
101 *Ibid.*, p. 520.
102 Aldous Huxley, *Grey Eminence*, p. 91.
103 *Ibid.*, p. 113.
104 *Ibid.*, p. 140.
105 *Ibid.*, p. 124.
106 *Ibid.*, p. 156.
107 *Ibid.*, p. 257.
108 *Ibid.*, p. 100.
109 *Ibid.*, p. 2.
110 *Ibid.*, p. 134.
111 *Ibid.*, p. 103.
112 *Ibid.*, p. 122.
113 *Ibid.*, pp. 160–161.
114 *Ibid.*, p. 151.
115 *Ibid.*, p. 152.
116 *Ibid.*, pp. 195–196.
117 *Ibid.*, p. 129.
118 *Ibid.*, p. 120.
119 *Ibid.*, p. 29.

120 *Ibid.*
121 *Ibid.*, p. 100.
122 *Ibid.*, p. 188.
123 *Ibid.*, p. 19.
124 *Ibid.*, p. 108.
125 *Ibid.*, p. 270.
126 *Ibid.*, p. 157.
127 *Ibid.*, p. 197.
128 *Ibid.*, p. 15.
129 *Ibid.*, p. 228.
130 *Ibid.*, p. 103.
131 *Ibid.*, p. 121.
132 *Ibid.*, p. 16.
133 *Ibid.*, p. 221.
134 *Ibid.*, p. 21.
135 *Ibid.*, p. 173.
136 *Ibid.*, p. 151.
137 *Ibid.*, p. 101.
138 *Ibid.*, p. 135.
139 *Ibid.*, p. 174.
140 *Ibid.*, p. 187.
141 *Ibid.*, p. 227.
142 *Ibid.*, p. 228.
143 *Ibid.*, p. 237.
144 *Ibid.*, pp. 158–159.
145 *Ibid.*, p. 259.
146 *Ibid.*, p. 188.
147 *Ibid.*, p. 21.
148 *Ibid.*, p. 22.
149 *Ibid.*, p. 269.
150 *Ibid.*
151 *Ibid.*, p. 23.
152 *Ibid.*, p. 225.
153 *Ibid.*, p. 236.
154 *Ibid.*, p. 227.
155 *Ibid.*, p. 260.
156 *Ibid.*, p. 261.
157 *Ibid.*, p. 4.
158 *Ibid.*, p. 8.
159 Ray F. Baumeister, *op. cit.*, p. ix.
160 Deanna Holtzman and Nancy Kulish, *op. cit.*, p. 2.
161 Karen Horney, *Neurosis and Human Growth*, New York: W. W. Norton & Company, 1950, p. 118.
162 Theodore Millon, *op. cit.*, p. 528.
163 *Ibid.*, p. 527.
164 Deanna Holtzman and Nancy Kulish, *op. cit.*, p. 5.
165 Aldous Huxley, *Grey Eminence*, p. 83.
166 *Ibid.*, p. 141.
167 *Ibid.*, p. 2.
168 *Ibid.*
169 *Ibid.*, p. 31.
170 *Ibid.*
171 *Ibid.*

172 Deanna Holtzman and Nancy Kulish, *op. cit.*, p. 1.
173 Theodore Millon, *op. cit.*, p. 525.
174 *Ibid.*
175 Aldous Huxley, *Grey Eminence*, p. 106.
176 *Ibid.*, p. 102.
177 *Ibid.*, p. 117.
178 *Ibid.*
179 *Ibid.*
180 *Ibid.*
181 William Langland, *Piers Plowman*, http://piers.iath.virginia.edu/index.html, e-text, accessed 7 January 2017.
182 Brian Smith, "Elements and Causes: Deducing the Present from the Past in Aldous Huxley's *Grey Eminence*," *Aldous Huxley Annual*, Vol. 12/13, Münster: Lit Verlag, 2013, p. 81.
183 See: Aldous Huxley, *Grey Eminence*, p. 251.
184 *Ibid.*
185 *Ibid.*
186 Milton Birnbaum, *Aldous Huxley: A Quest for Values*, New Brunswick and London: Transaction Publishers, 2009, p. 7.
187 *Letters by Aldous Huxley*, p. 444.
188 Karen Horney, *Neurosis and Human Growth*, p. 139.
189 Aldous Huxley, *Grey Eminence*, p. 102.
190 *Ibid.*, p. 106.
191 *Ibid.*, p. 156.
192 *Ibid.*, pp. 96–97.
193 *Ibid.*, p. 117.
194 *Ibid.*, p. 118.
195 *Ibid.*, p. 250.
196 *Ibid.*, p. 19.
197 *Ibid.*, p. 86.
198 *Ibid.*, p. 125.
199 *Ibid.*, p. 152.
200 *Ibid.*, p. 122.
201 *Ibid.*, p. 113.
202 *Ibid.*, p. 226.
203 *Ibid.*, p. 227.
204 *Ibid.*, p. 96.
205 *Ibid.*, p. 157.
206 *Ibid.*, p. 267.
207 *Ibid.*, p. 68.
208 Slavoj Žižek, *The Metastases of Enjoyment*, London and New York: Verso, 2005, p. 80.
209 Patrick, Grant, "Belief in Mysticism: Aldous Huxley, from *Grey Eminence* to *Island*," *Six Modern Authors and Problems of Belief*, London: Macmillan, 1979, p. 18.
210 Anthony De Mello, *Awareness*, https://archive.org/stream/Awareness-AnthonyDeMello/Awareness-AnthonyDeMello_djvu.txt, e-text, accessed 9 January 2017.
211 Karen Horney, *Neurosis and Human Growth*, p. 154.
212 William Maxwell, *So Long, See You Tomorrow*, London: The Harvill Press, 1997, p. 96.

7 Preacher of the Poisonwood Bible

Nathan Price and Antisocial Religiosity

Barbara Kingsolver's novel *The Poisonwood Bible* (1998) is told "not by one, not by two, but by five narrators, all female, one dead."[1] Despite such variety of narrative voices, the center stage in each of their stories is occupied by the monolithically dominant and inflexible character of their father and husband, Reverend Nathan Price, a Georgian Freewill Baptist Evangelist. The novel is primarily envisaged as a political narrative with an aim to expose the nature of the US interference in the Congo at the time it gained its independence and the events surrounding the assassination of its first president Patrice Lumumba. Most critics are preoccupied with this exact thread, and the author herself revealed that politics was the predominant motivation behind the book. However, the scope of the novel is much wider. For her research, Kingsolver "coordinated daily readings in the King James bible, with the diaries of missionaries, political handbooks, the Kikongo–French dictionary, and stacks of *Life*, *Look*, and *Saturday Evening Post* magazines dating from 1958 to 1961."[2] Apart from the fact that she had spent a large part of her childhood in the Congo, for the purposes of writing this novel she also went "into Western and Central Africa to live with the natives, shop in the local markets, and ask questions about history, religion, and African families."[3] After publication, the novel received numerous prestigious literary awards.

The story parallel to the tumultuous events in the newly independent state of Congo depicts the equally tumultuous events taking place within the Price household. There are "complex links between the private domestic story of the Price family and the public political narrative of US intervention in the Congo."[4] However, the political elements of the novel will be touched upon in our study only insofar as they relate to the major theme of our interest – the personality of the Reverent Nathan Price and the impact he had on his family and congregation.

The terms many critics use for this preacher (for example, the phrase that he was "a zealous, self-righteous fundamentalist"[5]) do outline his profile to a certain extent, but it seems that most of them fail to emphasize the full degree of madness and toxicity abiding in him. Based on the way he lived, acted, treated others, thought, and felt, it cannot but be assumed that he had an incorrigibly tenacious personality disorder, the nature of which is the theme of this chapter.

A Brief Biography of Nathan Price

Neither his early childhood nor his relationship with his parents are mentioned in the book, so his earliest experiences remain in the dark. The first mention we have of him is that of a successful quarterback on the high school football team, who "could not abide losing or backing down."[6] As a young man, he was already a charismatic, handsome, unusually self-assured preacher in tent revivals, whom people flock to see and hear. There is this paradox of "the intense charm of people who have no conscience, a kind of inexplicable charisma."[7] Orleanna, his future wife, seventeen and motherless, was intrigued by him, but also dismayed by his seriousness, for he only talked of religion when they were alone. Still, that was completely different from other young men she knew, whose main vocabulary consisted of lewd remarks to girls in the streets. After his repeated visits to her household to preach to her, life circumstances, rather than romantic emotions, brought them together before the altar.

Soon after the wedding, Nathan was drafted to fight in World War II. He spent some time in Asia where a shell hit him in the head, but he survived. All other soldiers from his unit died, which made him lose any shred of cheerfulness he might have had before the war and pushed him even more toward religion. Orleanna soon understood that he came back a different, much gloomier person and that the happy moments of their marriage had been irrevocably gone. Still, they went on to live together and procreate four girls.

In 1959, Price decided to uproot his family from the USA and move them to Africa, where he would quench his missionary zeal and pursue his obsessive objectives. Life for the wife and four girls in the new country was unbearably difficult, due to the harsh circumstances of the rural Congolese village of Kilanga, but much more to the abhorrent personality of their *paterfamilias*. It ended tragically, with one daughter dying, the wife and the rest of the children leaving Africa and returning to America, and Nathan resuming a reclusive life in the African jungle, still attempting to baptize as many black souls as possible. In these attempts, he once overturned a boat full of children, many of whom drowned in the river. In retaliation, the villagers burned him alive, and wild animals drew his remains apart.

Nathan Price and the Antisocial Personality Disorder

The novel clearly delineates Nathan Price's distancing from any decent humanistic norm, despite the fact that he did make personal sacrifices in order to achieve what in his skewed system represented higher values. His rigidity, lack of emotions, stubbornness, and almost any other feature he displayed mark him as highly advanced on the continuum of a personality disorder diagnosis. The exact type of disorder characteristic for him, however, is not easy to determine. There are in him elements of narcissism, paranoia, borderline rages, and sadism, but the way his life moved on and eventually ended up, propelled there by his own actions, irresistibly points toward antisocial personality disorder.

In his book *Personality Disorders in Modern Life*, Theodore Millon opens the chapter on antisocial personality disorder with a statement that in such people, "badness and madness seem to shade together."[8] Although the phrasing sounds laic, it accurately sums up the essential flaws associated with antisocials. The prescientific terms used for it were *la folie rasionannante* (Philippe Pinel, 1801) and "moral insanity" (James Cowles Prichard, 1835), while Hervey Cleckley, the pioneer in the modern area of personality disorders, called it "semantic aphasia" (1950). All of them imply Millon's "badness and madness." More precisely, the "badness" side of things involves being "tough, thick-skinned, and powerful,"[9] prone to coercing and manipulating others, instilling fear. These people are "devious, controlling, and punitive,"[10] basing their interactions on "pure interpersonal hostility."[11] The "madness" part refers to their utter lack of conscience, the proclivity to use superficial charm in order to achieve what they want, and their occasional "crimes [that] are so incomprehensible and morally repugnant that the act alone makes us doubt their sanity."[12] Besides, like in any personality disorder, the propensity to interpret reality very differently from its objective manifestation does point to elements of psychosis.

This particular kind of disorder is not easily linked with a religious vocation, but Kingsolver's literary portrait of Nathan Price makes for a very convincing case study of religious antisocial personality disorder. The following paragraphs will attempt to apply the DSM criteria of the diagnosis to this literary character.

One of the most obvious and most striking features that Price displays is his "irritability and aggressiveness,"[13] which is typical for antisocial personality disorder. Knowing very well how easy it was to make him cross, the family members were hostages of his temper. Nobody dared sit in his chair, talk back, or disobey him. They recognized the emerging signs of his rage – "the danger in his extremely calm speech, [...] the rising color creeping toward his hairline,"[14] and above all the tone of his voice, mentioned multiple times in the novel, that froze the blood in the veins of many a family and congregation member. He was an "atomic danger zone,"[15] a "Moses tromping off of Mount Syanide with ten fresh ways to wreck your life."[16] One time, his daughter Ruth May "peed in her pants just because Father coughed out on the porch."[17] He would beat the girls mercilessly for having their nails polished, for expressing a wish to leave Africa, or for any form of discontent. Once, when Orleanna had an opinion that slightly differed from his own, he grabbed a plate that she was holding in her hand and broke it on the kitchen table. Displacing his dissatisfaction in this way, he used the following explanation: "You were getting too fond of that plate. Don't you think I've noticed?" His look of "a mean boy fixing to smash puppies with a brick,"[18] of a "petulant [...] tough boy who's known too little love and is quick to blame others for his mistakes"[19] fits into the picture of antisocial personality disorder, peculiarly wrapped in a religious packing.

Another feature of this disorder is "impulsivity or failure to plan ahead,"[20] which is to be found in abundance in Reverend Nathan Price. He needed "permission only from the Savior" to act out on his impulses, and he always found ways to procure it. In conversation with others belonging to his own rank (primarily priests), "whenever he sees an argument coming, man oh man, does he get jazzed up."[21] He would get violent in church, too, like Elmer Gantry, "hit[ting] a man one time, who did not praise the Lord."[22] The unexpected outbursts of hostility and aggression would sometimes make his family lock themselves in the house and spend sleepless nights fearing his rage. One frightening night, "Ruth May put an aluminum saucepan on her head and slid two comic books down the seat of her jeans in case of a whipping."[23] However, as unexpected as his tantrums were, they sometimes just as equally unexpectedly disappeared, succeeded by sudden peacefulness. After a most horrible night of violence, the next morning Price "acted like nothing much had happened."[24] Such abrupt shifts in the overall mood are also associated with a disordered personality.

Where planning ahead is concerned, on the whole he did have a certain planning stratagem, but it was so inflexible and devoid of insight that his plans inevitably turned awry. He was fixated on his church, his garden, and baptizing. His determination to "save souls" even of those he considered unworthy (females, blacks, etc.) went rigidly on in most unfavorable circumstances and eventually cost him his life. Based on the aforesaid, instead of concluding that he had no plans at all, it is more appropriate to say he only had obsessions that drove him on. These appeared like plans on the surface, but beset by "the unthinking, unreflective stupidity,"[25] they did not have much chance of working out.

The criterion of "reckless disregard for safety of self or others"[26] is particularly emphasized in the so-called subcategory of a "risk-taking antisocial," that Millon describes as a combination of "antisocial and histrionic traits."[27] Nathan Price was extremely reckless and wanted to be seen as "unaffected by what almost anyone else would surely experience as dangerous or frightening."[28] The wife and the eldest daughter were trying to tell him "day in day out about how he is putting his own children in jeopardy of their lives, but he won't listen."[29] Nearing the end of the African ordeal, and after losing the youngest child Ruth May, the family felt "Nathan was something that happened to us, as devastating in its way as the burning roof that fell on the family Mwanza."[30]

"Consistent irresponsibility,"[31] also featuring in antisocial personality disorder, comes along with recklessness. People who have this disorder "not only [...] fail to learn self-care, but [...] also ha[ve] no awareness of the needs of others."[32] His family members, who were supposed to have been Price's first and foremost priority, were completely neglected by him. "He noticed children less and less. [...] Their individual laughter he couldn't recognize, nor their anguish."[33] The teenage daughter Leah reasoned: "For us to be here now, each day, was Father's decision and his alone. Yet he wasn't providing for us, but only lashing out at us more and more. He wasn't able to protect Mother and Ruth May from getting sick. If it's all up to him to decide our fate, shouldn't protection be part of the bargain?"[34] From a superficial point of view, he did display a sort of responsibility regarding his missionary goals, however malignant they were, but no logical prioritization of responsibilities was to be found on his horizon.

Like with any personality disorder, the emotional world of antisocials is extremely scarce and twisted. They seem to be unable to feel, "suffer[ing] an inborn inability to understand and express the meaning of emotional experience,"[35] and going through life "forever deprived of an authentic emotional intelligence."[36] Kevin Dutton uses the phrase "the refrigerated neurology,"[37] while Wayne E. Oates mentions a "taboo on tenderness."[38] Nathan Price fits into all of these descriptions. He never shows a single indication of love for his family. At the very opening of the novel, his wife Orleanna clearly spells out that she "married a man who could never love"[39] her. Unlike most sociopaths, who are sexual predators, Price's emotional confusion was strongly evident in his sex life, too. His wife's pregnancies embarrassed him profoundly, because they pointed to the ungodly fact of his wife "having a vagina and him having a penis."[40] After sex, during which he was feverish, he would feel unclean and guilty, blame his wife for being wanton, and turn into a tyrant.

The ban on tenderness was evidently in power also where children were concerned. The African babies he was baptizing meant nothing to him, their "little bald head[s] looked like [...] overripe avocado[s] he was prepared to toss away."[41] He would not hold his own child's hand "for the world,"[42] nor did he show any sign of distress when his wife and the youngest daughter Ruth May were "sick nigh unto death."[43] When one of his daughters broke an arm and had to be taken to a nearby town on a plane, he would not let his wife go with her, but boarded the aircraft himself, not because he would nurse his daughter on the way there, but because "he wanted to go walk on a city street in Stanleyville."[44] Most symptomatic of all, however, was his reaction to the death of his youngest daughter Ruth May from a snakebite. At first, he "seemed unable to grasp what had happened"[45] and "all he could think to say to his wife was 'This can't be'"[46] in an inappropriate, unfeeling manner. Still, his concern was not with the dead child, or the grieving mother, but with the fact that Ruth May was not baptized yet, so he held out her little body "for the sake of pageantry"[47] and went on to baptize her.

As much as Nathan Price lacked in emotional intelligence, he was equally deficient in social intelligence, too. Sociopaths are generally characterized by a "failure to conform to social norms."[48] The uncanny thing is that he did conform to some extrinsic norms of religious life, otherwise he could not have been a church representative, but on a more profound level, his social inadequacy was essential, as can be seen on the example of his interaction with family members and his congregation. "A mutual social covenant or contract between them and those to whom they are related is inoperative."[49] However, what differed him from classical sociopaths is that he did not "repeatedly perform[e] acts that are grounds for arrest,"[50] whether out of caution, righteousness, or awareness of his religious position. Still, it does not mean that deep down he did not have impulses toward unlawfulness. Very early on upon his arrival to Kilanga, he made an illegal purchase of dynamite from the dodgy pilot Eeben Axelroot. His aim was to put on "a high-horse show of force. He ordered men to go out in canoes and pitch dynamite in the river, stupefying everything within earshot."[51]

Eventually, when things fell apart and he left the village walking around the Congo on his missionary spree of madness, he disregarded social norms altogether, taking no care of personal hygiene, growing his hair and beard wild, and even claiming to have "swallowed a live snake."[52] Long before he slid into these extremely bizarre behaviors, Orleanna expressed the futility to do anything about her husband's "cold and cunning"[53] savageries: "There are no weapons for this fight. There are countless laws of man and nature, and none of these is on your side."[54] This indirectly expresses the fact that Price fell out of line from any social or natural harmony and that in him swarmed "elusive factors hidden beneath a veneer of social acceptability."[55]

The criterion of "deceitfulness, as indicated by repeating lying, use of aliases, or conning others for personal profit or pleasure"[56] is not particularly dominant in Price's personality. This does not mean that he did not have a deceitful bone in his body, for he was prone to carrying out his ideas disregarding the means employed. Still, what neutralized the antisocial tendency for double-dealing in his behavior was probably an unabashed righteousness, however grotesque and out of place it was. This righteousness sprang from a quality that most sociopaths lack, but that was very prominent in Nathan Price – the omnipresent feeling of overhanging guilt. Being ridden by guilt, or more precisely survivor's guilt, makes him slightly deviate from the antisocial norm that includes a "lack of empathy, guilt or remorse."[57] Of course, every human being deviates from any readymade formula; this is why diagnosing someone with a personality disorder does not mean meeting every single criterion of the disorder. Still, it was the sense of guilt that makes Price quite an uncharacteristic sociopath and that propels him further on onto a religious path.

As briefly mentioned earlier in this chapter, an episode that left a decisive mark on his adult personality was the war night in an Asian jungle when he was wounded by a shell but survived, while every other man in his unit lost their lives. He even earned a medal for it, but since it was not given him for heroism, but rather for the mere fact that he managed to stay alive, in his mind it rang with the loud notes of "Cowardice, Guilt, and Disgrace."[58] Such feelings compelled him to become even more devout than before, unreasonably so. When his wife saw him for the first time after the war and tried to kiss him, he pulled away from her saying: "Can't you understand the Lord is watching us?"[59]

The guilt for having survived turned "his steadfast disdain for cowardice [...] to obsession."[60] He was suspicious of it in his own self, and his quest to uproot it did not include only himself but also all family members, whom he "stamped [...] with a belief in justice, then drenched [...] in culpability."[61] With a hindsight, Orleanna reminisced that she "wouldn't wish such torment even on a mosquito."[62] While on one side, he was a child fraught with guilt before the face of God, on the other, he was a tyrant who imposed his irrational coercions on everybody around him. The decision to move the whole family to a jungle was most likely his attempt to be purged of the guilt of having been freed from the Asian war hell. Besides, his decision to stay in the Congo even after his family left, his wildness and eventual loss of life, sound more logical in the light of the idea that "he could not flee from the same jungle twice."[63]

Nathan Price's Religiosity

Switching the discussion to the field of spirituality, it is impossible to say that Reverend Nathan Price shared even a shred of it in his soul, for it was much cruder than the souls of many people who have no religious or missionary ambitions whatsoever. His failures were too serious and too many, even though he managed to make his wife believe that "God was on his side"[64] and to have some influence on the black congregation. However, this was short-lived, because both his family and the Africans turned either away from him or directly against him. It had taken them a while, but eventually they understood the extent of Price's detrimental influence.

Among many other things, he was also a misogynist and a racist. He hated the fact that he only had daughters. Even in his conversations with God, he complained about the "dull-witted, bovine females,"[65] not realizing that some of them were incomparably more intelligent and sophisticated than he was himself. He refused to send them to college, personally taking care of their education, "view[ing] himself as the captain of a sinking mess of female minds."[66] His oldest daughter Rachel was a typical teenage girl who wanted to enjoy her femininity, but in her father's mind, "makeup and nail polish are warning signals of prostitution, the same as pierced ears,"[67] and she would be severely punished for indulging in such lewdness. He saw his female children as commodities whose only goal in life was to get married, because "a girl who fails to marry is veering from God's plan."[68] If he had sons, he would not have treated them the way he treated his girls, "he might have been forced to respect them,"[69] as Rachel thought. However, he would make their life equally hard, but in a different way, probably forcing them to follow in his footsteps, which would perhaps be an even more serious ordeal for young boys.

Discriminating between genders has nothing to do with spirituality. However, many formal religions still express discriminatory attitudes. This is why this tendency in Nathan Price did not disqualify him from performing clerical service. In our context of mature spirituality, though, such attitude instantly and fully disqualifies him even from a semblance of it.

Very much in line with his misogyny was his racism, too. The decision to come to Africa and save as many souls as possible was the result of his personal urges and compulsions, not of a genuine desire to bring the good tidings to the tribes who were still unenlightened. All the while, he cherished an understanding that black people were different and he instructed his family to keep to their own. Religious grounds were used to perpetuate this idea: "Noah cursed all Ham's children to be slaves for ever and ever. That's how come them to turn out dark."[70]

In the pulpit, he tried to mesmerize, manipulate, frighten people out of sinning, and bring them back to Christ by force. At first he did manage to attract their attention, but gradually "their expressions had fallen in slow motion from joy to confusion to dismay."[71] In the end, brought to utter exasperation after he drowned those black children from a boat on the river, the locals "surrounded him in an old coffee field and he climbed up on one of those rickety watchtowers left over from the colonial days."[72] Then they burned him alive.

As might be expected, Reverend Nathan Price did not have any sensitivity to any religious traditions other than his own. It goes without saying that native faiths were to him, as to almost anyone else coming from the Christian world at that time, remnants of dark, pagan times, that only needed to be eradicated. However, he did not have a much better opinion of different Christian churches, too. "He'd say that the Irish and them are well known to be Catholic papists and worshippers of the false idols."[73] The previous tenant of the mission house in Kilanga was Brother Fowles, a Catholic missionary who was also a humanist. Fowles left a talking parrot in the house that the Prices inherited. When it occasionally uttered curses and swear words, such as "piss off," which made Nathan Price extremely uncomfortable, he'd say: "That [...] is a Catholic bird."[74] Dismissal of religious traditions other than the one to which a believer belongs is one of the most certain signs of religious immaturity.

On the whole, Rev Price's was an unexamined, psychologically stagnant existence, unfit for spiritual ministry. While "to live is to change,"[75] it is "hard to imagine a mortal man more unwilling to change [...] than Nathan Price."[76] Put in terms that from some other author's mouth might sound trite, Kingsolver says that he has "a stone in place of his heart."[77] Not a rolling stone, but a stone overgrown by moss. He believes that only he is right, his overall frame of reference is completely subjective, "he was a history book all to himself."[78] The result of the endless defenses he was erecting up against reality was the inability to comprehend that "the simple human relief of knowing you're doing wrong, and living through it"[79] is a miraculous gift of life.

Even when it becomes utterly ludicrous to preach, and when instead of followers he only has enemies, he keeps on preaching. Voices coming from anywhere else but his own head are mute to him. One of his daughters tragically understands that "father would sooner watch us all perish one by one than listen to anybody but himself."[80] People like that represent a threat in many ways, especially if they hold a position of power, and unfortunately many do. As shown in the novel, but also throughout history, such people bring on destruction to others and eventually perish amid their own destruction themselves.

The behaviors of people impervious to change are characterized by an absence of spontaneity in everyday life, as well as when it comes to their beliefs and values. Everything about Nathan Price lacks spontaneity, save for his outbursts of uncontrollable anger. He is a man who "won't usually answer a question straight. He always acts like there's a trap somewhere and he's not about to get caught in it."[81] There are no surprises for him, or rather he would not let on that anything has surprised him. If a theme he did not know anything about was mentioned in a conversation, he had to give an impression that he knew all about it. The values that he frantically pursues are inflexibly set in stone: righteousness and bravery; anything that wavers from them is unacceptable in his dichotomous world. Like with so many people with personality disorders, there is no other shade for Price but black or white.

The same lack of spontaneity is quite clearly evident in his religious behavior, too. He "love[s] to speak in parables"[82] and there is a strained quality of holiness in his words. "When he says anything at all, even a simple thing about a car or a plumbing repair, it tends to come out [...] as sacred."[83]

The essential insecurity in spiritual matters that religious fanatics harbor deeply beneath all their religious pomp and rigidity makes them unable to calmly and philosophically expose themselves to other people's doubts or even blasphemies. When a doctor who tended to his daughter's broken arm remarked that Lumumba had "a larger following than Jesus,"[84] the girl felt trepidation because she knew the reaction such a casual remark would bring about in her father's mind. "Saying anything is better than Jesus is a bad sin. Father looked up at the ceiling and out the window and tried not to hit anything."[85]

Based on the foundations described earlier, the religious practice of Nathan Price can in fact only be called religious malpractice. Similar to Elmer Gantry, he did manipulate the congregation with charismatic, but essentially void gestures, and he did "scare the dickens"[86] out of people to leave off sinning. The household punishment for his children was "the dreaded Verse"[87] – they had to copy a Verse from the Bible plus the ninety-nine subsequent verses for the whole afternoon, whereby the last verse would reveal the reason for the punishment. "Only upon reaching that one-hundredth verse do you finally understand you are being punished for the sin of insolence."[88] Price's good knowledge of the Scripture has to be acknowledged, though not a broad understanding of it. His quintessential misunderstanding of the Bible is neatly likened in the novel with his mispronunciation of the Kikongo word *bängala* when he declares "TATA JESUS IS BÄNGALA."[89] He wanted to say that Father Jesus "means something precious and dear. But the way he pronounces it, it means the poisonwood tree."[90] Hence the title of the novel, and hence the fact that, in his interpretation, "Jesus will make you itch like nobody's business."[91]

The rickety but menacing construction of Nathan Price's religion is rooted in numerous delusional and cognitively faulty ideas he held about the world and God, who in his murky mind is a magical caricature of a vindictive Old Testament Almighty. Price's Lord sends rain down to the earth, intervenes with health issues so no doctors are needed, and grants ultimate protection to him and his family for the very fact that they came to Africa in His service. Nathan's simplistic reasoning "that the Lord notices righteousness, and rewards it"[92] inevitably led to a simplistic conclusion that any suffering that took place in the family took place because one of the family members "had committed a failure of virtue."[93] His God was constantly "on the lookout for human failing"[94] which made Nathan squirm "desperately beneath the eyes of a God who will not forgive a debt."[95] Driven by an inner restlessness projected onto the outer divinity was an impossibly difficult existential position, persistently aggravated by the fact that truthfulness and reality were being barred from his mental world. The difference between him and his family members was that he lived immersed in his delusions, so things made more sense, but to them the enormous amount of suffering they had to endure was completely unnecessary and inexplicable. This made the whole story even more tragic.

The posttraumatic stress disorder that Nathan most likely suffered from after returning from the war spilled over into his religiosity, causing an incessant "holy war going on in [...][his] mind."[96] The unexamined challenges of his life merged into a frenzied urge to become God's instrument in the heart of black Africa, where "he has been singled out for a life of trial, as Jesus was."[97] When his family life came to an end, as well as his mission in the village, he "ran off to a hut in the woods he was calling the New Church of Eternal Life, Jesus Is Bängala." For him, the struggle had no end. It would continue on the metaphysical level one day, too, because in his mind, "the Kingdom of God [i]s an uncomplicated place, where tall, handsome boys fight on the side that always wins."[98]

A very astute phrase, the "deluded purveyor of Christian malpractice,"[99] that Nathan Price utters to describe the Catholic priest Fowles, is a perfectly worded projection that can only apply to his own self. Besides, the metaphor that Price walks around wearing "his faith like the bronzeplate of God's foot soldiers"[100] evokes an immediate suspicion about the authenticity of the values on such wide display, because true values that arise from the noetic depths are usually shrouded in a protective coating of shyness. What happens between one person's soul and God is a very private relationship and should be kept away from the eyes of others. On the other hand, others should also refrain from commenting on it. However, these rules are constantly being breached both in real life and in this book. The justification for commenting on the religiosity and spirituality of toxic personalities may be sought in the effect that their actions have on those around them. The influence Nathan Price had on his family and congregation is obviously damaging, but let us accentuate the extent to which this damaging effects went.

Nathan Price was overwhelmingly dominant. His wife and children feared him, even at the earlier stages when they still held some respect for and stood in awe of him. Orleanna would clamp her hands over her ears "to stop His words that rang in [...][her] head even when he was far away, or sleeping."[101] Gradually, they realized that, put very simply, he was "mean as a snake."[102] Instead of inspiring a profound sense of meaningfulness, love, and safety in his family and flock, he only stirred in them daydreams of violence against him, which was the only defense they were left with, but that poisoned their souls. His own daughters imagined killing him, not symbolically, but literally. Rachel was praying in her mind: "Oh, please God make a tree fall on him and smash his skull!"[103] while Adah "imagined getting the kerosene and burning him up in his bed."[104] After the family separated, the daughters never had the nerve to go and see him again, and the wife never remarried, having had enough of married life. Commenting on his savage demise, they were all in accord that "there's nothing he got that he didn't deserve."[105]

Due to the amount of hurt that he caused, and the inflexibly ludicrous path that he took, it is not surprising that the family members failed to evoke any feelings of pity for his cruel ending. He was supposed to enrich their spiritual lives, but he did just the opposite. In truth, he did something many problematic servants of God have done throughout history and continue to do to this day: he made others shun the religion altogether, or proverbially throw the baby with the bathwater. Due to the fact that religion was strongly associated with him, they wanted to sever any ties with whatever reminded them of him. Adah, the most spiritual of the children, "no longer believed in God,"[106] while for Rachel, later in life, "all those childhood lessons in holiness slid off [...] like hot butter off the griddle."[107] The deluded man who believed he was telling nothing but the truth in reality "set down for all time the Poisonwood Bible,"[108] and nothing else.

There is something repulsively reptilian in the way Nathan Price acted in his later life and in the way he died. "He'd gotten a very widespread reputation for turning himself into a crocodile and attacking children."[109] References to his snakelike meanness and Ruth May's demise by a snakebite have already been mentioned. This archetypal evil and coldheartedness, accompanied with a "lack of internal behavioral controls,"[110] could only have led to catastrophe. "This kind will always lose in the end."[111] Things might have been slightly different and less acute had he been able to develop at least the rudiments of "a sense of nurturing attachment,"[112] which represents the main therapeutic goal when working with people with the antisocial personality disorder. However, Reverend Price was closed off for change and warmth, and determinedly stubborn in accomplishing his religious mission, which in essence was only his unconscious compulsion toward destruction of others and of self.

Notes

1 Anne Marie Austenfeld, "The Revelatory Narrative Circle in Barbara Kingsolver's *The Poisonwood Bible*," *Journal of Narrative Theory*, Vol. 6, No. 2, Summer 2006, p. 293.
2 Mary Ellen Snodgrass, *Barbara Kingsolver: A Literary Companion*, Jefferson, NC and London: McFarland & Company, 2004, p. 23.
3 *Ibid.*
4 Susan Strehle, "Chosen People: American Exceptionalism in Kingsolver's *The Poisonwood Bible*," Critique: Studies in Contemporary Fiction, Vol. 49, No. 4, 2008, p. 413.
5 William F. Purcell, "The Gospel According to Barbara Kingsolver," *Logos: A Journal of Catholic Thought and Culture*, Vol. 12, No. 1, Winter 2009, p. 94.
6 Barbara Kingsolver, *The Poisonwood Bible*, London: Faber & Faber, 2000, p. 110.
7 Martha Stout, *The Sociopath Next Door*, New York: Harmony Books, 2006, p. 88.
8 Theodore Millon, *op. cit.*, p. 151.

9 Wayne E. Oates, *op. cit.*, p. 58.
10 *Ibid.*, p. 63.
11 Theodore Millon, *op. cit.*, p. 168.
12 *Ibid.*, p. 151.
13 *Diagnostic and Statistical Manual of Mental Disorders DSM-5*, Washington DC, London: American Psychiatric Publishing, 2013, p. 659.
14 Barbara Kingsolver, *op. cit.*, p. 378.
15 *Ibid.*, p. 152.
16 *Ibid.*, p. 31.
17 *Ibid.*, p. 388.
18 *Ibid.*, p. 193.
19 *Ibid.*, p. 225.
20 *DSM-5*, p. 659.
21 Barbara Kingsolver, *op. cit.*, p. 146.
22 *Ibid.*, p. 137.
23 *Ibid.*, p. 387.
24 *Ibid.*, p. 388.
25 Lorna Smith Benjamin, *Interpersonal Diagnosis and Treatment of Personality Disorders*, New York: The Guilford Press, 1996, p. 198.
26 *DSM-5*, p. 659.
27 Theodore Millon, *op. cit.*, p. 160.
28 *Ibid.*
29 Barbara Kingsolver, *op. cit.*, p. 201.
30 *Ibid.*, p. 436.
31 *DSM-5*, p. 659.
32 Lorna Smith Benjamin, *op. cit.*, p. 198.
33 Barbara Kingsolver, *op. cit.*, p. 111.
34 *Ibid.*, pp. 273–274.
35 Theodore Millon, *op. cit.*, p. 163.
36 Martha Stout, *op. cit.*, p. 191.
37 Kevin Dutton, *The Wisdom of Psychopaths*, New York: Scientific American/Farrar, Strauss and Giroux, 2012, p. 22.
38 Wayne E. Oates, *op. cit.*, p. 64.
39 Barbara Kingsolver, *op. cit.*, p. 8.
40 *Ibid.*, p. 225.
41 *Ibid.*, p. 426.
42 *Ibid.*, p. 206.
43 *Ibid.*, p. 246.
44 *Ibid.*, p. 135.
45 *Ibid.*, p. 419.
46 *Ibid.*
47 *Ibid.*
48 *DSM-5*, p. 659.
49 Wayne E. Oates, *op. cit.*, p. 61.
50 *DSM-5*, p. 659.
51 Barbara Kingsolver, *op. cit.*, p. 80.
52 *Ibid.*, p. 491.
53 Theodore Millon, *op. cit.*, p. 167.
54 Barbara Kingsolver, *op. cit.*, p. 217.
55 Lorna Smith Benjamin, *op. cit.*, p. 197.
56 *DSM-5*, p. 659.
57 Lorna Smith Benjamin, *op. cit.*, p. 195.
58 Barbara Kingsolver, *op. cit.*, p. 468.
59 *Ibid.*, p. 224.

60 *Ibid*., p. 110.
61 *Ibid*., p. 594.
62 *Ibid*.
63 *Ibid*., p. 468.
64 *Ibid*., p. 217.
65 *Ibid*., p. 85.
66 *Ibid*., p. 42.
67 *Ibid*., p. 18.
68 *Ibid*., p. 171.
69 *Ibid*., p. 383.
70 *Ibid*., p. 23.
71 *Ibid*., p. 33.
72 *Ibid*., p. 552.
73 *Ibid*., p. 278.
74 *Ibid*., p. 68.
75 *Ibid*., p. 438.
76 *Ibid*., p. 110.
77 *Ibid*., p. 111.
78 *Ibid*., p. 554.
79 *Ibid*., p. 594.
80 *Ibid*., p. 193.
81 *Ibid*., p. 147.
82 *Ibid*., p. 86.
83 *Ibid*., p. 47.
84 *Ibid*., p. 139.
85 *Ibid*.
86 *Ibid*., p. 375.
87 *Ibid*., p. 68.
88 *Ibid*., p. 69.
89 *Ibid*., p. 312.
90 *Ibid*.
91 *Ibid*.
92 *Ibid*., p. 227.
93 *Ibid*.
94 *Ibid*., p. 446.
95 *Ibid*., p. 468.
96 *Ibid*., p. 275.
97 *Ibid*., p. 49.
98 *Ibid*., p. 274.
99 *Ibid*., p. 292.
100 *Ibid*., p. 78.
101 *Ibid*., p. 218.
102 *Ibid*., p. 551.
103 *Ibid*., p. 193.
104 *Ibid*., p. 562.
105 *Ibid*., p. 551.
106 *Ibid*., p. 196.
107 *Ibid*., p. 584.
108 *Ibid*., p. 603.
109 *Ibid*., p. 551.
110 Theodore Millon, *op. cit*., p. 154.
111 Barbara Kingsolver, *op. cit*., p. 436.
112 Theodore Millon, *op. cit*., p. 183.

8 Case Studies of Minor Characters

The Holy Histrionics: Sister Jane and Sharon Falconer

Sister Jane

In his voluminous and memorable oeuvre, Aldous Huxley described many characters, both fictional and historical, that could easily be a part of this study. However, I am restricting myself to only two. Besides Father Joseph, analyzed in a previous chapter, another religiously peculiar personality, Sister Jane (Sœur Jeanne) of his historical biography *The Devils of Loudun* (1952), is now the subject of the unit on histrionic religiosity.

Very similar to *Grey Eminence*, it is also difficult to determine the genre of *The Devils of Loudun*. First of all, it is a history taking place in France at the time of Cardinal Richelieu and Father Joseph. It even mentions these two characters, who played certain roles in the Loudun events. However, "from start to finish the central theme of the book is never constant,"[1] it meanders between seventeenth-century mysticism, psychiatric practice of the time, witchcraft, demonology, and many more, "illustrat[ing] the fascinating range of Mr. Huxley's powers."[2] One of his most astute critics, George Woodcock, called it a "horrifying study of prejudice and superstition,"[3] which probably describes it best, since the center stage of the book is occupied by cumulative events of demonic possession in a French convent in the seventeenth century.

Based on a set of true events, the book has no central character. At least three of them enmeshed in these happenings share a similar kind of spotlight: the young Catholic parson Urbain Grandier, the mother superior of the Ursuline nuns in Loudun, Sister Jane, and the Jesuit exorcist Jean-Joseph Surin. They represent fascinating portraits of three persons with essentially different spiritual lives and idiosyncrasies – "the bewildering triptych of Loudun,"[4] as some put it. The emphasis in this chapter is fully on Sister Jane.

The events described in the book represent "one of the most fantastically strange stories in all French history."[5] Since we are primarily interested in the narrative of Sister Jane, the basic storyline will be presented from the perspective of her character. To begin with, she was born in 1602 as Jeanne del Belciel in "an ancient and eminent"[6] family from both her father's and her mother's side. However, the girl was physically misshapen, dwarfish, and with one shoulder higher than the other. Also, though intelligent, she had a difficult temper. The family basically attempted to keep her away as much as possible, first sending her to live with an aunt, then, when the aunt returned her, to a cloister, after which she ended up as Mother Superior in an Ursuline convent in Loudun, where she spent the rest of her life, excluding an episode of traveling that she conducted at the height of her controversial ecclesiastical glory.

In her childhood and youth, Jane did not receive a good education. When first sent to the cloister as a young girl, she was "so insubordinate, so wanting in zeal, so slack in the performance of her duties."[7] However, overnight she became extremely interested in mysticism; she applied herself to study and became "obedient, hard-working and devout."[8] This was but the first of many such abrupt changes in her life. Managing to convince many that she really was heart and soul devoted to religion, the dying mother superior of the Ursulines in Loudun appointed her as the successor. Sister Jane was only twenty five and she had seventeen nuns under her.

The interest in the world outside the cloister, the world off-limits to her, was very strong in Sister Jane. Talking in the parlor with many guests from the outside, she quickly learned about the talk of the town – a young, handsome pastor named Urbain Grandier, who was infamous for having ruined many a virgin and honest woman, thus pitting a large group of local enemies against himself. Sister Jane's imagination flew wild with stories of Grandier, and very soon he became her obsession. She yearned to meet him, but he always found a way to refuse to see her. She found this infuriating, and it kindled poisonous vengefulness in her soul, so deep that she soon declared Grandier a demon who flew into the convent at night and seduced her and other nuns in the sacristy. All but two or three other nuns were caught up in the infectious hysteria of demonic possession. The exorcisms were performed publicly, by several exorcists, and the craze gained such strength that Grandier was arrested, accused of sorcery, and burned alive. There were political reasons behind this act, too, but they are quite convoluted and not directly related to this analysis.

After Grandier's death, the devils still haunted the nuns, and only after six years of the possessions were all the demons finally chased out. This marked a new phase in Sister Jane's life – one of a living saint. Miracles started happening to her – the stigmatic names of saints cut into her skin, miraculous escapades from deadly illnesses, the sweetly scented unction that brought her back to life, angelic appearances, and much more. Some people were skeptical about all of these, and some were highly credulous, so credulous that she decided to go on a pilgrimage, see the masses unable to come to her, and visit all the high dignitaries on the way, letting them see these miracles for themselves. Many did she visit on this trip – archbishops, dukes, Richelieu, and the very Queen and King. Besides, thousands of people gathered every day from 4 AM to 10 PM to see the living saint, touch her, and get a blessing from her. For a while, she lived the life of a modern movie star, which perfectly suited her personality. After her return to the convent, she kept experiencing miracles almost up until until her death. When she passed away, her chemise, anointed with the holy unction, her head, placed "in a silver gift-box with crystal windows,"[9] and a large painting of the exorcism of Behemoth were all kept as reliquaries in the convent for eighty years, when a bishop ordered their removal, after which all of them disappeared.

The psychological outline of Sister Jane's life seems rather simple. What is probably the crucial set of elements that tipped her personality into disordered waters was being "an object either of repugnance or of pity"[10] in her childhood due to her deformity and physical unattractiveness. She only had beautiful eyes, which "everybody had always admired [...] – even her mother."[11] This is an oblique and poignant statement that she received no affection from the person most important in a child's life. Whether due to these circumstances or not, she did develop a personality that was "a trial to others and her own worst enemy."[12] Being disliked, she defensively disliked everybody else, was prone to attack, cherished "a chronic resentment,"[13] and eventually did not permit herself to be loved. The expressiveness of her emotionality was bizarre, characterized by "sudden sarcasms or strange outbursts of jeering laughter."[14] Huxley sees in her behavior a "craving for compensatory dominance"[15] and, using no specific labels of personality disorder, qualifies her as psychologically pathological: "Persons of Jeanne's character are apt to make a good deal of trouble, both for themselves and for other people."[16]

Many of the personality traits that Sister Jane shared were the common negative features that we find in most villains: she was a hypocrite who looked down on those below her and adulated those above her station, felt envy, hatred, contempt, and possessed a great "intensity of her native egotism."[17] Manipulation was second nature to her. She knew how to please when she expected some gain and she imposed herself on everyone and in all circumstances. Even when she was allegedly possessed by devils and unconscious, she never yet forgot about her immediate interests, and made sure not to be politically incorrect, such as to offend the king or Richelieu, while at the same time she blasphemed horribly against the Virgin or Jesus.

What predominantly colored her personality pathology, however, was a quality that used to be called hysteria several decades ago, that Huxley calls a condition of "the consummate actress,"[18] and that today goes mostly by the term histrionic. In anything that she did she needed a stage, an audience, and herself as the main protagonist everyone would focus on. Her roles had to be spectacular and supernatural, whether she was frolicking due to the possession by an incubus, whether she was being miraculously cured of fatal illnesses before the eyes of spectators, or whether she was touched by marks of saintliness, such as a bleeding cross on her forehead or the vision of an angel who revealed secrets to her. Her whole life turned out to be just a sensational role played by a mean, unhappy woman with frustrated sexuality and wild imagination. Behind the curtains she was lonely, empty, and bitter, and she did everything to keep apart the persona she longed to be and her true self.

The qualities that she possessed could have been redeeming had she exploited them to any significant extent. Her intelligence was indubitable, but constantly misused. She was also "highly sensitive"[19] the way some people with personality disorders are, having a strong intuition (like, for example, Perry Edward Smith, the murderer of the Clutter family described in Truman Capote's book *In Cold Blood*). Once after Grandier's death, she even showed genuine remorse for what she had done and was tearfully at the brink of committing a suicide. However, such moments of authentic conscientiousness were only fleeting and extremely rare. Eventually, all her potentialities remained unused.

Sister Jane is a complex psychological character. She definitely had a personality disorder, but the type of her pathology is not easy to determine. There were schizotypal elements in her personality structure, as well as narcissistic and antisocial ones, and possibly others, too. However, taking into account the overall picture, she does fit best into the slot of histrionic personality disorder: first of all, due to her urge to be an actress at the scene of life. Most of the eight DSM criteria of this disorder may be applied to her quite successfully. She is obviously "uncomfortable in situations in which [...] she is not the center of attention"[20] and "consistently uses physical appearance to draw attention to self."[21] Unlike textbook histrionics who use good looks to be flirtatious, Sister Jane used what she had at her disposal – angelic eyes, a distorted figure, hysterical writhing, and blaspheming laughter. The criterion that "interaction with others is often characterized by inappropriate sexually seductive or provocative behavior"[22] represents the foundation of the Loudun events, shrouded in the monastic, superstitious cloak of seventeenth-century France. It is also true that her style of speech was "excessively impressionistic"[23] and that she herself was "suggestible, i.e., easily influenced by others or circumstances."[24] The abrupt changes she was prone to correspond to the criterion of "rapidly shifting and shallow expression of emotions,"[25] and her obsession with Grandier may be seen as a propensity to "consider[...] relationships to be more intimate than they actually are."[26] Finally, besides admixtures of other types of personality disorders, what fully establishes her as histrionic is her constant need for "self-dramatization, theatricality, and exaggerated expression of emotion."[27] On top of everything else, what gives Sister Jane's histrionic character a special flavor is the religious framework within which she acted out all of her impure urges.

The age of superstition that the seventeenth century was represented a favorable soil for Sister Jane's religious charlatanism to flourish. The same age also engendered *bona fide* "directors of souls"[28] who "published extensive treatises on the problems of distinguishing false spirituality from the genuine article."[29] Huxley clearly states that Sister Jane would not have passed any of those tests of genuine spirituality had she been subjected to them, and wonders how come that she succeeded in "getting away with it"[30] for so long. Neither is this wonderment completely out of place in the twenty-first century too, where cases of flagrant spiritual fraud still manage to get away with it, despite all the alleged sophistication that the human race achieved throughout the centuries.

Sister Jane played at least three major religious roles in her lifetime. The first one represented her pretentions to become a mystical saint while still a young girl, when she overnight switched from being completely disinterested in anything spiritual into a voracious reader of mystical literature and a fervent contributor to religious discussions. As it usually happens, she did manage to trick some people into believing in her genuineness, while in reality, she was just impersonating St. Teresa and using her acting skills to achieve an ecclesiastical position of superiority and power.

After securing this position, her unresolved inner cravings naturally urged for more. Unable to exercise her sexual drives with the man she was obsessing about, the frustration took on an extremely powerful psychosomatic expression presented as being possessed by seven demons who abided in seven different parts of her body. The grotesque shows of diabolic presence in her bodily framework involved rolling of eyes, grinding of teeth, grunting, laughing, blaspheming, screaming, and writhing on the floor before spectators and exorcists. Such shows with basically the same repertoire of tricks lasted for six years. Once she even displayed false pregnancy after allegedly having been impregnated by Iscarion. Despite the clear judgment that "there was no genuine possession – only a sickness,"[31] it has to be admitted that the line between illusion, delusion, and fraud in the case of Sister Jane was confusingly thin.

Many were incredulous about the authenticity of the farce she was staging. In some parts of the spiritual autobiography she wrote years later, she even indirectly admits the fraud she was committing: "I perceived very clearly that in most instances I was the prime cause of my disorders, and that the devil only acted upon the cues I myself had given him."[32] The so-called seven devils corresponded to the fiendish traits in her character, and the root of her disorders was only within herself, without any need of "invoking extraneous causes."[33]

The last role that she played in her later years was that of a miracle-maker, during which she saw herself as a saint. She went on a tour across France to meet all the dignitaries and let the masses touch her. However, several instances reveal that her mission was as fraudulent as ever. First, after the reception by the royal couple, all subsequent receptions felt flat to her. No one else held a higher rank than the king and the queen, and so for someone like Sister Jane, the excitement of visiting dignitaries at lower ranks was expected to vane. Second, she used several tricks in order to deter curious minds from inspecting the nature of her chemise with the drops of the holy unction or the holy names inscribed on her skin. Third, in her autobiography, she made a single fleeting and unimportant comment about meeting Sister Jane Frances de Chantal, a true saint who had "a most embarrassing gift for looking through the persona at the real self behind the mask, and it may be that poor Sister Jane suddenly found herself spiritually naked before this formidably gentle old woman – naked and, all of a sudden – overpoweringly ashamed."[34]

The conclusion that is more or less unavoidable is that all her life Sister Jane "insisted on pretending to be someone else"[35] and thus failed to attain maturity in either psychological or spiritual sense, despite the fact that for over a century, she figured as a significant religious personality in France. Her idiosyncratic folly performed to impress the public does make her an outstandingly peculiar character in history, literature, cinematography (played brilliantly in Ken Russel's 1971 movie *The Devils* by Vanessa Redgrave), or opera (*Die Teufel von Loudun* by Krzysztof Penderecki), but where true spirituality is concerned, it seems that she almost had none at all to account for.

Sharon Falconer

Another histrionic "saint," but of a very different nature, is Sharon Falconer, a character described in the already analyzed novel *Elmer Gantry* by Sinclair Lewis. She was Elmer's bedazzling psychological counterpart whom the author based on Aimee Semple McPherson (1890–1944), a Canadian-born Pentecostal evangelist of the 1920s and 1930s who incorporated popular entertainment in her church sermons and became an impeccably stylish star of the mass media in North America. However, the character of Sharon Falconer is but loosely based on Aimee, so no tight connections between the two will be pursued here.

Elmer accidentally came across "the placard of a woman evangelist, one Sharon Falconer, a prophetess of whom he had heard."[36] He went to see her theatrical sermon and his infatuation boomed. At first, Sharon was resisting Elmer's blunt advances, but after a while, his charms worked on her and soon she took him on as a lover, a co-evangelist, and a confidant. Since both of them shared traits of personality disorders, their relationship was bound to be tumultuous, but, surprisingly enough, for most of the part, it went along rather smoothly. There were some signs that a tempest was on its way, but a real-life disaster cut their story short, so we do not know the course their relationship might have taken. The disaster was the fire in their newly built, glamorous temple above the water, where they were staging a sermon. Elmer emerged unscathed, while Sharon lost her life. However, their relationship is of secondary importance here, for our major interest lies with the personality of Sharon Falconer.

Biographically, we do not know terribly much about her. When she started opening up to Elmer, Sharon told him some basic facts of her life. First, she told him that she "did come from a frightfully old Virginia family,"[37] that she grew up in a mansion with servants who cared for her, that her parents were dead, and that she now owned the old plantation. She even took him there. However, in moments of utter honesty that she was occasionally prone to, she confessed that the Falconer family did not exist at all, and that her name was Katie Jonas, from Utica, NY, a daughter of a bricklayer, and a stenographer by profession. Still, she did not want to admit that her life was false in any way, for she exclaimed: "I AM Sharon Falconer now! I've made her – by prayer and by having a right to be her!"[38] This concocted identity represents the major framework for the role-playing principle she was employing on many different levels, including the religious one.

The claim that Sharon Falconer was a histrionic is corroborated by various remarks Sinclair Lewis adds about her throughout the novel (let us repeat the fact mentioned in the section on Elmer Gantry that the author wrote all of this years before the first studies on personality disorders were published). While Sister Jane was a nonstandard histrionic who drew attention to her stage role by the quirkiness of her personality, Sharon used the classical histrionic hook – a sophisticated "physical appearance to draw attention to self."[39] Always "beautiful and eloquent,"[40] with an "intense brooding femininity,"[41] the author remarks over half a dozen times on her attire, which is usually a combination of lace, fur, and satin, in white, crimson, or gold. Besides such flamboyant stage toilettes, on less formal occasions she would wear a "pleated white skirt, white shoes"[42] and a red tam o' shanter, and for after-midnight encounters, she would be enveloped in a "robe of deep crimson adorned with gold stars and crescents, swastikas and tau crosses."[43] Equally gaudy were her church stages or her personal abodes and private chapels. When Elmer saw her first at an evangelism, she appeared on "a pyramidal structure, of white wood with gilded legs,"[44] only to approach "a pulpit shaped like a shell and painted like a rainbow,"[45] adorned with "lilies, roses and vines."[46] Her own bedroom was similarly loud, only done in mock Oriental style: "a couch high on carven ivory posts, covered with a mandarin coat, unlighted brass lamps in the likeness of mosques and pagodas; gilt papier-mâché armor on the walls."[47] The overall ostentatiousness that characterized every aspect of her public life denoted her histrionic need for "self-dramatization, theatricality, and exaggerated expression of emotion."[48]

Sinclair Lewis occasionally refers to her urge for theatricality in very concrete terms. The arrival of Sharon and her troupe to a new town made as big a splash as if a movie star was visiting, "the walls and shop-windows were scarlet with placards"[49] and "sometimes a thousand people gathered at the station for her arrival."[50] The author ironically calls her "the greatest woman since Sarah Bernhardt"[51] and compares her preparations for evangelism with the behind-the-scene frenzy of a production of *Macbeth*. This irony constantly refers to the inauthenticity of the performance of her life, which was nothing but a series of diverse, incongruous roles: "sometimes she was a priestess and a looming disaster, sometimes she was intimidating in grasping passion, sometimes she was thin and writing and anguished with chagrined doubt of herself, sometimes she was pale and nun-like and still, sometimes she was a chilly business woman, and sometimes she was a little girl."[52] All this corroborates another classical trait of histrionic personality disorder: "rapidly shifting and shallow expression of emotions."[53]

Her style of speech could also be linked with the histrionic criterion of being "excessively impressionistic and lacking in detail."[54] She did not read anything "but the Bible and the advertisements of rival evangelists,"[55] and "it was impossible for her to originate any sentiment more profound than 'I'm unhappy.'"[56] Exaggerations and lies as space fillers of her inner emptiness were part of her persona, too. Sometimes, she talked about her imaginary grandfather Mr. Falconer as of "a bellicose and pious man,"[57] while on other occasions he was "General Falconer of Ole Virginny [...] the adviser and solace of General Robert E. Lee."[58] Following another disordered vein of "refrigerated neurology," Sharon could also have been moved only by intense things and events, hence her liking for Elmer. Once she admitted that she hated "the little vices – smoking, swearing, scandal, drinking [...]"[59] and loved "the big ones – murder, lust, cruelty, ambition!"[60] Lewis is again impeccable at describing different traits characteristic of some personality disorders and the way they manifest at the level of overall behavior.

The veneer of her stage persona was based on femininity, gentleness, and innocence. At the end of her sermons, she would "wave[...] her flaunting smile"[61] and beg to be forgiven for getting tired. Behind the scenes, however, her smile became "unsmiling"[62] and instead of a high priestess, she turned into a cold, raging businesswoman, whose major concern was "hit[ting] people for money, [...] and hitting 'em hard."[63] In no time, she would manipulate the crowds and "had them all crying, all aching to dash out and bring souls and dollars."[64] Besides, she was on the lookout for "any nice-looking young preachers,"[65] too. As a boss, she was particularly unfeeling and irresponsible: firing coworkers easily, paying poor wages, failing to pay the rent for the houses her troupe was staying in. No personal friends are ever mentioned around her, save for some sightless followers.

The fact that the person who managed to get closest to her was Elmer Gantry, the proverbial narcissists, speaks volumes about her, too. Only a person like him would be able to disregard all the falsities about Sharon, such as her lies that she kept an Old Ladies' Home (for which she was canvassing money), her histrionic urge to present herself as deeply sentimental ("No, I haven't Not a brain. All emotion. That's the trouble with me."[66]), or her reluctance to evangelize and a desire to "go out and spank a bald man on the head"[67] one minute, while the next she "was standing before the audience, rejoicing, 'Oh, my beloved, the dear Lord has a message for you tonight!'"[68]

The histrionic propensity of shallow affects, inconsistency, and intellectual patchiness made Sharon reveal her weaknesses to Elmer in quite frequent moments of honesty. Unlike the false love she was pretending to radiate on stage, she admitted to Elmer that she did not really like anyone, that no one could touch her soul, and that she was as fond of Elmer as much as she could be of anyone. The only poignant exception she felt true love for was the young Katie Jonas, her own real self, whom she abandoned and replaced with a theatrical construct. Killing the core of her true identity, she killed the possibility of happiness, despite the fact that she did become wealthy and famous. At various times, she clearly and insightfully admits to being vain, ambitious, ignorant, crazy, and lying. By the end of her life, she exclaims, "I'm just nobody,"[69] and summons Elmer to assuage her pathological loneliness by kissing her and lying to her some more. She senses how ramshackle the state of her construction was, feels more and more tired from playing inauthentic roles, which exacts enormous amounts of psychical and mental energy, and knows that the world she created is doomed to collapse sooner or later. Knowing that it could not last, she invited Elmer to make it last for her and begs him: "Don't let them take it away from me!"[70] This implicit knowledge of impending doom perhaps made her surrender to the fatal fire in the temple without striving to save herself at all.

The success of Sharon Falconer's ecclesiastical entourage was due to the sensationalism of her approach. She was always in the focus of the religious events that were meticulously planned "to throw a brighter limelight on Sharon."[71] She would either emerge slowly from behind the platform or run "down curving flower-wreathed stairs"[72] and flaunt her saintly smile at the mesmerized audiences, "pleading with them to find peace in salvation"[73] and "laying her shining hands on their heads."[74] She "floated forward, not human, a goddess, tears thick in lovely eyes."[75]

The religious ambitions that Sharon cherished corresponded with her personal megalomania and crudity. She relied heavily on what the mystics have always discouraged – tricks that are presented as manifestations of Divine Powers. Thus, she would have "four men and two women crawled about a pillar, barking like dogs, 'barking the devils out of the tree.'"[76] For her, these were the obvious miracles that corroborated her saintliness and direct connection with God. Likewise, she enacted healings of the sick, which were in fact expressions of collective euphoria during the events rather than actual medical changes. Intoxicated by the ecstasy of the crowd, the blind would admit to seeing even though they remained as blind as ever. However, such dubious elements propelled her ambitions further and further on. She planned to have a great national paper that would only be about religion and the Bible; she daydreamed about leading a new crusade (like Father Joseph), and allowed herself to think that "the next Messiah might be a woman."[77] The ambition that she did actualize was the building of an immense structure above water that was named The Waters of Jordan Tabernacle, with "an enormous revolving cross"[78] and "yellow and ruby electric bulbs."[79] The main purpose of this achievement was not the facilitation of spiritual solace for the masses, but the narcissistic delight that it was hers personally, and that it was "the only Christian tabernacle built out over the water."[80] Religion in her overall enterprise was just a crutch for her essentially histrionic personal needs.

Similar to her own ambiguous stance about her personality, where she was deluded one moment and then painfully honest the next, the same holds true for the experience of her own religiosity. In certain occasions, she was completely taken by the exultation of her spiritual specialness, while in others she revealed all the falsity of her devotion.

Ungrounded spiritual delusions involved the notions that she was "above sin, [...] really and truly sanctified,"[81] and that even if she did something that would be considered a sin in one unsanctified, in her "God will turn it to his glory."[82] She believed that she had a complete, mystical union with Jesus; that God talked to her, that she was God's right hand and "the reincarnation of Joan of Arc, of Catherine of Sienna."[83] The "aura of spirituality"[84] that she saw about herself was in fact not much more than an aura of unhinged and abusive feminine sentimentality.

The truth behind the evangelical gloss was that of an unhappy young woman with weary eyes, whose mouth would drop as soon as she was off the stage, and who essentially found enormous joy in all things human, but forced herself to live like a saint. The duplicity of her enactment involved cheating, manipulation, lying, irresponsibility, ignorance, absence of compassion, and enticing believers to sacrifice money. She "absolutely refuted the rising fad of evolution"[85] without even a clue of its scientific implications. Not only that she did not know science, she did not even know her theology. "I can talk my sermons beautifully ... but Cecil wrote most of 'em for me, and the rest I cheerfully stole."[86]

In the privacy of her home chapel, that was decorated with eclectic symbols from all faiths and cults, she prayed to heathen goddesses and what in Christianity would be considered false idols. Any semblance of religious consistency and integrity was compromised at every step of the way. In moments of lucid honesty, she even verbalized this in perfectly clear words such as "all our righteousness is filthy as rags"[87] or "we have sinned and come short of the glory of God."[88]

The last moments of Sharon's life, however, come as a surprise. What we would expect from a *bon vivant* such as she was would be similar to what Elmer did – run for the dear life. Unlike him, Sharon stayed on in the burning temple, urged people to walk out calmly and not be afraid, reminded them of God's protectiveness and the fact that nothing could happen to them in His house. She volunteered to lead them safely through the flames. In a "voice furious with mad sincerity,"[89] she reminded the audience that God was trying them and that their faith was at an ultimate test. Sharon died in that fire, either because she had eventually and completely put her trust in God, or more likely because she had resigned inwardly before the awareness that her life was a sham and that she had nowhere to go from there.

Based on a real evangelist, like most characters in Lewis's *Elmer Gantry*, Sharon Falconer is a perfect female counterbalance to the male protagonist of the novel. Her role in the 1960 movie was played by Jean Simmons; she has been enacted in theatre and opera and remains one of the most convincing religious histrionics in popular culture.

Reverend Collins: Obsessive-Compulsive Religiosity

The colossally antipathic Reverend Collins from Jane Austen's *Pride and Prejudice* (1813) is probably the best known of all the characters in this collection. The ampleness of his absurdity serves as one of the major elements of humor in the novel and he is, "for all the wrong reasons, one of the most memorable men in fiction."[90] There have been many diverse screen renditions of him, but his repellent nature breaks through in all of them based on the way he sees the world and the way his personality functions. Austen minutely described the grotesqueness of Mr. Collins over two hundred years ago; modern critics call him "an authentic monster,"[91] while a more psychologically informed analysis might reveal that he actually had a personality disorder. We take the risk here of associating his personality structure with the obsessive-compulsive variety.

Mr. Collins is a cleric related to the Bennet family, who has five unmarried daughters. The story is generally well-known, so suffice it to say that after Mr. Bennet passes away, Mr. Collins is to inherit the Longbourne estate where the family lives. The cleric has arrived to meet the Bennets for the first time. Both the readers of the novel and the Bennet family themselves are first introduced to Mr. Collins by means of a letter he writes to inform them of his visit. From this first written note (several more are to follow throughout the novel), it is obvious that the person behind it is strange, but the full scope of his strangeness is only to be discovered gradually. "Mr. Collins is at his dreadful best when it comes to his correspondence,"[92] but it takes more than just his letters to observe the overall extent of his dreadfulness. Let us pinpoint his unattractiveness in a more precise way and try to link it with the aforementioned personality disorder.

An obsessive-compulsive personality structure basically refers to people who are overly proper but cold, selfish, petty, meticulous, perfectionistic, inflexible, calculating, parsimonious, and stubborn. Lacking any charm or charisma, such people leave an impression of tediousness and exasperation, and if ever there was a literary character fitting the obsessive-compulsive personality structure, it is Mr. Collins. Despite the fact that he was created almost a century and a half before the first studies on personality disorders, and despite the fact that he does not meet every single criterion of the contemporary diagnosis of this illness, Mr. Collins does epitomize the obsessive-compulsive type of personality, as will be seen in the subsequent paragraphs.

One of the first impressions we get of Mr. Collins based on his written communication is that he is an exceptionally tedious human being. When we meet him, this impression only gets reinforced to such extreme extent that it becomes comical, and never leaves us until the end of the novel. It would be strange to include tediousness as a criterion for a personality disorder, but some authors do outright call people with obsessive-compulsive personality disorder "boring,"[93] mostly due to "their nonsuggestible and unimaginative style"[94] and "the deadly effect of literalism."[95] The style Mr. Collins employs in his letters and speeches is formal, detached, convoluted, lacking in emotion and substance, or put by Austen herself – full of "pompous nothings."[96] After reading the first letter, Elizabeth Bennet immediately commented that "he must be an oddity,"[97] which afterward turns out to be more than true. His "monotonous solemnity,"[98] bad dancing skills, endless thankfulness, and hairsplitting attitudes made everyone not only stop listening to him, but physically leave his company. Even his wife, Lizzy's friend Charlotte, arranged her schedule so as to spend as little time with him as possible, since "when Mr. Collins could be forgotten, there was really an air of great comfort throughout."[99]

Besides the immense boredom Mr. Collins provoked, he is guilty of another trait that is a criterion for obsessive-compulsive personality disorder – "rigidity and stubbornness."[100] These qualities are a general trademark of all disordered structures, but with the obsessive-compulsives, they are highly pronounced. Mr. Collins arrived to the Bennet household with only one purpose in mind – to find a wife. That was the aim he was stubbornly pursuing, which not even blunt rejections or unfavorable circumstances could derail. First he was interested in Jane Bennet, but when he learned that she was unavailable, "Mr. Collins had only to change from Jane to Elizabeth."[101] Proposing to Elizabeth is probably the most comical and the most exasperating scene in the whole novel – fully unaware of the way she sees him, he goes on naming all the wrong reasons for her to marry him. Her kind but very clear refusals, however, do not discourage him. Instead of taking in the sincerity of her words, he is convinced "that it is usual with young ladies to reject the addresses of the man whom they secretly mean to accept, when he first applies for their favour; and that sometimes the refusal is repeated a second, or even a third time. I am therefore by no means discouraged by what you have just said, and shall hope to lead you to the altar ere long."[102] Devoid of essential sincerity in his own life he fails to see it in others, too. He displays a kind of rigidity that Meissner described as "a tendency to adhere stubbornly to a particular line of thought, an inclination to be dogmatic, and a general oppositional quality of interaction."[103] When he finally does learn that Lizzy means what she says, he rationalizes that she would not make a good cleric's wife after all and proposes to her best friend Charlotte, who, alas, accepts. He made "two offers of marriage within three days,"[104] showing no embarrassment over the shiftiness of his arrangements, and, in the end, after the rejection by Lizzy, does not even shorten his visit with the Bennets. Only a highly insensitive mind, with "such perseverance in willful self-deception"[105] could have behaved in such a rigidly preconceived manner. There are numerous other instances where Mr. Collins shows his inflexibility and stubbornness, but his proposal to Lizzy is an unprecedented and iconic moment in all of English literature.

Such an important milestone as finding a life partner, where one expects emotions to play the crucial part, was in Collins's case utterly devoid of emotions. He does not even take them into the faintest consideration. Like with all people with a personality disorder, his emotional world is frighteningly barren. Probably growing up without much affection, his cognition recognizes feelings as "dangerous. After all, feelings cannot always be controlled,"[106] and his urge for control is paramount. Millon calls this emotional impoverishment an "isolation of affect. By stripping the emotions from ideas, the compulsive creates a mental working environment sterilized against the disorganizing influence of uncomfortable affects, while an awareness of the intellectual aspects of the ideas remains."[107]

In the obsessive-compulsive inner life, there is no room for spontaneity; everything is premeditated, calculated, secured, and deliberate. "They can tolerate little interference from others, or even from themselves, when it arises in the form of impulses that somehow escape willful control."[108] Part of this is also their propensity for punctuality. Mr. Collins is rigidly punctual, and even when altered circumstances ask for a change of plan, he never veers from his deeply entrenched course. In the age of letters and carriages, he informed the Bennets that he would arrive on "Monday, November 18th, by four o'clock, and shall probably trespass on your hospitality till the Saturday se'ennight following,"[109] and he did arrive at the exact hour and stay until the said day. As Theodore Millon put it, "efficiency, punctuality, a willingness to work hard, and orientation to detail are valued as necessary prerequisites to social and financial well-being."[110]

The major unattractiveness of obsessive-compulsive personality disorder comes from their tendency to calculate everything and only do things that bring them some kind of gain. As soon as he steps into the Bennet household, Mr. Collins shrewdly examines "the hall, the dining room, and all its furniture,"[111] because he will inherit it all one day and turn the Bennet widow and the girls out "before he [Mr. Bennet] is cold in his grave."[112] Collins knows that, in the mansion of his patroness Lady Catherine de Burgh, "the chimney piece alone had cost eight hundred pounds,"[113] and even though he once remarked "that he considered the money as a mere trifle,"[114] his actual attitude to it was diametrically opposite. Miserliness is one of the DSM criteria of this personality disorder, and it fits neatly into the tendency to calculate. Mr. Collins's compliments are also premeditated and he has a wide range of them ready for use. When Lizzy insightfully asks him whether "these pleasing attentions proceed from the impulse of the moment,"[115] he responds that "they arise chiefly from what is passing at the time, and though I sometimes amuse myself with suggesting and arranging such little elegant compliments as may be adapted to ordinary occasions, I always wish to give them as unstudied an air as possible."[116] This *sprezzatura* attitude only masks previous long laboriousness. One more absurd example of his computation is his announcement in person to Mr. Bennet: "Believe me, my dear sir, my gratitude is warmly excited by such affectionate attention; and depend upon it, you will speedily receive from me a letter of thanks for this, and for every other mark of your regard during my stay in Hertfordshire."[117] This is one of the reasons why the proverbially sarcastic Mr. Bennet intends to keep corresponding with Mr. Collins by the end of the novel and thus keep himself amused.

What comes to the absolute forefront of Mr. Collins's personality throughout the novel is his consistent and sickening condescension to his patroness, Lady Catherine de Burgh. This essentially arrogant and cold aristocratic woman is the overarching framework into whose dictate Mr. Collins places every observation and element of life – from such important choices such as a spouse, to trivialities such as the number of times her carriage has passed by his house. The attitude he takes toward her corresponds to what Len Sperry has to say about the interpersonal style of people with obsessive-compulsive personality disorder: "These individuals are exquisitely conscious of social rank and status and modify their behavior accordingly. That is, they tend to be deferential and obsequious to superiors, and haughty and autocratic to subordinates and peers."[118] Mr. Collins employs every single form of spineless subordination to his patroness, from confirming what she says, to flattery, praise, and glorification. He is overly and causelessly apologetic and frets greatly while visiting Lady Catherine whether his behavior is absolutely proper. Since nothing is left to spontaneity, and since no spontaneity is expected, the obsessive-compulsive propensity to formality is taken to an extreme in this novel.

Mr. Collins is an exaggerated picture of formality, "an excess of good breeding,"[119] or, as Millon puts it, "a caricature of order and propriety."[120] Everything about him is about "details, rules, lists, order, organization, or schedules."[121] There is no warmth in him, even when he is utterly polite. When the Bennets met him for the first time, his "air was grave and stately, and his manners were very formal"[122] and he was, in his own words, "cautious of appearing forward and precipitate."[123] Returning from a dinner once, he "ennumerat[ed] all the dishes at supper."[124] Minutiae, structure, and appearances are the only things that matter to obsessive-compulsives. Austen's was an age of pronounced formality, so besides depicting him as a disordered individual, Mr. Collins could also be understood as her satirical commentary on the current mores.

Beneath the glaze of Mr. Collins's politeness and propriety lurked not only coldness and calculation, but quite a sinister toxicity. This is a general characteristic of personality disorders, and these people are frequently trying to compensate for it using formation reaction or some other psychological defense mechanism. An obsessive-compulsive "overconforms to armor himself against impropriety."[125] However, the "wrongness" about them comes to the surface sooner or later.

What was so toxic about Mr. Collins? First of all, he was very touchy and easily offended when the good opinion he held about himself was in any way slighted, like, for example, when he was asked by the Bennet girls to stop reading a book of sermons aloud because his intonation was unbearably monotonous. His modesty, like everything about him, was false. Still, the full nature of his poisoned heart comes into play in a letter that he wrote to Mr. Bennet, commenting on the scandalous fact of the youngest daughter Lydia running away with an officer and living with him unmarried. His letter starts by consoling Mr. Bennet "on the grievous affliction [...] that no time can remove."[126] Instead in the tone of pastoral compassion, he goes on about the scandal, relishing the Bennets' misfortune as one would a dessert, accusing the parents of being too indulgent with the daughters, asking them who would marry the other girls after this, and constantly affirming between the lines his own moral superiority. "The death of your daughter would have been a blessing in comparison of this."[127] This clergyman concludes the letter with the following advice: "Dear sir, to console yourself as much as possible, to throw off your unworthy child from your affection for ever, and leave her to reap the fruits of her own heinous offense."[128] The righteous indignation characteristic of obsessive-compulsives permeates this address, as well as a thinly veiled delight in others' misfortune. Mr. Collins reacted in a similar way when it was revealed that Lizzy was going to marry Darcy, his patroness's nephew. Instead of congratulating the young couple in a Christian manner, he sends a communication full of poisonous disapproval.

When it comes to religiousness, which is only briefly referred to a few times in the novel, it is obvious that Rev. Collins is all about extrinsic formality and none about essential spirituality. In a veritably obsessive-compulsive manner, he is constantly conscious of his position as a clergyman and the duties that ensue therefrom – "christening, marrying, and burying his parishioners wherever it were required"[129] and "establish[ing] the blessing of peace in all families within the reach of […][his] influence."[130] Whether he managed to do the latter is dubious, since his grasp of reality and relationships was skewed and obscured, and when the Bennets are concerned, he certainly did not bring them any peace at all. His religious involvement is strictly delineated by taboos of formal nature – while on one hand "he never read novels"[131] (the truth is that he did not read even clerical books), on the other, he considered music "a very innocent diversion, and perfectly compatible with the profession of a clergyman."[132] Again, there is no temperamental inclination to things, only outer properness. When he mentions "the dictates of […] [his] conscience," he in fact displays behaviors that come from condescension and calculation, not from any noetic depths, because they are barred to him. At the same time, and due to his clerical position, he does have enough arrogance to consider himself above laity. His spiritual failure shows most openly at the end of the novel, in his letter about Lydia and her husband, where he gives advice to Mr. Bennet: "You ought certainly to forgive them, as a Christian, but never to admit them in your sight, or allow their names to be mentioned in your hearing."[133] Mr. Bennet could not but comment as follows: "That is his notion of Christian forgiveness!"[134] Lydia had broken a rule of propriety, something that to an obsessive-compulsive represents uttermost sacrilege, so she deserves no forgiveness of any kind.

The element that differentiates Mr. Collins from other characters in this analysis is an absence of zeal. However deluded it might have been, there was an abundance of it in Sister Jane or Nathan Price. Whereas they acted out on their madness, he has no recourse to the inner layers of his being at all, and all of his idiosyncrasies are being smothered by the obsessive-compulsive dictates of propriety. Jane Austen was brilliant enough to both ridicule and accurately portray somebody with this personality disorder many long decades before the first psychological discussions on this theme emerged in the modern psychiatric discourse.

Torquemada's Sadistic Religiosity

Even though sadistic personality disorder, similarly to the masochistic one, does not exist as a diagnosis in the *DSM-5*, and was only briefly suggested "as a provisional personality disorder requiring further study"[135] in an appendix to the third revised edition of the *DSM*, we have decided to include it in this book. The reason for this is that the sadistic personalities are "well known to history and contemporary society,"[136] that this is a particularly disturbing phenomenon within the religious context, and that a character synonymous with religious sadism has been described in a book of fiction – that of Thomas de Torquemada. This is why, despite obsolete psychological knowledge, we could not have missed a chance to devote a brief chapter to the world's most notorious inquisitor.

Howard Fast (1914–2003) was an unusually prolific American novelist and television writer best known for the novel *Spartacus* (1951) based on which the epic Hollywood movie was made. In 1966, he published the historical novel *Torquemada* which the reviewers rightfully called "ticky tacky,"[137] and which did not do great at sales either. However, the fact that it contains a graphic description of a religious sadist in action was intriguing enough for the context of this study. It is a fictionalized episode from the life of the Grand Inquisitor of Spain on one hand and of the Spanish knight Alvero on the other. The story takes place immediately after Torquemada's appointment to the position in 1483. "He is known to history primarily for his routine use of ingenuous forms of torture to induce confessions from those accused of various crimes."[138] The way he sets off on his licensed sadistic journey and then indulges his dark inner urges is the subject of the following paragraphs.

Plotwise, the novel unfolds at the very early days of Torquemada's new appointment, his visit to his friend Alvero's house, and a gradually developing suspicion on Torquemada's side that Alvero was guilty of supporting the then persecuted Jews. Coming from European Jewish background himself, one of Fast's purposes in this novel was to paint a picture "of anti-Semitism in the fifteenth-century Spain"[139] and give "a parable about the dangers of fanaticism."[140] Not only that Alvero was accused of protecting the Jews, his mortal sin was also having some Jewish blood in his family line. The irony is that Thomas de Torquemada's own "*converso* ancestry cannot [...] be doubted."[141] Exact ancestors who converted from Judaism to Christianity in his family tree were identified, but this did not hinder the Inquisitor to look for people guilty of the same sin and send them to the stake. Eventually, Alvero starts fearing his friend's growing suspicion, and his fears prove to be well grounded. As a traitor of the Catholic Church and a lover of Jews, Alvero falls into the hands of the Great Inquisition headed by Torquemada. The knight tries to preserve his human decency amid indescribable tortures during which he frequently loses consciousness, but the more ethical one is within a fanatical context such as the Holy Inquisition the more one opposes and irritates the dominant madness. The epilogue could hardly have been anything else but Alvero becoming one more among the numerous victims of one of the darkest religion's chapters in history.

Even before Torquemada becomes the leading Inquisitor, he is depicted as a person whose presence makes others uncomfortable. In one of the opening scenes, he encounters some children playing in the dust in the streets of Segovia. "When they looked up and saw Torquemada, they crossed themselves and fled."[142] It was not only children who cringed in his presence; many adults also felt "immediately uneasy in the presence of Torquemada,"[143] experienced fear and reluctance to be in his company, and usually became "taciturn and withdrawn."[144] To be around people like Torquemada was "a chilling experience, they lack humanity, beneath the opaque surface is a dark unknown sea of danger."[145] This reminds of the classical sociopathic trait that "there is an edgy and uncomfortable meanness to their personality in terms of the way psychopaths talk to other people, the ways that psychopaths treat other people, and they ways that psychopaths objectify other people."[146] Sociopathy, psychopathy, and sadistic personality disorder are different things, but even so Torquemada seems to have shared the psychopathic feature of making others feel tense in his proximity.

His general outlook was of a "stiff, very much self-contained"[147] person who was cold, vain, and proud, kept quiet, "ate sparingly,"[148] and was prone to sudden rages. Expressing emotions was a taboo because they were considered to be weaknesses, and a sadist "views kindness as a weakness,"[149] too. The fact that some children fled before him in fear "touched him and hurt him more than most people would imagine, and though his high-boned face did not change, he winced inwardly."[150]

Before becoming Inquisitor, his grimness was not so overpowering; he had friends, and occasionally "a slight smile play[ed] across his face and [gave] him an unusual charm."[151] Howard Fast notes astutely that the effect "when hard-faced and morose people smiled"[152] was extraordinary, which might be associated with the proverbial psychopathic charm. However, since being appointed to the grand position, Torquemada changed, became more serious and businesslike, "mocking and contemptuous."[153] He noticed the following almost with some melancholy: "I find little enough warmth from those I knew."[154] Convinced that he was doing good, he was perplexed why others did not see it, as if it were the most natural thing in the world to expect the victims to understand and accept their own sacrifice – but more on the theological justification of his cruelty later on in this chapter.

The ascetic façade he was maintaining was just that – a façade. In essence, he did enjoy good wine and was tempted in all other ways, too. Innocently embracing his friend Alvero's young daughter, unholy thoughts invaded his mind while "he felt her warm and pliable form against him."[155] The recognition of such unseemly urges made him see himself as weak and sinful, and "he promised himself that he would do penance for that."[156] Sin was something he obsessed about; he saw it on the faces of people around him. "It seemed to Torquemada that he could look at a man's face and see sin as a splash of purple paint."[157] Sometimes he even had to stifle his thought of sin, "knowing that if he allowed it to enlarge itself and dominate him, it would spoil his entire afternoon."[158] Becoming the leading Inquisitor, it seems that his obsession with sin did take over, and, coupled with a religious pretext, wreaked such infamous havoc as the very mention of the Spanish Inquisition immediately brings to mind.

The name of our hero has been historically synonymous with sadism, so it did not require too much thinking of which disorder Torquemada's personality falls into. The most general sign of sadism is "a pervasive pattern of cruel, demeaning, and aggressive behavior,"[159] which became a trademark of Torquemada's religious involvement. The gesture that epitomizes the beginning of the unleashing of his hitherto-suppressed sadistic drives was a seemingly harmless question he asked of Alvero as soon as he became the Inquisitor: "From where, Alvero? From where did you come?"[160] Alvero became wary, for he sensed that the question implied his potential Jewish background, but also because, when Torquemada asked it, "suddenly those blue eyes of his were cold as ice."[161] Alvero was a little confused and at first wondered why "as soon as he was appointed [...] Torquemada did not falter to provoke even his best friend."[162] He said: "You never asked me that before. Why, Thomas, why never before in twenty-five years?"[163] However, the officially sanctioned license to act out on his sadistic urges was too tempting to spare even his best friend, which testifies to the intensity of Torquemada's taste for cruelty. Soon afterward, Alvero falls into the hands of the Inquisition, where he was just one of many human subjects on which Torquemada and other religious sadists targeted their dark drives.

The very moment of Torquemada's clerical appointment also meant the end of his friendship with Alvero. Typical sadistic elements came into the picture of their reframed relationship, such as "the devolution, punishment, or humiliation,"[164] as well as intimidation. Torquemada wanted Alvero to collaborate in eliminating the local rabbi and burning down the synagogue, as well as to denounce a Dutch–Jewish tradesman who came to Segovia on business. Alvero refused all of this, but to little effect. Both the rabbi and the Dutchman were exterminated by the Inquisition, and the synagogue ended up in flames. Due to his refusal to cooperate, Alvero became the victim too. However, he might have been sacrificed even if he had shown readiness to help, for he figured on Torquemada's horizon and everything that was on it seems to have been doomed to be painfully destroyed, simply for the "sadistic pleasure in the accomplishment of seeing his violence rehearsed."[165] Torquemada even enjoyed his own suffering, so besides being an obvious sadist, there was also a strong masochistic streak in him, manifested occasionally when he would ask other monks to whip his naked back in his monastic cell at night.

What ensued for Alvero were indescribably painful tortures in the Inquisition's premises where screams were heard incessantly. "They pricked his skin with needles and they burned the flesh on his back with a hot iron, but it was enough to distort his time sense, and after that he had no idea nor was he ever truly to recollect how many additional times they took him to torture."[166] Losing his consciousness and coming to again, he could discern his former friend's face hovering above him. In a perversely intimate manner, they conversed at times, the topic of their conversation dancing obliquely around Torquemada's sadism.

Alvero asked: "Why? Why, Thomas? Why are you doing this to me? What devil drives you?"[167] He called the things by their proper names, just like when he said that Torquemada's witch hunt was "madness," or when he uttered: "What shall I tell you about pain, Thomas, my Father?"[168] Everything revolved around Torquemada's pleasure in the suffering of others, even though the Inquisitor's heavy defensiveness prevented him from facing the facts, so he asked in disbelief: "God in heaven, what do you think, Alvero? Do I love suffering? Am I a monster who feeds on death and misery?"[169] However, when Alvero started pleading for mercy, Torquemada's compulsive love of cruelty finally displayed itself in its fullness, since he said: "I cannot change it or stop it, Alvero. You know that. Don't think of what I would do or what I would not do."[170] This ultimate confession reveals the full scope of Torquemada's sadistic nature.

The general religious aura surrounding Torquemada was that of "the puritanical preacher, whose hellfire sermons are deliberately designed to force the flock onto the straight and narrow."[171] He was "a firm and angry servant of God,"[172] seemingly humble before his master, but in essence "enlarged and gratified."[173] The fact that the Inquisition partook "less of holiness than of greed"[174] did not bother him, nor did he find a mismatch between the faces of the victims submitted to torture and that of the "Crist on the cross which hung upon one wall of the torture room."[175] His attitude toward Jews and heretics reveals extreme religious intolerance, and when he explains how to tell which Christians are Jews at heart, he lists only the spiritually irrelevant, extrinsic elements such as the celebration of Sabbath, wearing clean garments, or lighting no fire on that day. For him, these are reasons enough "to call the fire of wrath"[176] upon them. All this shows that, despite utter dedication to the Church, Torquemada's faith was not just faulty, but diametrically opposite to what it should have been. The sad fact is that people with such dangerous religious convictions are sometimes embraced by religious institutions and appointed to high positions within them.

Just like anyone with a personality disorder, sadists also base their general functioning on defense mechanisms. The particular mechanisms characteristic of the sadistic personality disorder are "isolation, projection, rationalization, and displacement."[177] In case when a person with this type of disorder is religious, it usually happens that in their distorted world, religion becomes only a cog in the overall defensive machinery. This applies to Torquemada, too, whose bigoted and narrow-minded religious convictions do not have anything to do with what being religious in a mature way means. All of the aforementioned defense mechanisms are evident in his twisted clerical engagements.

In order to torture his best friend and send him to the stake, Torquemada had to separate any friendly feelings he might have had toward him from the conviction that Alvero was sinful and deserving of earthly punishment. "You spoke of friendship before, Alvero. I will open my arms and my heart but shall I weaken my faith for you?"[178] Thus, in isolating humanness from alleged religiosity, Torquemada in fact shows that the essence of religion, i.e. the spirit of the golden rule, is completely alien to him. In other instances, the principles of projection are more than obvious, like when he calls a rabbi "the devil's handyman,"[179] when he accuses Alvero of being a Jew, or when he preaches that the mortal body consists only of "filth, dirt and sin."[180]

However, the most powerful defensive pattern that Torquemada subjugated religion to is that of rationalization. In fact, it seems that his religion was nothing but one huge rationalization for his sinister urges. The starting point of his theology was the notion that the body is sinful and that the soul is pure, and that in order to purify the soul, the sinful body should be burnt away, which is an ultimate "act of faith."[181] So, instead of seeing his witch hunt for what it was, he rationalized that despite the fact that these people suffer at the hands of the Holy Inquisition, at least "their souls live naked and clean."[182] Not cringing from the most gruesome acts of torture and murder on the one hand, he was allegedly "horrified at the thought of a soul imperiled"[183] on the other. In a similar vein, he philosophized that "a man's life is a moment,"[184] using this trite piece of wisdom only to substantiate his notion of the relative unimportance of earthly life, particularly for those who fall into the Inquisition's grip. Finally, the platform at which the convicted sinners were burned was called "the pedestal of faith."[185] It is amazing how history has at times turned religion into its very demonic opposite.

Another crucial element in this epic scaffolding of religious rationalizations was the conviction that "the Inquisition is God's arm."[186] Torquemada and other inquisitors pretended that they were doing God's job, and managed to convince the wider society that that was the case. Confusing sadistic exultation for religious rapture at "purging souls," Torquemada "felt alive and excited – close to God – closer to God than he had ever been before."[187]

To be certain of whom God is and what He wants has been detrimental so many times in human history. Torquemada's position was that it wasn't he who was performing those atrocious acts, but rather that he was only obeying higher authority – almost a Stanley Milgram situation. Thus, it was "God's will that the synagogue be burned to the ground."[188] If someone denounced a Jew, "that way, cunningly, you will trap him and clothe your own immortal souls in specific grace."[189] To serve Spain was the same as to serve your soul (in Father Joseph's version, it was France). The Inquisitor did hear people talking that he was a monster, but in his defensive manner, he asked a hypothetical question – "Do monsters serve God?"[190] Also, when people expressed fear before him, he again used the same kind of logic and commented that "they don't fear me. They fear God, and in me they fear only what is God's purpose."[191]

One of the things that Howard Fast's novel *Torquemada* reminds us of is that "the letter killeth, but the spirit giveth life,"[192] and even if this has not been a novel idea, the humankind seems to keep forgetting it over and over again. Substantiated by the mere letter, even extreme sadists such as Torquemada may find religious grounding for their devilish missions, throwing the spirit completely out of the window.

Margaret White: The Exaggerated Borderline Fanatic

The final in the line of characters included in this study is Margaret White, the cruel mother of the teenage girl Carrie from Stephen King's eponymous 1974 debut novel. The novel and the film versions of it have become an unavoidable part of popular American culture, and even though the book was published more than four decades ago, "after all these years [it] still holds its own as a riveting story in its own."[193] It is a Cinderella-like tale of a religiously fundamentalist mother who suffocates her daughter with extremist restrictions of freedom and sexuality. The girl's response to these fetters is the budding awakening of her telekinetic powers. Proportionate to her mother's fundamentalist sadism is the cataclysmic havoc that Carrie wreaks in the final scenes of the book. The symbolism of her parapsychological might has been the focus of many analyses, but what interests us here is the nature of her mother's religiosity.

Margaret White is the least believable of all the literary characters discussed so far. In fact, she might be taken more as a wildly exaggerated metaphor of religious fanaticism than as a human being. Presented in a psychologically chunky way with no nuances, as frequently is the case in horror fiction, the attempt to analyze her personality structure seems a little redundant. Still, the popularity of this story, the thematic fit into our study, and the distant possibility to talk about a specific personality disorder related to Margaret White were sufficient factors to take her character into account here. Besides, perhaps it makes sense to conclude this gallery of portraits on such a roaring note. But also despite the wildness of the story, "in *Carrie*, as in most of King's work, fictional horror and the supernatural are indeed the lies that tell the truth."[194] Notwithstanding the fact that this is a horror novel, it still "deals with the familiar milieu of cruel parents, a faceless high school, and painful rituals of conformity."[195]

Based on what King gives us in the novel, on the one hand it is possible to outline the major events of Margaret White's life, but on the other, there is no sufficient substance for genuine psychological insight – so we will go with what we have. First of all, Margaret's grandmother had telekinetic powers. "She had been able to light the fireplace without even stirring from her rocker by the window."[196] However, not much is said about her, or about Margaret's parents for that matter, other than that they were quite well-to-do, and "owned a prosperous night spot [...] called The Jolly Roadhouse."[197] The father was shot in a bar accident in 1959, when Margaret was almost thirty. She continued to live with her mother and "began attending fundamentalist prayer meetings."[198] When the mother found a new partner, Margaret accused her of adultery and living in sin, but refused to leave the parental home. She left only when she met her own partner, Ralph White, at a revival meeting and eventually got married.

Ralph is a figure even hazier than she, but a fundamentalist match to Margaret. "He always looked mean. And you didn't meet his eyes, not ever."[199] He was a construction worker and always carried two things to work – the Bible and a gun. "The Bible was for his coffee break and lunch. The .38 was in case he met Antichrist on the job."[200] They lived "without sin" most of the time, apart from one time (or maybe a few more) when they did have intercourse. The result was the birth of their baby Carrie in 1963, but Ralph had died seven months earlier at a work accident. Margaret gave birth to the child alone at home and basically hated the girl from the very first day. She had thought that her pregnancy had been a stomach cancer, but when she realized that it was a reminder of her sin, she had a knife ready to kill the baby. The knife as a leitmotif to kill her own child reappears several times in the novel, until the very end.

At the time when the major events of the novel took place, Carrie was almost seventeen and Margaret worked in a laundry. She "was a very big woman, and she always wore a hat. Lately her legs had begun to swell, and her feet always seemed on the point of overflowing her shoes. [...] Her eyes were blue and magnified behind rimmed bifocals."[201] The head had once been beautiful, and perhaps still was "in a weird, zealous way."[202] In the novel, her life ends on the night of the prom disaster – first, she tries to kill Carrie with a knife, but then Carrie uses her telekinetic powers to stop her mother's heart. In the movie, though, Carrie crucifies her "with kitchen utensils in a prolonged death throe that is a comically grotesque mixture of agony and sexual ecstasy."[203] In any case, the biographical facts are there, but subtler insights into developmental processes are sorely missing.

What permeates the book is an oversaturated picture of both religious fanaticism and fundamentalism, and Margaret White is its center stage symbol. She has been described by critics as a "raving psychoreligious, psychosexual lunatic,"[204] and by Stephen King himself as one of the "religious nuts"[205] plagued by "religious mania."[206] Without a shred of warmth, compassion, or philosophy, she treads on obsessed by sin and pictures of an angry God of punishment and dread. Let us take a quick look into the world of her religious ideation.

Margaret White's religion has no denomination. She has her own altar and chapel at home, and she herself conducts all services sometimes lasting up to three hours, with Carrie being her only congregation member. She and Ralph "had been Baptists once but had left the church when they became convinced that the Baptists were doing the work of the Antichrist."[207] One critic pinpointed her religion as "a fanatical blend of evangelical Protestantism (her literal reliance on scripture and belief that every woman and all forms of sexual expression are inherently sinful) and Catholicism (the cathedral-like environment she constructs in her home),"[208] but the bottom line is that she dissented from all known branches of Christianity and adhered to her own version of things.

Anything pleasant was sinful in Margaret's mind. Her paramount obsession was sexuality. It was not only that any form of sexual expression was a deadly sin in her eyes; "even simply having the body parts is enough to condemn a young girl to hell forever."[209] She is angry at Carrie when the girl has her first period and forces her to "pray to Jesus for our woman-weak, wicked, sinful souls."[210] Besides this, the Christian youth camps where Carrie wanted to go were in, Margaret's mind, "Sin and Backsliding"[211] since they were run by "Methodists and Baptists and Congregationalists."[212] The rigidity and obsessiveness characteristic of religious fundamentalism are at their extreme here.

Since even accepted religions figure as sinful in Margaret's mind, it is only too easy to guess what she thinks of the secular world. The laundry she worked at "was Godless,"[213] and "Satan had reserved a special blue corner of Hell"[214] for her boss. Satan is also in rock and roll music, in parking lots, and especially in roadhouses, which she mentions multiple times. Anyone who advocates Darwin's theory of evolution is a Devil. Even people who smoke cigarettes fall in that same category. However, it seems that she saw Satan most epitomized in Carrie and her powers. In her mad, projective logics, she equates the killing of her child with the salvation of the world from evil. "Thou shalt not suffer a witch to live."[215] Even in more moderate cases of personality disorder, people find it difficult to see their real selves. In this literary example, it could not have been expected of Margaret White to realize that it was she who was the witch.

As opposed to the Devil, what did then God look like in her religious understanding? Again, never once associated with love, forgiveness, acceptance, or tolerance, but a God of wrath, exorcising demons with his avenging terror. "If thine right eye offend thee, pluck it out."[216] She has extracted such a picture of the religious realm that aligns with her mental climate and abounds in angels with swords, scorpions, crushing boulders, Jesus's wounds, drowning sinners, and the burning of Sodom and Gomorrah. Her prayers were eerie, her Yahweh angry, her Christ "a terrible Jesus of blood and righteousness."[217]

All the elements of religious immaturity mentioned in the introductory chapters of this book seem to have been grossly embodied in the literary character of Margaret White.

The reiteration of the notion that there is no sufficient psychological substratum in the novel means no disrespect of the book. The story is captivating on many different levels, despite the fact that this psychological roundedness is missing. Still, we will attempt to give a sketch of Margaret White's psychological life, based on the scanty information from the book itself and partly also based on our own imaginative effort.

One fact is clear – Mrs. White was "a fanatic, a freak, but at least she was predictable."[218] This suggests that she had created a tightly controlled world, within which she was isolated but functional, which is a characteristic of people with personality disorders, rather than those with schizophrenia, major depression, or other mental illnesses. Besides this, she had an extremely rigid mind and imposed her worldviews with utmost intensity, which again features in people with personality disorders. If we accept the possibility that she had a severe personality disorder, the next step would be an attempt to classify it. The major features of her behavior were abhorrence of sexuality, paranoia, sadism, self-harm, sudden rages, and obsessiveness. Of all the variants described in literature, Margaret White seems to be in some way closest to borderline personality disorder (BPD), perhaps also because "borderline pattern overlaps nearly every other personality disorder."[219] Generally, people diagnosed with it tend to have "unstable relationships and emotional reactions. Everything about them seems frantic, chaotic, and impulsive."[220] As deep as it can go, this literary character matches several criteria for this disorder, as is shown next.

Out of the nine DSM criteria for this disorder, Margaret clearly does not meet some, such as impulsivity in spending, sex, reckless driving, suicidal behavior, and the like. However, there are quite a few that she does meet. The most obvious are her short temper and raging moods, or, as psychological literature puts it, "emotional dysregulation (angry outbursts, emotional instability)."[221] The intensity of her rage has more than once been described with the picture of her nostrils, which "flared like those of a horse that has heard the dry rattle of a snake."[222] (The trigger for this extreme anger was merely Carrie's statement that she was going to go to the prom.) Another time, when Carrie was only three and saw the next door neighbor in a bathing suit, Margaret went ballistic. "She just whooped. Rage. Complete, insane rage. Her face went just as red as the side of a fire truck and she curled her hands into fists and whooped at the sky. She was shaking all over. I thought she was having a stroke. Her face was all scrunched up, and it was a gargoyle's face."[223] This quote overdoes it and corroborates the statement that King's characters here are not believable but, at the same time, emphasizes a trait that might be taken as a symptom of borderline personality disorder.

Margaret White is prone to another borderline trait – self-harming. It "refers to harm inflicted upon the body, usually as a means of relieving emotional distress, and can take many forms."[224] Some studies show that "54 percent of women with BPD reported engaging in deliberate self-harm."[225] When she realized that she was unable to have it her own way, Margaret "bayed at the sky. And then started to ... to hurt herself, scourge herself. She was clawing at her neck and cheeks, making red marks and scratches. She tore her dress."[226] On another, more extreme occasion, she "hooked her right hand into claws and ripped it across her own cheek, bringing thin blood. [...] She made her right hand into a fist and struck herself in the moth, bringing blood."[227] As grotesque as it sounds, this still represents behavior characteristic of many diagnosed with BPD.

Being paranoid is another trait that features in this disorder, and our character has paranoid ideation, too. She was convinced that "all politicians were crooks and sinners and would eventually give the country over to the Godless Reds who would put all the believers of Jesus – even the Catholics – up against the wall."[228]

Not exclusive to borderlines, but present in personality disorders in general, are sadistic and obsessional behaviors, and Margaret engages in both. She is sadistic first of all in her relationship with her daughter, because she does not actually have any other relationships in her life. Carrie is often punished by being mercilessly shut in a small closet behind the altar where she would be kept for hours, sometimes even for over a day. Once Margaret threw a cup of tea in Carrie's face, and more than once she reached for her husband's knife to deal with the devil in her daughter. While hurting Carrie in different ways on one hand, on the other she encouraged her "symbiotic clinging"[229] and raged at any stir toward autonomy, although it is a normal developmental achievement. The persistent abuse of the girl resulted in a far-reaching catastrophe, which may be taken as almost a Shakespearean symbol of the pathology of home life and the disastrousness of its consequences.

Where obsessions are concerned, it has already been noted that Margaret White was for some reason traumatized by sexuality and mere bodily functions. In her mind, these were horrible sins. "She never hung any undies on the back line. Not even Carrie's, and she was only three back then. Always in the house."[230] Making love meant to be terribly bad. She called breasts "dirtypillows," thought that being naked was evil, that women who wore swimming suits in public were "sluts and strumpets,"[231] and that boys chasing girls were like dogs sniffing at a blood trail, "grinning and slobbering, trying to find out what that smell is."[232] It is not quite clear where this abhorrence of anything sexual came from, particularly since she had not had a puritanical background. Furthermore, her rejection of sexuality seems to be in line with the borderline proneness to splitting: "Good and bad images of objects are actively separated."[233] In Margaret White's twisted world, there was nothing good in sexuality. To make the matters slightly more perverse, her terrible confession to Carrie about how she conceived with Ralph included the highlight that she enjoyed doing it – an unforgiveable sin that has been repaid by having a child with demonic powers.

In the context of borderline personality disorder, Theodore Millon states that people diagnosed with it "fail to acquire inner resources from which they can draw sustenance,"[234] which is so true of Margaret White, and which is so true of personality disorders in general. When looking at these people from a spiritual perspective, in case they decide to be religious, it seems that they use religion only as a crutch for their inner disabilities, without any understanding of its subtle, genuine nature. Having no recourse to the noetic levels of their being, or to their "inner sources" as Millon puts it, makes them sadly disabled for the real richness and beauty of life. When they are not affecting others, we may feel sorry for the emptiness that they are generally filled with. But when others are victims of their personal misfortune, as is often the case, especially when everything is done with a religious pretext, then not only do we not feel sorry for them, but we remain amazed and shocked by their abuse of and disservice to religion.

Notes

1 Angus Wilson, *Aldous Huxley – The Critical Heritage*, p. 384.
2 *Ibid.*, p. 385.
3 George Woodcock, *The Dawn and the Darkest Hour*, London: Faber and Faber, 1972, p. 245.
4 Lilly Zähner, *op. cit.*, p. 119.
5 *The Letters of Aldous Huxley*, p. 480.
6 Aldous Huxley, *The Devils of Loudun*, New York: Harper & Brothers, 1953, p. 96.
7 *Ibid.*, p. 97.
8 *Ibid.*
9 *Ibid.*, p. 279.
10 *Ibid.*, p. 96.
11 *Ibid.*, p. 104.

12 *Ibid.*, p. 96.
13 *Ibid.*
14 *Ibid.*
15 *Ibid.*, p. 97.
16 *Ibid.*
17 *Ibid.*, p. 114.
18 *Ibid.*, p. 102.
19 *Ibid.*, p. 183.
20 *DSM-5*, p. 667.
21 *Ibid.*
22 *Ibid.*
23 *Ibid.*
24 *Ibid.*
25 *Ibid.*
26 *Ibid.*
27 *Ibid.*
28 *Ibid.*, p. 101.
29 *Ibid.*
30 *Ibid.*, 102.
31 *Ibid.*, p. 138.
32 *Ibid.*, p. 230.
33 *Ibid.*, p. 242.
34 *Ibid.*, pp. 272–273.
35 *Ibid.*, pp. 278–279.
36 Sinclair Lewis, *op. cit.*
37 *Ibid.*
38 *Ibid.*
39 *DSM-5*, p. 667.
40 Sinclair Lewis, *op. cit.*
41 *Ibid.*
42 *Ibid.*
43 *Ibid.*
44 *Ibid.*
45 *Ibid.*
46 *Ibid.*
47 *Ibid.*
48 *DSM-5*, p. 667.
49 Sinclair Lewis, *op. cit.*
50 *Ibid.*
51 *Ibid.*
52 *Ibid.*
53 *DSM-5*, p. 667.
54 *Ibid.*
55 Sinclair Lewis, *op. cit.*
56 *Ibid.*
57 *Ibid.*
58 *Ibid.*
59 *Ibid.*
60 *Ibid.*
61 *Ibid.*
62 *Ibid.*
63 *Ibid.*
64 *Ibid.*

65 *Ibid.*
66 *Ibid.*
67 *Ibid.*
68 *Ibid.*
69 *Ibid.*
70 *Ibid.*
71 *Ibid.*
72 *Ibid.*
73 *Ibid.*
74 *Ibid.*
75 *Ibid.*
76 *Ibid.*
77 *Ibid.*
78 *Ibid.*
79 *Ibid.*
80 *Ibid.*
81 *Ibid.*
82 *Ibid.*
83 *Ibid.*
84 *Ibid.*
85 *Ibid.*
86 *Ibid.*
87 *Ibid.*
88 *Ibid.*
89 *Ibid.*
90 Susannah Fullerton, *Celebrating Pride and Prejudice*, Minneapolis, MN: Voyageur Press, 2013, p. 100.
91 Harold Bloom, "Introduction," *Jane Austen's Pride and Prejudice*, ed. Harold Bloom, Philadelphia, PA: Chelsea House, 2004, p. 8.
92 Susannah Fullerton, *op. cit.*, p. 98.
93 "dosadni," Snezana Milenkovic, *op. cit.*, p. 119.
94 Len Sperry, *Handbook of Diagnosis and Treatment of DSM-IV-TR Personality Disorders*, p. 172.
95 Ivor Morris, *Mr Collins Considered*, London and New York: Routledge and Kegan Paul, 1987, p. 142.
96 Jane Austen, *Pride and Prejudice*, London: Penguin, 1994, p. 58.
97 *Ibid.*, p. 52.
98 *Ibid.*, p. 56.
99 *Ibid.*, p. 123.
100 *DSM-5*, p. 679.
101 Jane Austen, *op. cit.*, p. 58.
102 *Ibid.*, p. 86.
103 William W. Meissner, "The Phenomenology of Religious Psychopathology," *Bulletin of the Menninger Clinic*, Vol. 55, p. 287.
104 Jane Austen, *op. cit., p.* 101.
105 *Ibid.*, p. 88.
106 Lorna Smith Benjamin, *op. cit.*, p. 246.
107 Theodore Millon, *op. cit.*, p. 26.
108 William W. Meissner, *op. cit.*, p. 287.
109 Jane Austen, *op. cit.*, p. 52.
110 Theodore Millon, *op. cit.*, p. 227.
111 Jane Austen, *op. cit.*, p. 53.
112 *Ibid.*, p. 220.

113 *Ibid.*, p. 61.
114 *Ibid.*, p. 67.
115 *Ibid.*, p. 55.
116 *Ibid.*
117 *Ibid.*, pp. 99–100.
118 Len Sperry, *Handbook of Diagnosis and Treatment of DSM-IV-TR Personality Disorders*, p. 171.
119 Jane Austen, *op. cit.*, p. 60.
120 Theodore Millon, *op. cit.*, p. 249.
121 *DSM-5*, p. 678.
122 Jane Austen, *op. cit.*, p. 53.
123 *Ibid.*
124 *Ibid.*, p. 68.
125 Theodore Millon, *op. cit.*, p. 226.
126 Jane Austen, *op. cit.*, p. 227.
127 *Ibid.*
128 *Ibid.*
129 *Ibid.*, p. 52.
130 *Ibid.*, p. 51.
131 *Ibid.*, p. 56.
132 *Ibid.*, p. 82.
133 *Ibid.*, p. 280.
134 *Ibid.*
135 Theodore Millon, *op. cit.*, p. 530.
136 *Ibid.*
137 Gerald Sorin, *Howard Fast, Life and Literature in the Left Lane*, Bloomington: Indiana University Press, 2012, p. 339.
138 William Lowell Putnam, *Torquemada Revisited: The Power of Effective Persuasion on Intellectual Freedom and Racism*, Flagstaff: Light Technology Publishing, 2006, e-book.
139 Gerald Sorin, *op. cit.*, p. 339.
140 *Ibid.*
141 Henry Karmen, *Inquisition and Society in Spain in the Sixteenth and Seventeenth Centuries*, Bloomington: Indiana University Press, 1985, p. 19.
142 Howard Fast, *Torquemada*, Open Road Media, 2011, Kindle edition, e-book.
143 *Ibid.*
144 *Ibid.*
145 *Ibid.*
146 Matt Delisi, *Psychopathy as Unified Theory of Crime*, New York: Palgrave Macmillan, 2016, p. 228.
147 Howard Fast, *op. cit.*
148 *Ibid.*
149 Theodore Millon, *op. cit.*, p. 532.
150 Howard Fast, *op. cit.*
151 *Ibid.*
152 *Ibid.*
153 Lynn S. Chancer, *Sadomasochism in Everyday Life: The Dynamics of Power and Powerlessness*, New Brunswick, NJ: Rutgers University Press, 1992, p. 49.
154 Howard Fast, *op. cit.*
155 *Ibid.*
156 *Ibid.*

157 *Ibid.*
158 *Ibid.*
159 Theodore Millon, *op. cit.*, quoted from the *Diagnostic and Statistical Manual of Mental Disorders*, Third Edition Revised, American Psychiatric Association, 1987, p. 531.
160 Howard Fast, *op. cit.*
161 *Ibid.*
162 *Ibid.*
163 *Ibid.*
164 Henry Kellerman, *Dictionary of Psychopathology*, New York: Columbia University Press, 2009, p. 221.
165 Claire Raymond, *Witnessing Sadism in the Texts of the American South*, Farnham: Ashgate, 2014, p. 29.
166 Howard Fast, *op. cit.*
167 *Ibid.*
168 *Ibid.*
169 *Ibid.*
170 *Ibid.*
171 Theodore Millon, *op. cit.*, p. 532.
172 Howard Fast, *op. cit.*
173 *Ibid.*
174 *Ibid.*
175 *Ibid.*
176 *Ibid.*
177 Theodore Millon, *op. cit.*, p. 535.
178 Howard Fast, *op. cit.*
179 *Ibid.*
180 *Ibid.*
181 *Ibid.*
182 *Ibid.*
183 *Ibid.*
184 *Ibid.*
185 *Ibid.*
186 *Ibid.*
187 *Ibid.*
188 *Ibid.*
189 *Ibid.*
190 *Ibid.*
191 *Ibid.*
192 2 Corinthians 3:6.
193 George Beahm, *Stephen King from A to Z*, Kansas City: Andrews McMeal Publishing, 1998, p. 29.
194 James Arthur Anderson, *The Linguistics of Stephen King*, Jefferson, NC: McFarland & Company, 2017, p. 18.
195 Garry Hoppenstand and Ray B. Browne, *The Gothic World of Stephen King: Landscape of Nightmares*, Bowling Green, OH: Bowling Green State University Popular Press, 1987, p. 51.
196 Stephen King, *Carrie*, London: Hodder & Stoughton, 2007, Kindle edition, e-book.
197 *Ibid.*
198 *Ibid.*
199 *Ibid.*
200 *Ibid.*

201 *Ibid.*
202 *Ibid.*
203 Toni Magistrale, *Hollywood's Stephen King*, New York: Palgrave MacMillan, 2003, p. 24.
204 Louis H. Gresh and Robert Weinberg, *The Science Of Stephen King*, Hoboken, NJ: John Wiley & Sons, 2007, p. 7.
205 Stephen King, *op. cit.*
206 *Ibid.*
207 *Ibid.*
208 Toni Magistrale, *op. cit.*, p. 24.
209 Louis Gresh, *op. cit.*, p. 8.
210 Stephen King, *op. cit.*
211 *Ibid.*
212 *Ibid.*
213 *Ibid.*
214 *Ibid.*
215 *Ibid.*
216 *Ibid.*
217 *Ibid.*
218 *Ibid.*
219 Theodore Millon, *op. cit.*, p. 483.
220 *Ibid.*, p. 516.
221 Valerie Porr, *Overcoming Borderline Personality Disorder*, Oxford: Oxford University Press, 2010, p. 8.
222 Stephen King, *op. cit.*
223 *Ibid.*
224 Anthony W. Bateman and Roy Krawitz, *Borderline Personality Disorder*, Oxford: Oxford University Press, 2013, p. 10.
225 Alexander L. Chapman and Kim L. Gratz, *The Borderline Personality Disorder Survival Guide*, Oakland, CA: RHYW, 2007, p. 137.
226 Stephen King, *op. cit.*
227 *Ibid.*
228 *Ibid.*
229 Theodore Millon, *op. cit.*, p. 494.
230 Stephen King, *op. cit.*
231 *Ibid.*
232 *Ibid.*
233 Theodore Millon, *op. cit.*, p. 492.
234 *Ibid.*, p. 506.

Bibliography

Psychology and Psychological Biography

Allport, Gordon, *Pattern and Growth in Personality*, New York: Holt, Rinehart and Wilson, 1961.

Bateman, Anthony W. and Roy Krawitz, *Borderline Personality Disorder*, Oxford: Oxford University Press, 2013.

Baumeister, Ray F., *Masochism and the Self*, New York and London: Psychology Press, 1989.

Benjamin, Lorna Smith, *Interpersonal Diagnosis and Treatment of Personality Disorders*, New York: The Guilford Press, 1996.

Butcher, James, Jill M. Hooley and Susan M. Mineka, *Abnormal Psychology*, Boston, MA: Pearson, 2004.

Chancer, Lynn S., *Sadomasochism in Everyday Life: The Dynamics of Power and Powerlessness*, New Brunswick, NJ: Rutgers University Press, 1992.

Chapman, Alexander L. and Kim L. Gratz, *The Borderline Personality Disorder Survival Guide*, Oakland, CA: RHYW, 2007.

Cleckley, Harvey, *The Mask of Sanity*, Augusta, GA: Emily Cleckley, private printing, 1988.

Colapinto, John, *As Nature Made Him: The Boy Who Was Raised as a Girl*, New York: HarperCollins, 2013.

Delisi, Matt, *Psychopathy as Unified Theory of Crime*, New York: Palgrave Macmillan, 2016.

De Mello, Anthony, *Awareness*, https://archive.org/stream/Awareness-AnthonyDeMello/Awareness-AnthonyDeMello_djvu.txt, e-text, accessed at 9 January 2017.

Diagnostic and Statistical Manual of Mental Disorders DSM-5, Washington, DC and London: American Psychiatric Publishing, 2013.

Dully, Howard and Charles Fleming, *My Lobotomy*, New York: Three Rivers Press, 2008.

Dutton, Kevin, *The Wisdom of Psychopaths*, New York: Scientific American/Farrar, Strauss and Giroux, 2012.

Erikson, Erik, *Identity and the Life Cycle*, New York: W. W. Norton & Company, 1994.

Frankl, Viktor, *Man's Search for Meaning*, New York: Pocket Books, 1985.

Frankl, Viktor, *Man's Search for Ultimate Meaning*, New York: Basic Books, 2000.

Frankl, Viktor, *On the Theory and Therapy of Mental Disorders*, tr. James M. Dubois, New York: Brunner-Routledge, 2005.

Frankl, Viktor, *Psychotherapy and Existentialism*, New York: Washington Square Press, 1967.

Frankl, Viktor, *The Doctor and the Soul*, New York: Vintage Books, 1973.

Frankl, Viktor, *The Unheard Cry for Meaning*, New York: Touchstone, 1979.

Frankl, Viktor, *The Will to Meaning*, New York: A Meridian Book, 1988.

Freud, Sigmund, "On Narcissism: An Introduction," *General Psychological Theory: Papers on Metapsychology*, ed. Philip Rieff, New York: A Touchstone Book, 2008.

Freud, Sigmund, *The Future of an Illusion*, tr. and ed. James Starchey, New York: W. W. Norton, 1961.

Fromm, Erich, *Man for Himself: An Inquiry into the Psychology of Ethics*, New York: Rinehart & Co, 1947.

Graber, V. Ann, *Viktor Frankl's Logotherapy*, Lima, OH: Wyndham Hall Press, 2010.

Holtzman, Deanna, and Nancy Kulish, "Introduction: The Suffering of Sisyphus," *The Clinical Problem of Masochism*, eds. Deanna Holtzman and Nancy Kulish, Lanham, MD: Jason Aronson, 2012, pp. 1–14.

Horney, Karen, *Neurosis and Human Growth*, New York: W. W. Norton & Company, 1950.

Horney, Karen, *Our Inner Conflicts*, Abingdon: Routledge, 2001.

Kagan, Jerome, *The Human Spark: The Science of Human Development*, New York: Basic Books, 2013.

Kellerman, Henry, *Dictionary of Psychopathology*, New York: Columbia University Press, 2009.

Kübler-Ross, Elizabeth, *On Children and Death*, New York: Touchstone, 1997.

Lewis, Michael, *The Rise of Consciousness and the Development of Emotional Life*, New York, London: The Guilford Press, 2014.

Lowen, Alexander, *Narcissism: Denial of the True Self*, New York: Touchstone, 2004.

Maslow, Abraham, *O zivotnim vrednostima*, tr. Aleksandar Dimitrijevic, Belgrade: Zarko Albulj, 2001.

May, Rollo, *Psihologija i ljudska dvojba*, tr. Anita Sujoldzic, Zagreb: Naprijed, 1980.

Millon, Theodore, *Personality Disorders in Modern Life*, Hoboken, NJ: Wiley, 2004.

Porr, Valerie, *Overcoming Borderline Personality Disorder*, Oxford: Oxford University Press, 2010.

Sacks, Oliver, *The Man Who Mistook His Wife for a Hat*, New York: Harper & Row, 1987.

Seefeldt, Carol, and Barbara A. Wasik, *Early Education*, Upper Saddle River, NJ: Pearson/Merrill/Prentice Hall, 2006.

Solomon, Andrew, *The Noonday Demon*, New York: Scribner, 2001.

Sperry, Len, *Handbook of Diagnosis and Treatment of DSM-IV-TR Personality Disorders*, New York: Brunner-Routledge, 2005.

Sperry, Len, "Integrating Spiritual Direction Functions in the Practice of Psychotherapy," *Journal of Psychology and Theology*, Vol. 31, No. 1, 2003, pp. 3–13.

Spranger, Eduard, *Types of Men: The Psychology and Ethics of Personality*, Halle: M. Niemeyer, 1928.

Stoddard, W. H. B., *Mind and Its Disorders*, London: H. K. Lewis, 1908.

Stojiljkovic, Srboljub, *Psihijatrija, sa medicinskom psihologijom*, Belgrade and Zagreb: Medicinska knjiga, 1979.

Stout, Martha, *The Sociopath Next Door*, New York: Harmony Books, 2006.

Timothy F. Murphy, "Experiments in Gender: Ethics at the Boundaries of Clinical Practice and Research," *Ethics and Intersex*, ed. Sharon E. Systma, Dordecht: Springer, 2006.

Yalom, Irvin, *Becoming Myself*, New York: Basic Books, 2017, Kindle edition, e-book.

Religion and Mythology

Armstrong, Karen, *A History of God*, New York: Ballantine Books, 1994.

Armstrong, Karen, *A Short History of Myth*, Edinburgh: Canongate, 2005, Kindle edition, e-book.

Armstrong, Karen, *The Spiral Staircase*, London: Harper Perennial, 2005, Kindle edition, e-book.

Armstrong, Karen, *Through the Narrow Gate*, London: Flamingo, 1998.

Armstrong, Karen, *Twelve Steps to a Compassionate Life*, London: The Bodley Head, 2011.

Bakrac, Vladimir, *Religija i mladi: Religioznost mladih u Crnoj Gori*, Podgorica: Narodna knjiga, 2013.

Barrett, Justin L., *Born Believers: The Science of Children's Religious Belief*, New York: Free Press, 2012.

Bhagavad Gītā As It Is, purported by Swami Prabhupada, New York: Collier Books, 1972.

Carse, James P., *The Religious Case against Belief*, London: Penguin, 2008.

Chödzin, Sherab, "Foreword," Chögyam Rinpoche, *Crazy Wisdom*, ed. Sherab Chödzin, Boston, MA: Shambala, 2001.

Cox, Michael, *Mysticism, the Direct Experience of God*, Wellingborough: The Aquarian Press, 1983.

Dalryple, William, *Nine Lives: In Search of the Sacred in Modern India*, London: Bloomsbury, 2009.

DiValerio, David M., *The Holy Madmen of Tibet*, New York: Oxford University Press, 2015.

Eliade, Mircea, *Vodic kroz svetske religije*, tr. Andjelka Cvijic, Belgrade: Narodna knjiga, Alfa, 1996.

Feuerstein, Georg, *Holy Madness: The Shock Tactics and Radical Teachings of Crazy-Wise Adepts, Holy Fools, and Rascal Gurus*, New York: Paragon House, 1991.

Ghose, Sisirkumar, *Mystics and Society*, London: Asia Publishing House, 1968.

Heller, Dana, "Holy Fools, Secular Saints, and Illiterate Saviors in American Literature and Popular Culture," *CLCWeb: Comparative Literature and Culture*, Vol. 5, No. 3, 2003. doi:10.7771/1481-4374.1193.

Hesse, Hermann, *Moja vera*, tr. Jasmina Burojevic, Belgrade: Narodna knjiga – Alfa, 1999.

Hunt, Priscilla, "Holy Foolishness as a Key to Russian Culture," *Holy Foolishness in Russia: New Perspectives*, eds. Priscilla Hunt and Svitlana Kobets, Bloomington, IN: Slavica Publications, 2001.

James, William, *The Varieties of Religious Experience*, Harmondsworth: Penguin, 1987.

Kester, Monique, "Karen Armstrong: Don't Do to Others As You Don't Want Others to Do to You," *Academy Magazine,* Autumn 2007, https://www.speakersacademy.com/files/karenarmstrong_pdf.pdf

Otto, Rudolph, *The Idea of the Holy*, Oxford: Oxford University Press, 1958.

Robson, William, *The Life of Cardinal Richelieu*, London: George Routledge, 1854.

Roose, Kevin, *The Unlikely Disciple: A Sinner's Semester at America's Holiest University*, New York: Grand Central Publishing, 2009, Kindle e-book.

Rosen, Christine, *Preaching Eugenics: Religious Leaders and the American Eugenics Movement*, Oxford: Oxford University Press, 2004.

Rydén, Lennart, "Introduction," *The Life of St. Andrew the Fool*, ed. Lennart Rydén, Uppsala: Acta Universitatis Upsaliensis, Studia Byzantina Upsalensia, Vol. 4, No. 1, 1995.

Sawyer, Dana, *Huston Smith: Wisdomkeeper*, Louisville, KY: Fons Vitae, 2014.

Sen, K. M., *Hinduizam*, tr. Vesna Mladenovic, Belgrade: Decja knjiga, 1990.

Smith, Huston, *Forgotten Truth*. New York: Harper Colophon Books, 1977.

Smith, Huston, *The World's Religions*, New York: Harper One, 2009.

Smith, Huston and Jeffrey Paine, *Tales of Wonder: Adventures Chasing the Divine*, New York: Harper One, 2009.

Smith, Marion, "Religious Education," *Lawrence Kohlberg: Consensus and Controversy*, eds. Sohan Modgil and Celia Modgil, New York: Routledge, 2011.

Trollinger, William Vance Jr., *God's Empire: William Bell Riley and Midwestern Fundamentalism*, Madison: The University of Wisconsin Press, 1990.

Upanisads, tr. Patrick Olivelle, Oxford: Oxford University Press, 1996.

Walton, Alan Hull, "Introduction," *Ashvaghosa – The Awakening of Faith*, tr. Timothy Richard, New Hyde Park, NY: University Books, 1961, pp. 7–25.

Psychology and Religion

Allport, Gordon, *The Individual and His Religion*, New York: Macmillan, 1962.

Coric, Simun Sito, *Psihologija religioznosti*, Jasterbarsko: Slap, 2003.

Dacquino, Giacomo, *Religioznost i psihoanaliza*, tr. Silvana Trosanski-Mircevic, Belgrade: Plato, 2005.

Firman, John and Ann Gila, *Psychosynthesis: A Psychology of the Spirit*, Albany: State University Of New York Press, 2002, p. 19.

Frankl, Viktor, *Bog podsvesti*, tr. D. Petrovic, Belgrade: Zarko Albulj, 2001.

Frankl, Viktor, *Man's Search for Ultimate Meaning*, New York: Basic Books, 2000.

Fromm, Erich, *Psychoanalysis and Religion*, New Haven, CT: Yale University Press, 1955.

Fuller, Andrew Reid, *Psychology and Religion: Eight Points of View*, London: Littlefield Adams, 1994.

Grof, Stanislav and Hal Zina Bennett, *The Holotropic Mind*, New York: Harper Collins, 1993.

Meissner, William W., "The Phenomenology of Religious Psychopathology," *Bulletin of the Menninger Clinic*, Vol. 55, pp. 281–298.

Milenkovic, Snezana, *Psihoterapija i duhovnost*, Belgrade: Cigoja stampa, 2002.

Oates, Wayne E., *Behind the Masks: Personality Disorders in Religious Behaviour*, Louisville, KY: The Westminster Press, 1987.

Wulff, David M., *Psychology of Religion, Classic and Contemporary Views*, New York: Wiley, 1991.

Zivkovic, Ilija and Suzana Vuletic, "Ekleziogene neuroze u psihopatoloskim oblicima religioznosti," *Zagreb: Drustvena Istrazivanja*, Vol. 6, No. 92, 2007, pp. 1263–1285.

Fiction and Literary Criticism

Anderson, James Arthur, *The Linguistics of Stephen King*, Jefferson, NC: McFarland & Company, 2017.

Austen, Jane, *Pride and Prejudice*, London: Penguin, 1994.

Austenfeld, Anne Marie, "The Revelatory Narrative Circle in Barbara Kingsolver's *The Poisonwood Bible*," *Journal of Narrative Theory*, Vol. 6, No. 2, Summer 2006, pp. 293–305.

Beahm, George, *Stephen King from A to Z*, Kansas City, MO: Andrews McMeal Publishing, 1998.

Birnbaum, Milton, *Aldous Huxley: A Quest for Values*, New Brunswick, NJ and London: Transaction Publishers, 2009.

Bloom, Harold, "Introduction," *Jane Austen's Pride and Prejudice*, ed. Harold Bloom, Philadelphia, PA: Chelsea House, 2004, pp. 7–9.

Brown, Russel M. and Donna A. Bennet, "Magnus Eisengrim: The Shadow of the Trickster in the Novels of Robertson Davies," *Jungian Literary Criticism*, ed. Richard P. Sugg, Evanston, IL: Northwestern University Press, 1992, pp. 285–301.

Cordell, Richard, *Somerset Maugham*, London: Heinemann, 1961.

Curtis, Anthony, *Somerset Maugham*, Windsor: Profile Books, 1982.

Davies, Robertson, *Fifth Business*, London: Penguin, 2001, Kindle edition, e-book.

Fast, Howard, *Torquemada*, Open Road Media, 2011, Kindle edition, e-book.

Fullerton, Susannah, *Celebrating Pride and Prejudice*, Minneapolis, MN: Voyageur Press, 2013.

Grant, Patrick, "Belief in Mysticism: Aldous Huxley, from *Grey Eminence* to *Island*," *Six Modern Authors and Problems of Belief*, London: Macmillan, 1979, pp. 17–38.

Gresh, Louis H. and Robert Weinberg, *The Science Of Stephen King*, Hoboken, NJ: Wiley, 2007.

Hastings, Selina, *The Secret Lives of Somerset Maugham*, London: John Murray, 2010.

Heidenreich, Rosmarin, *The Postwar Novel in Canada: Narrative Patterns and Reader Response*, Waterloo, ON: Wilfrid Laurier University Press, 1989.

Hoppenstand, Garry and Ray B. Browne, *The Gothic World of Stephen King: Landscape of Nightmares*, Bowling Green, OH: Bowling Green State University Popular Press, 1987.

Huxley, Aldous, *Ape and Essence*, London: Chatto & Windus, 1978.Huxley, Aldous, "Foreword," Hubert Benoit, *The Supreme Doctrine*, Psychological Studies in Zen Buddhism, New York: Pantheon Books, 1955.

Huxley, Aldous, *Grey Eminence*, London: Chatto & Windus, 1949.

Huxley, Aldous, *Letters by Aldous Huxley*, ed. Grover Smith, London: Chatto & Windus, 1969.

Huxley, Aldous, *Proper Studies*, London: Chatto & Windus, 1927.

Huxley, Aldous, "Shakespeare and Religion," *Aldous Huxley, a Memorial Volume*, ed. Julian Huxley, London: Chatto & Windus, 1965, pp. 161–175.

Huxley, Aldous, *The Devils of Loudun*, New York: Harper & Brothers, 1953.

Huxley, Aldous, *The Perennial Philosophy*, London: Chatto & Windus, 1946.

Huxley, Aldous, *Time Must Have a Stop*, London: Chatto & Windus, 1945.

James, William Closson, *Locations of the Sacred: Essays on Religion, Literature, and Canadian Culture*, Waterloo, ON: Wilfred Laurier University Press, 1998.

King, Stephen, *Carrie*, London: Hodder & Stoughton, 2007, Kindle edition, e-book.

Kingsolver, Barbara, *The Poisonwood Bible*, London: Faber & Faber, 2000.

Knight, Mark, *An Introduction to Religion and Literature*, New York: Continuum, 2009.

Lanes, Victor J., *Aspects of Robertson Davies' Novels*, New York: Peter Lang Publishing, 2009.

Langland, William, *Piers Plowman*, http://piers.iath.virginia.edu/index.html, e-text, accessed at 7 January 2017.

Lea, James, "Sinclair Lewis and the Implied America," *American Fiction between the Wars*, ed. Harold Bloom, New York: Chelsea House, 2005.

Lewis, Sinclair, *Elmer Gantry*, A Project Gutenberg of Australia eBook, 0300851, May 2003.

Marlowe, Christopher, *The Tragical History of Dr. Faustus*, www.gutenberg.org/files/779/779-h/779-h.htm, e-text, accessed 9 August 2017.

Maugham, Somerset, *The Razor's Edge*, London: Heinemann, 1964.

Maxwell, William, *So Long, See You Tomorrow*, London: The Harvill Press, 1997.

Meyers, Jeffrey, *Somerset Maugham, A Life*, New York: Alfred A. Knopf, 2004.

Milton, John, *Paradise Lost, the English Poems of John Milton*, Ware: Wordsworth, 2004.

Moriarty, Michael G., *The Perfect Ten: The Blessings of Following God's Commandments in a Postmodern Way*, Grand Rapids, MI: Zondervan, 1999.

Morris, Ivor, *Mr Collins Considered*, London and New York: Routledge and Kegan Paul, 1987.

Palmer, Robert A., *A Literary Cavalcade II*, self-published, 2013.

Purcell, William F., "The Gospel According to Barbara Kingsolver," *Logos: A Journal of Catholic Thought and Culture*, Vol. 12, No. 1, Winter 2009, pp. 93–116.

Quinn, Edward, *History in Literature: A Reader's Guide to 20th Century History and the Literature It Inspired*, New York: Facts on File, 2004.

Raymond, Claire, *Witnessing Sadism in the Texts of the American South*, Farnham: Ashgate, 2014.

Roper, Gordon, "Robertson Davies' *Fifth Business* and 'That Old Fantastical Devil of Dark Corners, C. G. Jung'," *The Canadian Novel Here and Now: A Critical Anthology*, Vol. 1, ed. John Moss, Toronto, ON: New Canada Publications, 1983, pp. 53–66.

Schorer, Mark, "Sinclair Lewis," *Seven Modern American Novelists, an Introduction*, ed. William Van O'Connor, Minneapolis: The University of Minnesota Press, 1964.

Shakespeare, William, *Hamlet*, http://shakespeare.mit.edu/hamlet/full.html, e-text, accessed 30 July 2014.

Shakespeare, William, *A Midsummer Night's Dream*, www.shakespeare-online.com/plays/mids_5_1.html, e-text, accessed at 21 July 2014.

Shakespeare, William, *The Winter's Tale*, http://shakespeare.mit.edu/winters_tale/full.html, e-text, accessed at 13 July 2014.

Smith, Brian, "Elements and Causes: Deducing the Present from the Past in Aldous Huxley's Grey Eminence," *Aldous Huxley Annual*, eds. Bernfried Nugel, Jerome Meckier, Vol. 12/13, Münster: Lit Verlag, 2013, pp. 81–103.

Snodgrass, Mary Ellen, *Barbara Kingsolver: A Literary Companion*, Jefferson, NC and London: McFarland & Company, 2004.

Sorensen, Sue, *The Collar: Reading Christian Ministry in Fiction, Television, and Film*, Eugene, OR: Cascade Books, 2014.

Sorin, Gerald, *Howard Fast: Life and Literature in the Left Lane*, Bloomington: Indiana University Press, 2012.

Sova, Down B., *Banned Books: Literature Suppressed on Social Grounds*, New York: Facts on File, 2006.

Strehle, Susan, "Chosen People: American Exceptionalism in Kingsolver's *The Poisonwood Bible*," *Critique: Studies in Contemporary Fiction*, Vol. 49, No. 4, 2008, pp. 413–429.

Swift, Jonathan, *Gulliver's Travels*, London: Penguin, 1994.

Warwick, Ellen D., "The Transformation of Robertson Davies," *The Canadian Novel Here and Now: A Critical Anthology*, Vol. 1, ed. John Moss, Toronto, ON: New Canada Publications, 1983, pp. 67–78.

Wedgwood, C. V., "The Mystic and the World," *Aldous Huxley, the Critical Heritage*, ed. Donald Watt, London and New York: Routledge, 2005, pp. 335–337.

Woodcock, George, *The Dawn and the Darkest Hour*, London: Faber and Faber, 1972.

Responsibility Foundation, "The Statue of Responsility is the One Thing that Changes Everything" www.mystatueofresponsibility.com/.

Zähner, Lilly, *Demon and Saint in the Novels of Aldous Huxley*, Bern: Francke Verlag, 1975.

General and Reference

The Bible, 2 Corinthians 3:6.

"2012 Republican Party of Texas Report of Platform Committee," word document downloaded from: www.texasgop.org/about-the-party/, accessed at 10 July 2014.

Aupperle, Kenneth E. and Deane Van Pham, "An Expanded Investigation into the Relationship of Corporate Social Responsibility and Financial Performance," *Employee Responsibilities and Rights Journal*, Vol. 2, No. 4, New York: Springer, 1989, pp. 263–274.

Bruce, Fein, "Hustler Magazine v. Falwell: A Mislitigated and Misreasoned Case," *William and Mary Law Review*, Vol. 30, No. 4, Williamsburg, VA: 1989, pp. 905–917.

Haubrich, William S., *Medical Meanings: A Glossary of Word Origins*, Philadelphia, PA: American College of Physicians, 2003.

Karmen, Henry, *Inquisition and Society in Spain in the Sixteenth and Seventeenth Centuries*, Bloomington: Indiana University Press, 1985.

Putnam, William Lowell, *Torquemada Revisited: The Power of Effective Persuasion on Intellectual Freedom and Racism*, Flagstaff: Light Technology Publishing, 2006, e-book.

Wiegand, Wayne, "Collecting Contested Titles: The Experience of Five Small Public Libraries in the Rural Midwest, 1893–1956," *Libraries and Culture*, Vol. 30, No. 3, Summer 2005, pp. 368–384.

Zizek, Slavoj, *The Metastases of Enjoyment*, London and New York: Verso, 2005.

Index